Dearest Jeff

    In hoping this will enhance your intellectual curiosity and development as a great scholar. . . .

    Merry Christmas,

      Love Grisele

        XOXOXO

        Dec 1989.

VIDEO CULTURE
A Critical Investigation

VIDEO CULTURE
A Critical Investigation

Edited by John G. Hanhardt

Gibbs M. Smith, Inc.
Peregrine Smith Books
in association with
Visual Studies Workshop Press, 1986

Designed by Joan Lyons
Typeset by Susan Cergol at Visual Studies Workshop
Cover design and plates by Philip Zimmermann,
Zimmermann Multiples, Rhinebeck, NY

This book has been supported in part by grants from the National Endowment for the Arts, a Federal Agency, and the New York State Council on the Arts.

Visual Studies Workshop Press
31 Prince Street, Rochester, New York 14607

Distributed to the trade by
Gibbs M. Smith, Inc., Peregrine Smith Books
P.O. Box 667, Layton, Utah 84041

1986

Library of Congress Cataloging-in-Publication Data

Main entry under title:
Video culture.

   "Peregrine Smith Books."
   Bibliography: p.
   Includes index.
   1. Video art—Addresses, essays, lectures.
2. Television broadcasting—Addresses, essays, lectures.
3. Mass media—Addresses, essays, lectures.
I. Hanhardt, John G.
PN1992.8.V5V535 1986   700'.9'04   85-40821
ISBN 0-87905-222-8
ISBN 0-89822-044-0 (Visual Studies Workshop Press)

Acknowledgments

Grateful acknowledgment is made for permission to reprint the following essays:

Walter Benjamin: "The Work of Art in the Age of Mechanical Reproduction." From *Illuminations*, translated by Harry Zohn. (New York: Schocken Books, 1969). Reprinted by permission of Harcourt Brace Jovanovich, Inc.

Bertolt Brecht: "The Radio as an Apparatus of Communication." From *Brecht on Theatre*, edited and translated by John Willett. (New York: Hill and Wang, 1964). Copyright © 1957, 1963, 1964 by Suhrkamp Verlag Frankfurt am Main. This translation and notes © by John Willett. Reprinted by permission of Farrar, Straus & Giroux, Inc.

Louis Althusser: "Ideology and Ideological State Apparatuses (Notes Towards an Investigation)." From *Lenin and Philosophy*, translated by Ben Brewster. (New York: Monthly Review Press, 1971). Copyright © 1971 by NLB. Reprinted by permission of the Monthly Review Foundation.

Hans Magnus Enzensberger: "Constituents of a Theory of the Media." From *The Consciousness Industry*, translated by Stuart Hood. (New York: Seabury Press, 1974). Reprinted by permission of The Continuum Publishing Company.

Jean Baudrillard: "Requiem for the Media." From *For a Critique of the Political Economy of the Sign*, translated by Charles Levin. (St. Louis, MO: Telos Press, 1981). Reprinted by permission of Telos Press.

David Antin: "Video: The Distinctive Features of the Medium." From *Video Art*, edited by Ira Schneider and Beryl Korot. (New York: Harcourt Brace Jovanovich, 1976). Reprinted by permission of the Institute of Contemporary Art, University of Pennsylvania, from the catalogue to the exhibition "Video Art," 1975.

David Ross: "Truth or Consequences: American Television and Video Art." From *The Luminous Image (Het Lumineuze Beeld)*. (Amsterdam: Stedelijk Museum, 1984). Reprinted by permission of the author.

Rosalind Krauss: "Video: The Aesthetics of Narcissism." From *New Artists Video*, edited by Gregory Battcock. (New York: E.P. Dutton, 1978). Reprinted by permission of the author.

Stanley Cavell: "The Fact of Television." From *Daedalus*, vol. III, no. 4 (Fall 1982). Reprinted by permission of *Daedalus*.

Nam June Paik: "La Vie, Satellites, One Meeting—One Life." From *Nam June Paik—Mostly Video*, translated by Yumiko Yamazaki. (Tokyo: The Tokyo Metropolitan Art Museum, 1984). Reprinted by permission of the author.

Gene Youngblood: "Art, Entertainment, Entropy." From *Expanded Cinema*. (New York: E.P. Dutton and Co. Inc., 1970). Copyright © 1970 by Gene Youngblood. Reprinted by permission of E.P. Dutton, a division of New American Library.

Jack Burnham: "Art and Technology: The Panacea That Failed." From *The Myths of Information: Technology and Postindustrial Culture*, edited by Kathleen Woodward.(Madison, Wisconsin: Coda Press, 1980). Distributed by Indiana University Press. Reprinted by permission of the author.

John Ellis: "Cinema and Broadcast TV Together." From *Visible Fictions: Cinema: Television: Video*. (London, Boston: Routledge & Kegan Paul PLC, 1982). Reprinted by permission of Routledge & Kegan Paul PLC.

Douglas Davis: "Filmgoing/Videogoing: Making Distinctions." From *Artculture: Essays on the Post-Modern*. (New York: Harper and Row, 1977). Reprinted by permission of Harper and Row.

Contents

Dedicated to my parents
Arthur M. and Helene G. Hanhardt.

This selection of essays was developed out of courses and lectures on the history of video art delivered at a number of colleges and museums around the country. In particular I enjoyed the opportunity to teach at Middlebury College and develop two workshops at the Visual Studies Workshop. In both cases these essays provoked stimulating discussion and opened up the issue of video art to a complex of social, technological, and aesthetic issues. It is my hope that putting these essays together will help students, teachers, and artists to reexamine video art today. I have added a bibliography to suggest further readings.

The original footnotes for each essay have been retained. This results in some confusion, especially in the first section where the authors cite different editions and translations of the same works. Since several of these works are reprinted in this anthology, I have referred the reader to the pages in this text where they appear.

I want to thank Ted Perry of Middlebury College for inviting me to be Christian A. Johnson Visiting Professor of Art in Winter Term 1984. In particular I want to extend my appreciation to Nathan Lyons, Director, Visual Studies Workshop, who suggested that my reading list could be made into a book, and Joan Lyons, Director of the Visual Studies Workshop Press, for leading this project through to its completion.

Special thanks to Callie Angell for assistance in the preparation of the manuscript.

John G. Hanhardt

Introduction

John G. Hanhardt

THIS ANTHOLOGY brings together a wide range of critical, theoretical and historical writings on film, video, and television. My aim is to provide the reader with a collection that will address issues pertaining to art and technology and, more specifically, the definition of a "video culture" as it is determined by the distinctive features of the medium and the forces acting on its history.

The first section, *Theory and Practice*, contains key essays which have informed the critical debates involving the creative potential and political implications of the mass media of radio, film, and television. Walter Benjamin (1892-1940), the German critic and philosopher, first published "The Work of Art in the Age of Mechanical Reproduction" in 1936. It is a seminal inquiry into film and photography and their means of reproduction which he suggests will undermine the authority of art and remove the aura of the fine art object. Benjamin's essay serves as the basis for an appreciation of film as a potent force in modernism. Bertolt Brecht's (1898-1956) "The Radio as an Apparatus of Communication" (1932) examines radio's potential as a means for true communication, not as a standardized one-way means of entertainment controlled by the state. The implications of Brecht's essay for alternative television has given it a broad meaning for artists' use of television. The controls exercised by the state through the institutions of law, education, and communication are addressed in the French philosopher Louis Althusser's powerful critique of the modern state. Althusser's concept of the "Ideological State Apparatus" has been an influential analytical tool in examining television's role in society. The forms of intervention that artists might make in affecting social and cultural institutions are treated in Hans Magnus Enzensberger's "Constituents of a Theory of the Media," in which the author, a leading German poet and essayist, seeks to liberate the potential of the media as a positive instrument for cultural/social change and expression. The French sociologist Jean Baudrillard's "Requiem for the Media" posits a post-modern skepticism towards the previous programs of media alternatives. Baudrillard rejects the media as a means to overturn the dominance of the state and looks to alternative interventions that question and subvert the traditional ideological structures from within.

The history of video as an art form has often been perceived in terms of its relationship to television. The second group of essays, *Video and Television*, begins with poet and critic David Antin's "Video: The Distinctive Features of the Medium," an early look at how video art and its strategies contradicted the norms of television. Antin argues that video art could be defined by the total absence of those features which define television. David Ross, currently Director of the Institute of Contemporary Art, Boston, examines the strategies of video artists who deliberately exploit television's techniques and styles. Art historian Rosalind Krauss turns to the process of video production, the camera and screen, as a conduit for exploring the self of the artist and relates this strategy to the "process art" of the early 1970s. The experience of television and its pervasive presence are examined by the philosopher Stanley Cavell, who focuses on how we adapt to television and how the fulfillment of our expectations of the medium creates an uneasiness in our relationship to its technology. Nam June Paik is an artist who has played a key role in video art's history. His exuberant speculations on global television as a metaphor for art point to the need for a dialogue between technology and art, between video and television.

The third group of essays, *Film and Video: Differences and Futures*, contrasts video to film and examines how both have been viewed as utopian projects. Gene Youngblood's "Art, Entertainment, Entropy" is an excerpt from his book-length study of film, video and multimedia experiments entitled *Expanded Cinema*. In this section Youngblood offers an optimistic view of a cognitive interchange between technologies in the multi-media projects of the late 1960s. Art historian Jack Burnham reflects on those hopes and questions those who rely on technology without examining the full ramifications of the medium as a sustained form of expression and inquiry. John Ellis's examination of the difference between broadcast television and filmmaking and Douglas Davis's speculations on the viewing experience as defined by both media provide a critical perspective on the changes taking place in film and video today.

From Cinema to Video Culture

As we approach the last decade of the twentieth century there is a sense of profound change that is affecting our interaction and perception of the world around us. The transitional nature of our time is reflected in the very labels we invent—post-industrial and post-modern—to identify the social, economic, and cultural forces at work in our society. The common prefix, "post-", lays emphasis on the idea that we are leaving something behind but have not progressed so far as to effectively identify the new paradigm and give it its own name.

Today we are witnessing a dialectical pull between a post-modernism that self-consciously replays figurative expressionism or neo-classical formalism, and an opposed body of art works which offer meta-critical discourses on the history of modernism. The ultimate question of how a truly post-modern paradigm will emerge from these activities has yet to be answered. The self-consciousness of the art world and its increasingly uncritical preoccupation with the marketplace[1] suggests that we ask another question: What are artists for? This is the question implicitly and directly raised in the essays collected here. What is the artist's relationship to society and the broader culture? This issue is made more complex by artists working with film and video, the technologies of the mass media. The following pages historically survey how film and video artists, by stripping modern technology of its false ideology, question technology's means and methods of perception and thus ultimately consider how these inventions contribute to shaping our world.

The History of the American Avant-Garde Film: Origins and Models

The precursors and models for American avant-garde cinema are the avant-garde films produced in Europe during the 1920s and 1930s and the cinema of the Soviet Union produced in the late 1920s. Made by artists who, for the most part, had reputations in other media, the films were independent productions created outside the ascending mainstream of commercial film production and distribution. The European avant-garde demonstrated how the tenets and strategies of modernist art could be re-articulated in the medium of film. As Standish Lawder has written in *The Cubist Cinema*:

> The avant-garde film movement of the twenties is that chapter in the history of film created, for the most part, by painters and poets whose principal medium of expression was not film. Their films were non-commercial undertakings, and usually non-narra-

tive in form. Through the medium of film they sought to give concrete plastic shape to inner visions rather than manipulate images of external reality for dramatic effect. In its broadest outlines, the avant-garde film movement followed a course similar to modern painting in the twenties, that is, from a rigorously geometric and abstract style, as in De Stijl or Bauhaus aesthetic, to the hallucinatory content of surrealism in the late twenties.[2]

These filmmakers were concerned with the properties of filmic movement, editing, and the fantastic juxtapositions and *gestalts* that could be created through manipulation of photography or the graphic animation of abstract forms. Such films as Robert Weine's *Das Cabinet des Dr. Caligari (The Cabinet of Dr. Caligari)* (1920), Fernand Léger's *Ballet Méchanique* (1924), Hans Richter's *Rhythmus 21* (1921), and Luis Buñuel and Salvador Dali's *Un Chien Andalou* (1929) reflect the diversity of concerns in the European avant-garde films and point to the variety of forms which would be manifested in the American avant-garde.

The Soviet cinema as represented by Sergei Eisenstein and Dziga Vertov entered into a dialogue with the European avant-garde film through mutual influence and a shared concern with the expressive potential of the medium of film. Eisenstein's importance in a consideration of the avant-garde resides in his films (*Potemkin* was a favorite of the surrealists) and in his theoretical writings, which elaborated his ideas about editing (montage), composition, and a range of other basic issues. Standish Lawder discusses an interesting and remarkable passage from Eisenstein film *Old and New*, which indicates the possible influence of the European avant-garde on the Soviet director:

> It is tempting to see in Eisenstein's *Old and New* of 1929 certain echoes of *Ballet Méchanique*. In the cream separator scene, for instance, the patterns of machinery in motion—seen through the eyes of the skeptical peasants who ask, "Will it work?"—are transformed into a dazzling arabesque of light playing on metallic surfaces. Even closer to the spirit of...Léger is the freedom with which Eisenstein edited this visually sensuous passage, for intercut with these poetic images are spectacular shots of pirouetting shafts of light which, on closer inspection, can be seen to be nothing more than a spinning bicycle wheel! This passage in Eisenstein's film is by far the most abstract he ever made, and quite likely he was stimulated to experiment along these lines by the European avant-garde films that Ehrenburg had shown him in 1926.[3]

It is important to remember, however, that for Eisenstein abstract imagery was used only in service of the narrative, not as an end in itself.

Dziga Vertov's *The Man with the Movie Camera* is on one level a day in the life of a Soviet cameraman. The film shows him at work, experimenting with his equipment and creating a dialectic between his experience and the medium of film. The viewer witnesses the procedures of filming, processing, editing and projecting the film. The very complexity of the film in terms of editing, idea and ideology suggests an ontology of film through its self-referential strategies. Vertov's film is especially important in a discussion of the avant-garde film since it came out of Soviet Russia at a time when the interaction among artists working in all media had achieved a euphoria of mutual exploration. Constructivism's abstraction, employment of materials, and activization of space, and formalism's examination of literary texts in formal and structural terms both influenced the Soviet cinema. Thus Vertov's film was created in a context of change, in which process and method were part of the social and aesthetic/artistic enterprise. The radical Soviet cinema is similar to the avant-garde film of Europe in the 1920s and of America in the 1940s and later insofar as it operated within contexts of modernism and radical ambitions.

In a seminal appreciation of *The Man with the Movie Camera*, Annette Michelson writes:

> ... If the filmmaker is, like the magician, a manufacturer of illusions, he can, unlike the prestidigator and in the interests of instruction of a heightening of consciousness, destroy illusion by that other transcendentally magical procedure, the reversal of time by the inversion of action. He can develop, as it were, "the negative of time" for "the communist decoding of reality." This thematic interplay of magic, illusion, labor, and filmic techniques and strategy, articulating a theory of film as epistemological inquiry is the complex central core around which Vertov's greatest work develops.[4] ... In a sense most subtle and complex, he was, Bazin to the contrary, one of those directors "who put their faith in the image;" that faith was, however, accorded to the image seen, recognized as an image and the condition of that faith or recognition, the consciousness, the subversion through consciousness, of cinematic illusionism.[5]

The European avant-garde directly confronted the medium of film by engaging the issues of its illusionism and its temporal and material qualities while maintaining an appreciation of the iconography of the popular entertainment film, especially comedy and melodrama (e.g. the surrealists' enthusiasm for the comedies of Chaplin and the serial adventure of the French director Louis Feuillades). However, outside the cineclubs and special expositions the films were seldom shown, and they were seldom presented in a gallery or museum context, which might have affirmed their origins in the other arts and thereby validated and encouraged the aesthetic issues they raised. Failing to affirm a world view congruent with that of film historians, critics, museum curators, and general viewers, the avant-garde films of the 1920s became curiosities in the film histories and problems in some film theories.

The possibilities for an alternative cinema in America were opened up by a technical development that enabled the filmmaker to work without a large staff or expensive, cumbersome equipment. In the early 1940s a portable motion picture camera was introduced. The Bolex 16mm camera was sturdy and easy to use, with flexible focal lengths that permitted the filmmaker to shift quickly from close-ups to long shots and to manipulate the film image by altering the camera's speed—the rate at which images were being recorded.

The 16mm camera heralded the beginning of an alternative cinema in America, a cinema that began with the film *Meshes of the Afternoon* (1943) by Maya Deren in collaboration with Alexander Hammid. This film was to become emblematic of the first decade of the American independent cinema, a period shaped by Deren and filmmakers Sidney Peterson, James Broughton, Kenneth Anger, Willard Maas, Marie Menken, Douglas Crockwell, and Gregory Markopoulos, and others. P. Adams Sitney opens his book *Visionary Film*, a history of the American independent cinema, with a discussion of *Meshes of the Afternoon*. He locates its aesthetic in European twentieth-century modernism and the avant-garde art movements of constructivism, surrealism, and expressionism. The often reproduced still of Deren from the film stands as a symbol of her position in the history of independent film. We see her hands pressed against a membrane of window glass that reflects the outside world; as she stares through that reflecting surface, as if into the camera's lens or through a film screen out into the world, she becomes a reflection of herself mediated by the projected film image. It is the relation of the artist to the projected dreamworld of film that dominated the first ten years of the independent cinema. As Deren describes *Meshes of the Afternoon*, it "is concerned with the interior experiences of an individual. It does not record an event which will be witnessed by other persons. Rather, it reproduces the way in which the subconscious of an individual will develop, interpret and elaborate an apparently simple and casual incident into a critical emotional experience."[6]

The film depicts a woman moving through the interior spaces of a house, an action repeated in a silent dreamlike scenario. *Meshes of the Afternoon,* as Deren notes, "is still based on a strong literary-dramatic line as a core, and rests heavily upon the symbolic value of objects and situations."[7] In Deren's film, a formation of the artistic self is articulated in the expression of the dream state, a dream narrative within a dream film, in which a psychological presence is created within the illusionistic film space. This attitude—the articulation of subconscious experience along a narrative line—became a powerful focus for early avant-garde film and continues to function today as a genre within independent filmmaking.

The decades of the 1950s and 1960s constitute a formative period in the history of the American independent film. It was a time of transition, during which major changes occurred involving both aesthetic issues and such practical matters as how and where films should be distributed and exhibited. One outcome of these controversies was that the filmmakers and filmmaker-run organizations took on an activist role, as a result of which independent film fashioned a new presence for itself in American culture and received greater public attention. As had happened in American jazz and the off-Broadway theater, the independent filmmaker established an indigenous, new art form which expressed radical changes taking place in American culture. The films being produced and distributed in these turbulent years did not comprise a single school of filmmaking whose progress and influence are easily charted; rather, the film community was a competitive and vociferous group of individuals joined by friendships and loose affiliations to meet specific needs or voice particular ideological and aesthetic goals.

Beginning in the late 1950s the relationship of the film image to the cinematic apparatus (camera, film, projection system) shifted: instead of projecting a symbolic, hallucinatory dream state representing the unconscious along narrative lines, filmmakers from Stan Brakhage and Bruce Connor to Robert Breer and Andy Warhol focused on the direct acknowledgment of the material properties of film and of the artifice of the production process. The art of the film confronted and ultimately dismantled a cinema predicated on surrealist aesthetic models and replaced it with an eclectic and distinctly American film culture.

In addition, filmmakers discarded the taboos defining what should and should not be seen on film as judged by the defenders of public morality. The independent film, like the off-Broadway theater, gained in notoriety as more work was produced and exhibited. Controversy— caused on the one hand by censorship, on the other by the outraged response that often greeted new forms of cinematic representation— abounded both within and outside the film community. Thus the

American independent film stood poised against the dominant morality of its time and the public's expectation of what a film was as entertainment and art. The independent cinema achieved a cultural celebrity
that was to give the filmmaker a new prominence in the 1960s and
1970s.

This brief survey of the early history of the avant-garde cinema leads
to the emergence of video art in the mid-1960s. It was against the background of television and the historical precedent of the independent
cinema that the video art movement was to develop. Although communication between film and video artists was limited during the 1960s
and 1970s, today the dialogue between artists and art forms is developing, as the aesthetics of film and video respond to the pressures of
changing technologies.

Television, Video, and the Art World

The beginnings of video art can be traced to the early 1960s and Wolf
Vostell's and Nam June Paik's incorporation of the television set into
their artworks; however, it was in the middle of that decade, when the
Sony Corporation introduced its portable video recorder into the
American market, that video began to grow as an art form. This "Portapak" system released the medium from the economic, ideological, and
aesthetic confines of the television studio and placed it in the hands of
individual artists. The immediate appeal of video was the ease and flexi-
bility of its operation. It did not require crews and specialists to operate; one could work with it by oneself in the studio/loft and out-of-
doors; what was being recorded by the camera on videotape could
immediately be seen on the monitor's screen. The electronic recording
capability of video was such that, unlike film, there was no wait for the
videotape to be processed before seeing what had been shot with the
camera. The subsequent rapid development of video technology—the
introduction of color, more sophisticated editing systems, and im-
proved cameras—in part accounts for video's dramatic rise in such a
short time. But there was also the fact that artists already working in
other art forms were attracted to the medium. They came to video with
ideas which were further elaborated by the capacities of this new
medium, and which, in turn, helped shape video's aesthetic discourse.

The artists who pioneered the development of video as an art form—
Nam June Paik, Wolf Vostell, Bruce Nauman, Vito Acconci, Richard
Serra, Nancy Holt, Peter Campus, Juan Downey, Frank Gillette, Ira
Schneider, among others—came to the medium from other fields such
as music, performance, dance, and sculpture. Some were interested in

subverting the dominant model of television while others wanted to see their work distributed on television. The context in which they worked was the art world, and they were ultimately attracted to the conceptual properties of the medium, to the fact that within its time-based image-recording capacities one could explore visual and sound relationships with a whole new set of options. These options were in part guided by the intertextual nature of the medium: while exploring its unique capacities for recording and transforming imagery, artists could combine video with other art forms. Not only was video a two-dimensional screen of black and white (and later color) sequences, but one could write and compose for the soundtrack. Artists could also direct the camera at themselves and express and explore personal narratives and body art; they could take it out-of-doors and record and interpret events and create video landscapes. The image transformation properties of video came in part from the very nature of the medium: one could create effects and later, with the development of the colorizer and video synthesizer, transform these pre-recorded images into wholly abstract sequences.

The question, "Is video art real art?" implies that the medium must somehow legitimize itself as an art form. But the real question is not whether video is an art form but how video changes definitions of art. Walter Benjamin's influential essay, "The Work of Art in the Age of Mechanical Reproduction," stated the same proposition in examining the challenge of photography and film in the later nineteenth and twentieth centuries. As with any new medium, the traditions within art resist a new technology that appears to simply record reality rather than transform it through an artist's vision or aesthetic. However, the argument that film, and by extension video, simply reproduces what is before the camera has been proven false. By extension, video art is ontologically different from film and the other visual arts: yet, as I noted, it does not exist in a vacuum unaffected by the aesthetic concerns of painting, sculpture, performance art, film, music, theater, and dance. It appropriates aspects of these forms and transforms them into a richly suggestive and complex iconography of genres and styles.

Video art is not only single-channel videotapes created for gallery and/or broadcast. It also has its expanded forms: sculptural installation pieces that engage multi-media and formal issues within gallery spaces. It is on this work that I would like to focus, because it addresses a set of issues and questions intrinsic to our understanding of video's creative use, and it re-examines the basic ontology of video, its distinction from television, and its intertextual nature. The eleven pieces I will discuss represent historically the forms that were part of video art from its beginning. They demonstrate how flexible video is both in terms of its technology and our conceptualization of it. In these projects a whole series of issues is raised regarding the relationship of the image on the monitor's screen to the monitor or television set. Both the screen and its container are taken as integral elements in a whole: that whole reshapes video into a plastic form that suggest the full experience of the medium. This plasticity is also apparent in projected video where the monitor is absent as a physical presence and the image becomes an enlarged surface.

Certainly the key figure in the history of video art is Nam June Paik, who was given a comprehensive retrospective exhibition in 1982 at the Whitney Museum of American Art and whose work has explored all areas and forms of video. In 1963, in an exhibition entitled "Exposition of Music-Electronic Television," at the Galerie Parnass, in Wuppertal, West Germany, Paik presented prepared televisions—sets whose components had been altered to produce unexpected effects—as part of his performance and installation. It was the first time Paik had appropriated television technology and it signalled the beginning of a lifelong effort to deconstruct and demystify television. With sets randomly distributed in all positions around the gallery, each television became an instrument, removed from its customary context, handled and manipulated in a direct and physical way. The exteriors were marked up and cluttered with bottles and other objects, while chairs were scattered about the space. The scanning mechanisms in some televisions were magnetically manipulated, affecting the reception of broadcast images. Paik's prepared televisions were his first video sculptures. Just like his prepared pianos, Paik's first television sculptures displayed the residues of use (and abuse), and were thus radically transformed into sculptural objects. In the process, Paik changed our perception of television as a cultural form. The origin of Paik's attitude toward both the high art instrument of the piano and the popular cultural icon of the television comes in part from fluxus, the anarchic, anti-high art movement founded by George Maciunas. Like Wolf Vostell, who also incorporated television in his contribution to Allan Kaprow's Yam Festival in New York in 1963, Paik shared in fluxus' aggressive attack on all forms and attitudes of culture.

The transformation of television in a post-modern art form came about through Paik's understanding of the social presence and meaning of television. To Paik the popular perception of television as only a mass commodity of entertainment, or as simply a radio with pictures, was shortsighted, and he set out as an artist to both demystify and change it. As he stated in his writings, teaching, and, later, videotapes, television represented a new communications technology of enormous potential and signalled the beginning of a post-industrial age where manufacturing, the organization of society, and the making of art would be merged and transformed. Paik saw the electronic medium of television as a discourse that functioned in social, cultural, political, and economic ways. Like the computer and other developments in science, television had initiated a change of a magnitude close to that of the Industrial Revolution. In his art he sought to comment on that discourse, to create a complex aesthetic text that would reconceive television through an array of formal strategies.

In 1969 the Howard Wise Gallery in New York organized an exhibition entitled "TV as a Creative Medium" which included the work of twelve artists. This was a seminal event in the history of video art. By suggesting a utopian and McLuhanesque vision of a "global village" of instant communication and expression now possible through the medium of video/television, this exhibition offered a new view of ourselves, our society, and our customs. One of the key works which expressed this revisionary view of the television was *Wipe Cycle* (1969), created by Ira Schneider and Frank Gillette. Facing a bank of nine monitors the viewer saw himself and the space he viewed from different vantage points, at different points in time, all intercut with programming from television to create what was called at the time a "media ecology" out of the production and distribution of images and information. Both Schneider and Gillette were to continue to create work individually; Schneider's *Manhattan Is an Island* (1974) and *Time Zones* (1980) established formal metaphors for television and the geography of image making; Gillette's *Aransas: Axis of Observation* (1978) and *Oracle* (1981-83) expressed complex semiotic models for the ecology of the environment. Closed-circuit video, in which one can see immediately in real time what the camera is recording, was to be employed in a variety of forms in installations.

One of the key works Paik developed in 1965 was the *Magnet TV*, shown at his exhibition at the New School for Social Research in New York City. A large magnet was placed on the exterior of a television set; as the magnet was moved around, it generated interference with the electronic signal. The result was the distortion of received signals and the creation of abstract patterns of light on the screen's surface.

Paik's later sculpture/installations were to transform our customary view of the medium by creating powerful and witty metaphors that altered the entire viewing process and removed the medium from its customary contexts and function. In *TV Garden* (1974-78), approximately thirty television sets of all sizes were positioned in a darkened gallery space, surrounded by plants and TVs. As viewers entered the gallery and walked around the *TV Garden* they saw different groupings of video images as their point of view changed. Television sets were placed on their backs, sides, upside down, upright, partly covered by ferns and plants. The resulting video environment, or landscape, transformed the sets into a kind of electronic flora. On the sets the videotape *Global Groove* was displayed, a pulsating collage of images and sounds that had been created on the Paik-Abe Video Synthesizer, which layered and colorized pre-recorded images in dazzling displays of shapes and colors.

Schneider and Gillette's radical approach to video as communication system and ideology was shared by Juan Downey. With Gillette and Schneider, Downey was an original member of the Raindance collective. Together they explored what message the medium of video had the potential to deliver. Downey's *Plato Now* (1973), exhibited at the Everson Museum, Syracuse, New York, involved the spectator in the production process. The performers sat in meditation and attempted to produce alpha waves. Their brain activity would control the recurrence of pre-recorded quotations from Plato's dialogues. This fusion of the human brain with video suggested a biological metaphor for technology and created an engaging model of communication and dialogue. Downey was to continue in his installations and videotapes to explore culture (*Video Trans Americas*, 1976), the politics of representation in Western art (*The Looking Glass*, 1981), and the politics of global power (*The Chicago Boys*, 1984).

Bruce Nauman employed video in a fashion which reflected the origins of his aesthetic in minimalism and conceptual art. Nauman's *Corridor* (1969-70) is one of his best known works. Nauman found in video new options for expression not available within the conventional parameters of sculptural material or film. In *Corridor* we see a passageway perceived from, and mediated by, the video camera's viewpoint. This viewpoint shapes our perception of the space as a sculptural form and poses an epistemological inquiry into real time and space, and the flattening of that space (as information) on the monitors.

The strategy of turning the video camera onto a space and thus causing the viewer to perceive that space differently was part of a complex phenomenological inquiry into the ontology of materials and one's own presence when viewing, experiencing, the aesthetic text. Peter Campus, in a number of installations, including *mem* (1975), turned the video camera onto the body of the spectator and then projected the image of the spectator onto the gallery wall at an angle; the viewer was then confronted with a distorted and ambiguous image of himself mysteriously appearing in the darkness. In this and other works, such as his *Three Transitions* (1973), Campus employed the unique properties of video to create an evocative portrait and interpretation of the self. Campus's strategy is to place the viewer into the very artwork he is perceiving and thus invoke a vivid and reflexive self-encounter.

The transformation of reality through the medium of video has also been explored in Bill Viola's *He Weeps for You* (1977). In this work a closed-circuit video camera projects a close-up of water dripping from a pipe. This enlarged image is seen on a screen; and the sound of water slowly dripping is amplified. This richly poetic work takes a mundane object and in magnifying it into a large-scale image creates a vividly detailed and shocking presence. As with all of his art, including the videotapes *Chott el-Djerid* (1979) and *Hatsu Yume* (1981), Viola's attention to the mysterious in the ordinary and the sublime in the natural environment displays a potent visual sensibility and ability to create images that synthesize subject matter and video technique.

Concurrent with the projects which employed live closed-circuit video were multi-monitor and multi-channel installations in which artists utilized video to compose visual interpretations of places. One of the seminal works in this form of video was Beryl Korot's *Dachau 1974* (1975). A two-channel, four-monitor installation, it presented, in black and white videotape, a meditation on the Nazi concentration camp at Dachau. The silent images conveyed by the subtly unfolding perspectives and shifting points of view reveal the empty architectural shell of this institution of death. Korot's work effectively uses the medium's ability to articulate shifting points of view and imagery to depict a powerful landscape of desolation. By masking the monitor's dials, Korot has made the surface of the monitor's screen the focus of our attention and has stripped the video image of the connotations of the television set.

Shigeko Kubota's *Three Mountains* (1977-79) employs a subtle interpretation and treatment of the monitor within an allegorical sculptural form. *Three Mountains* presents three elaborations on the form of a mountain. Within these angular structures are fitted monitor screens whose images of desert and mountain landscapes of the American Southwest are doubled and distorted into a variety of prismatic patterns. Situated in front of the two larger pieces is a truncated triangular shape. By leaning forward and looking into its center, the viewer can observe a pool of video images. This action by the viewer is similar to looking over a rocky ledge or into a stream, but in this instance one can see rectangles of video imagery that are reflected among actual rocks placed on the mirrored surface.

The strength of these structures rests partly on their scale and partly on their physical angularity, which does not imitate mountains but instead creates a subtle metaphorical experience in which video appears as fissures in the wood's surface. As in a Japanese or Romantic landscape these pieces conjure up images of terrains past and present, with openings like crystalline deposits at the base of the mountains in which we see evoked the video impressions of the landscape. Kubota refers in her writing to the ancient geological land bridge between the Asian and North American continents as a source of spiritual and linguistic inter-relationship between herself and the Native Americans of the South-west. Looking at this video sculpture one perceives in action the dialec-tical process of two cultures expressed in a total sculptural *gestalt* be-tween the technology of video images and the material structures of the sculptures.

The last two works I shall discuss demonstrate how contemporary video artists are simultaneously engaging the latest technologies of video production techniques and capabilities while focusing on issues central to video art-making. By using commercial television as a source of imagery, Dara Birnbaum's *P.M. Magazine* (1982) articulated a pow-erful critique of television's overt and hidden agendas. In this vivid fusion of television commercials and popular news programming Birnbaum creates a synthesized and dialectical approach to the seduc-tive and subliminally sexist subtext of commercial television.

In Birnbaum's videotapes, which are the basis of the *P.M. Magazine* installation, she refashions television's popular images through a vari-ety of editing and image processing strategies to expose the hidden meanings within narrative and commercial programs. The three panels into which the monitors are inserted each present a static image from the videotapes which, in their juxtaposition with the moving images contribute to a layered text of meanings. The pulsating action of the commercials and the introductions to the *P.M. Magazine* program con-trasts with the illusory two-dimensional space of the photograph. This kaleidoscopic juxtaposition of sound and word and image, both frozen and moving, not only creates a complex visual surface, but exposes the dark side of broadcast television. *P.M. Magazine* thus engages the issues of representation in television entertainment and advertising.

Mary Lucier's *Ohio at Giverny* (1983) is a lyrical and eloquent evoca-tion of two landscapes which fuses her birthplace in Ohio to Monet's garden in Giverny, France. The two sites are joined into a visually com-pelling evocation of place and time. Lucier places her monitors into a series, framed by a walled surface which masks the dials of the moni-tors' display; on this white wall several different-sized screens jux-taposed in different positions display two channels of video. A sound-track composed by Earl Howard resonates through the space as images of flowers, fields, streets, and houses are joined in a work of hypnotic power. *Ohio at Giverny* uses movement and time, through the jux-taposition of monitors and image sequences, to create a genuine video landscape that confronts and challenges conventional notions of painting and sculpture.

This brief description of these eleven individual projects outlines the first twenty years of video art's history through the variety of forms and issues expressed in installation and sculptural work. To chart video art's distinctive features we must first recognize that that history is defined by many artists and individual artworks. By commenting on these works, we can identify a body of work that, although it has yet to be fully examined, has already challenged critical and historical interpretations of twentieth century art. It is a medium that is constantly evolving through the development of its technologies and the changing aesthetics of its artists. As the post-industrial, technologized age creates a new paradigm for our culture the home viewer and the gallery goer are confronted by changing home entertainment and a transformed museum exhibition space. Just as the industrial revolution introduced photography and film, so the age of electronic technology has brought forth video. The future of this medium will affect how we perceive the world around us and ultimately how we refashion and preserve it. The artist, forever participating in and charting change, will create new works and ideas from the resources of his/her vision, the critical debates surrounding its history, and the future forms that the "moving image" technologies will take in our society/culture.

NOTES
1. Rosalyn Deutsche and Cara Gendel Ryan. "The Fine Art of Gentrification." *October* 31 (Winter 1984): 91-111.
2. Standish Lawder. *The Cubist Cinema*. (New York: New York University Press, 1975), p. 36.
3. Ibid., p. 188.
4. Annette Michelson. *"The Man with the Movie Camera:* From Magician to Epistemologist," *Artforum* (March 1972): 66.
5. Ibid., p. 69.
6. Maya Deren, quoted in P. Adams Sitney, *Visionary Film: The American Avant-Garde*. (New York: Oxford University Press, 1974), p. 9.
7. Ibid.

THEORY AND PRACTICE

The Work of Art in the Age of Mechanical Reproduction

Walter Benjamin

Our fine arts were developed, their types and uses were established, in times very different from the present, by men whose power of action upon things was insignificant in comparison with ours. But the amazing growth of our techniques, the adaptability and precision they have attained, the ideas and habits they are creating, make it a certainty that profound changes are impending in the ancient craft of the Beautiful. In all the arts there is a physical component which can no longer be considered or treated as it used to be, which cannot remain unaffected by our modern knowledge and power. For the last twenty years neither matter nor space nor time has been what it was from time immemorial. We must expect great innovations to transform the entire technique of the arts, thereby affecting artistic invention itself and perhaps even bringing about an amazing change in our very notion of art. [1]

—Paul Valéry, *Pièces sur l'Art*,
"La Conquète de l'ubiquité," Paris.

Preface

When Marx undertook his critique of the capitalistic mode of production, this mode was in its infancy. Marx directed his efforts in such a way as to give them prognostic value. He went back to the basic conditions underlying capitalistic production and through his presentation showed what could be expected of capitalism in the future. The result was that one could expect it not only to exploit the proletariat with increasing intensity, but ultimately to create conditions which would make it possible to abolish capitalism itself.

The transformation of the superstructure, which takes place far more slowly than that of the substructure, has taken more than half a century to manifest in all areas of culture the change in the conditions of production. Only today can it be indicated what form this has taken. Certain prognostic requirements should be met by these statements. However, theses about the art of the proletariat after its assumption of power or about the art of a classless society would have less bearing on these demands than theses about the developmental tendencies of art under present conditions of production. Their dialectic is no less noticeable in the superstructure than in the economy. It would therefore be wrong to underestimate the value of such theses as a weapon. They brush aside a number of outmoded concepts, such as creativity and genius, eternal value and mystery—concepts whose uncontrolled (and at present almost uncontrollable) application would lead to a processing of data in the fascist sense. The concepts which are introduced into the theory of art in what follows differ from the more familiar terms in that they are completely useless for the purposes of fascism. They are, on the other hand, useful for the formulation of revolutionary demands in the politics of art.

I

In principle a work of art has always been reproducible. Man-made artifacts could always be imitated by men. Replicas were made by pupils in practice of their craft, by masters for diffusing their works, and, finally, by third parties in the pursuit of gain. Mechanical reproduction of a work of art, however, represents something new. Historically, it advanced intermittently and in leaps at long intervals, but with accelerated intensity. The Greeks knew only two procedures of technically reproducing the works of art: founding and stamping. Bronzes, terra cottas, and coins were the only art works which they could produce in quantity. All others were unique and could not be mechanically reproduced. With the woodcut graphic art became mechanically reproducible for the first time, long before script became reproducible by print. The enormous changes which printing, the mechanical reproduction of writing, has brought about in literature are a familiar story. However, within the phenomenon which we are here examining from the perspective of world history, print is merely a special, though particularly important, case. During the Middle Ages engraving and etching were added to the woodcut; at the beginning of the nineteenth century lithography made its appearance.

With lithography the technique of reproduction reached an essentially new stage. This much more direct process was distinguished by the tracing of the design on a stone rather than its incision on a block of wood or its etching on a copperplate and permitted graphic art for the first time to put its products on the market, not only in large numbers as hitherto, but also in daily changing forms. Lithography enabled graphic art to illustrate everyday life, and it began to keep pace with printing. But only a few decades after its invention, lithography was surpassed by photography. For the first time in the process of pictorial reproduction, photography freed the hand of the most important artistic functions which henceforth devolved only upon the eye looking into a lens. Since the eye perceives more swiftly than the hand can draw, the process of pictorial reproduction was accelerated so enormously that it could keep pace with speech. A film operator shooting a scene in the studio captures the images at the speed of an actor's speech. Just as lithography virtually implied the illustrated newspaper, so did photography foreshadow the sound film. The technical reproduction of sound was tackled at the end of the last century. These convergent endeavors made predictable a situation which Paul Valéry pointed up in this sentence: "Just as water, gas, and electricity are brought into our houses from far off to satisfy our needs in response to a minimal effort, so we shall be supplied with visual or auditory images, which will appear and disappear at a simple movement of the hand, hardly more than a sign."[2] Around 1900 technical reproduction had reached a standard that not only permitted it to reproduce all transmitted works of art and thus to cause the most profound change in their impact upon the public; it also had captured a place of its own among the artistic processes. For the study of this standard nothing is more revealing than the nature of the repercussions that these two different manifestations—the reproduction of works of art and the art of the film—have had on art in its traditional form.

II

Even the most perfect reproduction of a work of art is lacking in one element: its presence in time and space, its unique existence at the place where it happens to be. This unique existence of the work of art determined the history to which it was subject throughout the time of its existence. This includes the changes which it may have suffered in physical condition over the years as well as the various changes in its ownership.[3] The traces of the first can be revealed only by chemical or physical analyses which it is impossible to perform on a reproduction; changes of ownership are subject to a tradition which must be traced from the situation of the original.

The presence of the original is the prerequisite to the concept of authenticity. Chemical analyses of the patina of a bronze can help to establish this, as does the proof that a given manuscript of the Middle

Ages stems from an archive of the fifteenth century. The whole sphere of authenticity is outside technical—and, of course, not only technical—reproducibility.[4] Confronted with its manual reproduction, which was usually branded as a forgery, the original preserved all its authority; not so *vis à vis* technical reproduction. The reason is twofold. First, process reproduction is more independent of the original than manual reproduction. For example, in photography, process reproduction can bring out those aspects of the original that are unattainable to the naked eye yet accessible to the lens, which is adjustable and chooses its angle at will. And photographic reproduction, with the aid of certain processes, such as enlargement or slow motion, can capture images which escape natural vision. Secondly, technical reproduction can put the copy of the original into situations which would be out of reach for the original itself. Above all, it enables the original to meet the beholder halfway, be it in the form of a photograph or a phonograph record. The cathedral leaves its locale to be received in the studio of a lover of art; the choral production, performed in an auditorium or in the open air, resounds in the drawing room.

The situations into which the product of mechanical reproduction can be brought may not touch the actual work of art, yet the quality of its presence is always depreciated. This holds not only for the art work but also, for instance, for a landscape which passes in review before the spectator in a movie. In the case of the art object, a most sensitive nucleus—namely, its authenticity—is interfered with whereas no natural object is vulnerable on that score. The authenticity of a thing is the essence of all that is transmissible from its beginning, ranging from its substantive duration to its testimony to the history which it has experienced. Since the historical testimony rests on the authenticity, the former, too, is jeopardized by reproduction when substantive duration ceases to matter. And what is really jeopardized when the historical testimony is affected is the authority of the object.[5]

One might subsume the eliminated element in the term "aura" and go on to say: that which withers in the age of mechanical reproduction is the aura of the work of art. This is a symptomatic process whose significance points beyond the realm of art. One might generalize by saying: the technique of reproduction detaches the reproduced object from the domain of tradition. By making many reproductions it substitutes a plurality of copies for a unique existence. And in permitting the reproduction to meet the beholder or listener in his own particular situation, it reactivates the object reproduced. These two processes lead to a tremendous shattering of tradition which is the obverse of the contemporary crisis and renewal of mankind. Both processes are intimately connected with the contemporary mass movements. Their most powerful agent is the film. Its social significance, particularly in its most positive form, is inconceivable without its destructive, cathartic aspect, that is, the liquidation of the traditional value of the cultural heritage. This phenomenon is most palpable in the great historical films. It extends to ever new positions. In 1927 Abel Gance exclaimed enthusiastically: "Shakespeare, Rembrandt, Beethoven will make films ... all legends, all mythologies and all myths, all founders of religion, and the very religions ... await their exposed resurrection, and the heroes crowd each other at the gate."[6] Presumably without intending it, he issued an invitation to a far-reaching liquidation.

III

During long periods of history, the mode of human sense perception changes with humanity's entire mode of existence. The manner in which human sense perception is organized, the medium in which it is accomplished, is determined not only by nature but by historical circumstances as well. The fifth century, with its great shifts of population, saw the birth of the late Roman art industry and the Vienna Genesis, and there developed not only an art different from that of antiquity but also a new kind of perception. The scholars of the Viennese school, Riegl and Wickhoff, who resisted the weight of classical tradition under which these later art forms had been buried, were the first to draw conclusions from them concerning the organization of perception at the time. However far-reaching their insight, these scholars limited themselves to showing the significant, formal hallmark which characterized perception in late Roman times. They did not attempt—and, perhaps, saw no way—to show the social transformations expressed by these changes of perception. The conditions for an analogous insight are more favorable in the present. And if changes in the medium of contemporary perception can be comprehended as decay of the aura, it is possible to show its social causes.

The concept of aura which was proposed above with reference to historical objects may usefully be illustrated with reference to the aura of natural ones. We define the aura of the latter as the unique phenomenon of a distance, however close it may be. If, while resting on a summer afternoon, you follow with your eyes a mountain range on the horizon or a branch which casts its shadow over you, you experience the aura of those mountains, of that branch. This image makes it easy to comprehend the social bases of the contemporary decay of the aura. It rests on two circumstances, both of which are related to the increasing significance of the masses in contemporary life. Namely, the desire of contemporary masses to bring things "closer" spatially and humanly, which is just as ardent as their bent toward overcoming the uniqueness of every reality by accepting its reproduction.[7] Every day the urge grows stronger to get hold of an object at very close range by way of its likeness, its reproduction. Unmistakably, reproduction as offered by picture magazines and newsreels differs from the image seen by the un-armed eye. Uniqueness and permanence are as closely linked in the lat-ter as are transitoriness and reproducibility in the former. To pry an ob-ject from its shell, to destroy its aura, is the mark of a perception whose "sense of the universal equality of things" has increased to such a de-gree that it extracts it even from a unique object by means of reproduc-tion. Thus is manifested in the field of perception what in the theoreti-cal sphere is noticeable in the increasing importance of statistics. The adjustment of reality to the masses and of the masses to reality is a pro-cess of unlimited scope, as much for thinking as for perception.

IV

The uniqueness of a work of art is inseparable from its being imbedded in the fabric of tradition. This tradition itself is thoroughly alive and ex-tremely changeable. An ancient statue of Venus, for example, stood in a different traditional context with the Greeks, who made it an object of veneration, than with the clerics of the Middle Ages, who viewed it as an ominous idol. Both of them, however, were equally confronted with its uniqueness, that is, its aura. Originally the contextual integration of art in tradition found its expression in the cult. We know that the ear-liest art works originated in the service of a ritual—first the magical, then the religious kind. It is significant that the existence of the work of art with reference to its aura is never entirely separated from its ritual function.[8] In other words, the unique value of the "authentic" work of art has its basis in ritual, the location of its original use value. This ritualistic basis, however remote, is still recognizable as secularized ritual even in the most profane forms of the cult of beauty.[9] The secular cult of beauty, developed during the Renaissance and prevailing for three centuries, clearly showed that ritualistic basis in its decline and the first deep crisis which befell it. With the advent of the first truly rev-olutionary means of reproduction, photography, simultaneously with the rise of socialism, art sensed the approaching crisis which has be-come evident a century later. At the time, art reacted with the doctrine of *l'art pour l'art*, that is, with a theology of art. This gave rise to what might be called a negative theology in the form of the idea of "pure" art, which not only denied any social function of art but also any categorizing by subject matter. (In poetry, Mallarmé was the first to take this position.)

An analysis of art in the age of mechanical reproduction must do justice to these relationships, for they lead us to an all-important insight: for the first time in world history, mechanical reproduction emancipates the work of art from its parasitical dependence on ritual. To an ever greater degree the work of art reproduced becomes the work of art designed for reproducibility.[10] From a photographic negative, for example, one can make any number of prints; to ask for the "authentic" print makes no sense. But the instant the criterion of authenticity ceases to be applicable to artistic production, the total function of art is reversed. Instead of being based on ritual, it begins to be based on another practice—politics.

V

Works of art are received and valued on different planes. Two polar types stand out: with one, the accent is on the cult value; with the other, on the exhibition value of the work.[11] Artistic production begins with ceremonial objects destined to serve in a cult. One may assume that what mattered was their existence, not their being on view. The elk portrayed by the man of the Stone Age on the walls of his cave was an instrument of magic. He did expose it to his fellow men, but in the main it was meant for the spirits. Today the cult value would seem to demand that the work of art remain hidden. Certain statues of gods are accessible only to the priest in the cella; certain Madonnas remain covered nearly all year round; certain sculptures on medieval cathedrals are invisible to the spectator on ground level. With the emancipation of the various art practices from ritual go increasing opportunities for the exhibition of their products. It is easier to exhibit a portrait bust that can be sent here and there than to exhibit the statue of a divinity that has its fixed place in the interior of a temple. The same holds for the painting as against the mosaic or fresco that preceded it. And even though the public presentability of a mass originally may have been just as great as that of a symphony, the latter originated at the moment when its public presentability promised to surpass that of the mass.

With the different methods of technical reproduction of a work of art, its fitness for exhibition increased to such an extent that the quantitative shift between its two poles turned into a qualitative transformation of its nature. This is comparable to the situation of the work of art in prehistoric times when, by the absolute emphasis on its cult value, it was, first and foremost, an instrument of magic. Only later did it come to be recognized as a work of art. In the same way today, by the absolute emphasis on its exhibition value the work of art becomes a creation with entirely new functions, among which the one we are conscious of, the artistic function, later may be recognized as incidental.[12] This much is certain: today photography and the film are the most serviceable exemplifications of this new function.

VI

In photography, exhibition value begins to displace cult value all along the line. But cult value does not give way without resistance. It retires into an ultimate retrenchment: the human countenance. It is no accident that the portrait was the focal point of early photography. The cult of remembrance of loved ones, absent or dead, offers a last refuge for the cult value of the picture. For the last time the aura emanates from the early photographs in the fleeting expression of a human face. This is what constitutes their melancholy, incomparable beauty. But as man withdraws from the photographic image, the exhibition value for the first time shows its superiority to the ritual value. To have pinpointed this new stage constitutes the incomparable significance of Atget, who, around 1900, took photographs of deserted Paris streets. It has quite justly been said of him that he photographed them like scenes of crime. The scene of a crime, too, is deserted; it is photographed for the purpose of establishing evidence. With Atget, photographs become standard evidence for historical occurrences, and acquire a hidden political significance. They demand a specific kind of approach; free-floating contemplation is not appropriate to them. They stir the viewer; he feels challenged by them in a new way. At the same time picture magazines begin to put up signposts for him, right ones or wrong ones, no matter. For the first time, captions have become obligatory. And it is clear that they have an altogether different character than the title of a painting. The directives which the captions give to those looking at pictures in illustrated magazines soon become even more explicit and more imperative in the film where the meaning of each single picture appears to be prescribed by the sequence of all preceding ones.

VII

The nineteenth-century dispute as to the artistic value of painting versus photography today seems devious and confused. This does not diminish its importance, however; if anything, it underlines it. The dispute was in fact the symptom of a historical transformation the universal impact of which was not realized by either of the rivals. When the age of mechanical reproduction separated art from its basis in cult, the semblance of its autonomy disappeared forever. The resulting change in the function of art transcended the perspective of the century; for a long time it even escaped that of the twentieth century, which experienced the development of the film.

Earlier much futile thought had been devoted to the question of whether photography is an art. The primary question—whether the very invention of photography had not transformed the entire nature of art—was not raised. Soon the film theoreticians asked the same ill-considered question with regard to the film. But the difficulties which photography caused traditional aesthetics were mere child's play as compared to those raised by the film. Whence the insensitive and forced character of early theories of the film. Abel Gance, for instance, compares the film with hieroglyphs: "Here, by a remarkable regression, we have come back to the level of expression of the Egyptians. . . . Pictorial language has not yet matured because our eyes have not yet adjusted to it. There is as yet insufficient respect for, insufficient cult of, what it expresses." [13] Or, in the words of Séverin-Mars: "What art has been granted a dream more poetical and more real at the same time! Approached in this fashion the film might represent an incomparable means of expression. Only the most high-minded persons, in the most perfect and mysterious moments of their lives, should be allowed to enter its ambience." [14] Alexandre Arnoux concludes his fantasy about the silent film with the question: "Do not all the bold descriptions we have given amount to the definition of prayer?" [15] It is instructive to note how their desire to class the film among the "arts" forces these theoreticians to read ritual elements into it—with a striking lack of discretion. Yet when these speculations were published, films like *L'Opinion publique* and *The Gold Rush* had already appeared. This, however, did not keep Abel Gance from adducing hieroglyphs for purposes of comparison, nor Séverin-Mars from speaking of the film as one might speak of paintings by Fra Angelico. Characteristically, even today ultrareactionary authors give the film a similar contextual significance —if not an outright sacred one, then at least a supernatural one. Commenting on Max Reinhardt's film version of *A Midsummer Night's Dream*, Werfel states that undoubtedly it was the sterile copying of the exterior world with its streets, interiors, railroad stations, restaurants, motorcars, and beaches which until now had obstructed the elevation of the film into the realm of art. "The film has not yet realized its true meaning, its real possibilities . . . these consist in its unique faculty to express by natural means and with incomparable persuasiveness all that is fairylike, marvelous, supernatural."[16]

VIII

The artistic performance of a stage actor is definitely presented to the public by the actor in person; that of the screen actor, however, is presented by a camera, with a twofold consequence. The camera that presents the performance of the film actor to the public need not respect the performance as an integral whole. Guided by the cameraman, the camera continually changes its position with respect to the performance. The sequence of positional views which the editor composes from the material supplied him constitutes the completed film. It comprises certain factors of movement which are in reality those of the camera, not to mention special camera angles, close-ups, etc. Hence, the performance of the actor is subjected to a series of optical tests. This is the first consequence of the fact that the actor's performance is presented by means of a camera. Also, the film actor lacks the opportunity of the stage actor to adjust to the audience during his performance, since he does not present his performance to the audience in person. This permits the audience to take the position of a critic, without experiencing any personal contact with the actor. The audience's identification with the actor is really an identification with the camera. Consequently the audience takes the position of the camera; its approach is that of testing.[17] This is not the approach to which cult values may be exposed.

IX

For the film, what matters primarily is that the actor represents himself to the public before the camera, rather than representing someone else. One of the first to sense the actor's metamorphosis by this form of testing was Pirandello. Though his remarks on the subject in his novel *Si Gira* were limited to the negative aspects of the question and to the silent film only, this hardly impairs their validity. For in this respect, the sound film did not change anything essential. What matters is that the part is acted not for an audience but for a mechanical contrivance—in the case of the sound film, for two of them. "The film actor," wrote Pirandello, "feels as if in exile—exiled not only from the stage but also from himself. With a vague sense of discomfort he feels inexplicable emptiness: his body loses its corporeality, it evaporates, it is deprived of reality, life, voice, and the noises caused by his moving about, in order to be changed into a mute image, flickering an instant on the screen, then vanishing into silence. . . . The projector will play with his shadow before the public, and he himself must be content to play before the camera."[18] This situation might also be characterized as follows: for the first time—and this is the effect of the film—man has to operate with his whole living person, yet foregoing its aura. For aura is tied to his presence; there can be no replica of it. The aura which, on the stage, emanates from Macbeth, cannot be separated for the spectators from that of the actor. However, the singularity of the shot in the studio is that the camera is substituted for the public. Consequently, the aura that envelopes the actor vanishes, and with it the aura of the figure he portrays.

It is not surprising that it should be a dramatist such as Pirandello who, in characterizing the film, inadvertently touches on the very crisis in which we see the theater. Any thorough study proves that there is indeed no greater contrast than that of the stage play to a work of art that is completely subject to or, like the film, founded in, mechanical reproduction. Experts have long recognized that in the film "the greatest effects are almost always obtained by 'acting' as little as possible. . . ." In 1932 Rudolf Arnheim saw "the latest trend . . . in treating the actor as a stage prop chosen for its characteristics and . . . inserted at the proper place."[19] With this idea something else is closely connected. The stage actor identifies himself with the character of his role. The film actor very often is denied this opportunity. His creation is by no means all of a piece; it is composed of many separate performances. Besides certain fortuitous considerations, such as cost of studio, availability of fellow players, décor, etc., there are elementary necessities of equipment that split the actor's work into a series of mountable episodes. In particular, lighting and its installation require the presentation of an event that, on the screen, unfolds as a rapid and unified scene, in a sequence of separate shootings which may take hours at the studio; not to mention more obvious montage. Thus a jump from the window can be shot in the studio as a jump from a scaffold, and the ensuing flight, if need be, can be shot weeks later when outdoor scenes are taken. Far more paradoxical cases can easily be construed. Let us assume that an actor is supposed to be startled by a knock at the door. If his reaction is not satisfactory, the director can resort to an expedient: when the actor happens to be at the studio again he has a shot fired behind him without his being forewarned of it. The frightened reaction can be shot now and be cut into the screen version. Nothing more strikingly shows that art has left the realm of the "beautiful semblance" which, so far, had been taken to be the only sphere where art could thrive.

X

The feeling of strangeness that overcomes the actor before the camera, as Pirandello describes it, is basically of the same kind as the estrangement felt before one's own image in the mirror. But now the reflected image has become separable, transportable. And where is it transported? Before the public.[20] Never for a moment does the screen actor cease to be conscious of this fact. While facing the camera he knows that ultimately he will face the public, the consumers who constitute the market. This market, where he offers not only his labor but also his whole self, his heart and soul, is beyond his reach. During the shooting he has as little contact with it as any article made in a factory. This may contribute to that oppression, that new anxiety which, according to Pirandello, grips the actor before the camera. The film responds to the shriveling of the aura with an artificial build-up of the "personality" outside the studio. The cult of the movie star, fostered by the money of the film industry, preserves not the unique aura of the person but the "spell of the personality," the phony spell of a commodity. So long as the movie-makers' capital sets the fashion, as a rule no other revolutionary merit can be accredited to today's film than the promotion of a revolutionary criticism of traditional concepts of art. We do not deny that in some cases today's films can also promote revolutionary criticism of social conditions, even of the distribution of property. However, our present study is no more specifically concerned with this than is the film production of Western Europe.

It is inherent in the technique of the film as well as that of sports that everybody who witnesses its accomplishments is somewhat of an expert. This is obvious to anyone listening to a group of newspaper boys leaning on their bicycles and discussing the outcome of a bicycle race. It is not for nothing that newspaper publishers arrange races for their delivery boys. These arouse great interest among the participants, for the victor has an opportunity to rise from delivery boy to professional racer. Similarly, the newsreel offers everyone the opportunity to rise from passer-by to movie extra. In this way any man might even find himself part of a work of art, as witness Vertov's *Three Songs About Lenin* or Ivens's *Borinage*. Any man today can lay claim to being filmed. This claim can best be elucidated by a comparative look at the historical situation of contemporary literature.

For centuries a small number of writers were confronted by many thousands of readers. This changed toward the end of the last century. With the increasing extension of the press, which kept placing new political, religious, scientific, professional, and local organs before the readers, an increasing number of readers became writers—at first, occasional ones. It began with the daily press opening to its readers space for "letters to the editor." And today there is hardly a gainfully employed European who could not, in principle, find an opportunity to publish somewhere or other comments on his work, grievances, documentary reports, or that sort of thing. Thus, the distinction between author and public is about to lose its basic character. The difference becomes merely functional; it may vary from case to case. At any moment the reader is ready to turn into a writer. As expert, which he had to become willy-nilly in an extremely specialized work process, even if only in some minor respect, the reader gains access to authorship. In the Soviet Union work itself is given a voice. To present it verbally is part of a man's ability to perform the work. Literary license is now founded on polytechnic rather than specialized training and thus becomes common property.[21]

All this can easily be applied to the film, where transitions that in literature took centuries have come about in a decade. In cinematic practice, particularly in Russia, this change-over has partially become established reality. Some of the players whom we meet in Russian films are not actors in our sense but people who portray *themselves*—and primarily in their own work process. In Western Europe the capitalistic exploitation of the film denies consideration to modern man's legitimate claim to being reproduced. Under these circumstances the film industry is trying hard to spur the interest of the masses through illusion-promoting spectacles and dubious speculations.

XI

The shooting of a film, especially of a sound film, affords a spectacle unimaginable anywhere at any time before this. It presents a process in which it is impossible to assign to a spectator a viewpoint which would exclude from the actual scene such extraneous accessories as camera equipment, lighting machinery, staff assistants, etc.—unless his eye were on a line parallel with the lens. This circumstance, more than any other, renders superficial and insignificant any possible similarity between a scene in the studio and one on the stage. In the theater one is well aware of the place from which the play cannot immediately be detected as illusionary. There is no such place for the movie scene that is being shot. Its illusionary nature is that of the second degree, the result of cutting. That is to say, in the studio the mechanical equipment has penetrated so deeply into reality that its pure aspect freed from the foreign substance of equipment is the result of a special procedure, namely, the shooting by the specially adjusted camera and the mounting of the shot together with other similar ones. The equipment-free aspect of reality here has become the height of artifice; the sight of immediate reality has become an orchid in the land of technology.

Even more revealing is the comparison of these circumstances, which differ so much from those of the theater, with the situation in painting. Here the question is: How does the cameraman compare with the painter? To answer this we take recourse to an analogy with a surgical operation. The surgeon represents the polar opposite of the magician. The magician heals a sick person by the laying on of hands; the surgeon cuts into the patient's body. The magician maintains the natural distance between the patient and himself; though he reduces it very slightly by the laying on of hands, he greatly increases it by virtue of his authority. The surgeon does exactly the reverse; he greatly diminishes the distance between himself and the patient by penetrating into the patient's body, and increases it but little by the caution with which his hands move among the organs. In short, in contrast to the magician— who is still hidden in the medical practitioner—the surgeon at the decisive moment abstains from facing the patient man to man; rather, it is through the operation that he penetrates into him.

Magician and surgeon compare to painter and cameraman. The painter maintains in his work a natural distance from reality, the cameraman penetrates deeply into its web.[22] There is a tremendous difference between the pictures they obtain. That of the painter is a total one, that of the cameraman consists of multiple fragments which are assembled under a new law. Thus, for contemporary man the representation of reality by the film is incomparably more significant than that of the painter, since it offers, precisely because of the thoroughgoing permeation of reality with mechanical equipment, an aspect of reality which is free of all equipment. And that is what one is entitled to ask from a work of art.

XII

Mechanical reproduction of art changes the reaction of the masses toward art. The reactionary attitude toward a Picasso painting changes into the progressive reaction toward a Chaplin movie. The progressive reaction is characterized by the direct, intimate fusion of visual and emotional enjoyment with the orientation of the expert. Such fusion is of great social significance. The greater the decrease in the social significance of an art form, the sharper the distinction between criticism and enjoyment by the public. The conventional is uncritically enjoyed, and the truly new is criticized with aversion. With regard to the screen, the critical and the receptive attitudes of the public coincide. The decisive reason for this is that individual reactions are predetermined by the mass audience response they are about to produce, and this is nowhere more pronounced than in the film. The moment these responses become manifest they control each other. Again, the comparison with painting is fruitful. A painting has always had an excellent chance to be viewed by one person or by a few. The simultaneous contemplation of paintings by a large public, such as developed in the nineteenth century, is an early symptom of the crisis of painting, a crisis which was by no means occasioned exclusively by photography but rather in a relatively independent manner by the appeal of art works to the masses.

Painting simply is in no position to present an object for simultaneous collective experience, as it was possible for architecture at all times, for the epic poem in the past, and for the movie today. Although this circumstance in itself should not lead one to conclusions about the social role of painting, it does constitute a serious threat as soon as painting, under special conditions and, as it were, against its nature, is confronted directly by the masses. In the churches and monasteries of the Middle Ages and at the princely courts up to the end of the eighteenth century, a collective reception of paintings did not occur simultaneously, but by graduated and hierarchized mediation. The change that has come about is an expression of the particular conflict in which painting was implicated by the mechanical reproducibility of paintings. Although paintings began to be publicly exhibited in galleries and salons, there was no way for the masses to organize and control themselves in their reception.[23] Thus the same public which responds in a progressive manner toward a grotesque film is bound to respond in a reactionary manner to surrealism.

XIII

The characteristics of the film lie not only in the manner in which man presents himself to mechanical equipment but also in the manner in which, by means of this apparatus, man can represent his environment. A glance at occupational psychology illustrates the testing capacity of the equipment. Psychoanalysis illustrates it in a different perspective. The film has enriched our field of perception with methods which can be illustrated by those of Freudian theory. Fifty years ago, a slip of the tongue passed more or less unnoticed. Only exceptionally may such a slip have revealed dimensions of depth in a conversation which had seemed to be taking its course on the surface. Since the *Psychopathology of Everyday Life* things have changed. This book isolated and made analyzable things which had heretofore floated along unnoticed in the broad stream of perception. For the entire spectrum of optical, and now also acoustical, perception the film has brought about a similar deepening of apperception. It is only an obverse of this fact that behavior items shown in a movie can be analyzed much more precisely and from more points of view than those presented on paintings or on the stage. As compared with painting, filmed behavior lends itself more readily to analysis because of its incomparably more precise statements of the situation. In comparison with the stage scene, the filmed behavior item lends itself more readily to analysis because it can be isolated more easily. This circumstance derives its chief importance from its tendency to promote the mutual penetration of art and science. Actually, of a screened behavior item which is neatly brought out in a certain situation, like a muscle of a body, it is difficult to say which is more fascinating, its artistic value or its value for science. To demonstrate the identity of the artistic and scientific uses of photography which heretofore usually were separated will be one of the revolutionary functions of the film.[24]

By close-ups of the things around us, by focusing on hidden details of familiar objects, by exploring commonplace milieus under the ingenious guidance of the camera, the film, on the one hand, extends our comprehension of the necessities which rule our lives; on the other hand, it manages to assure us of an immense and unexpected field of action. Our taverns and our metropolitan streets, our offices and furnished rooms, our railroad stations and our factories appeared to have us locked up hopelessly. Then came the film and burst this prison-world asunder by the dynamite of the tenth of a second, so that now, in the midst of its far-flung ruins and debris, we calmly and adventurously go traveling. With the close-up, space expands; with slow motion, movement is extended. The enlargement of a snapshot does not simply render more precise what in any case was visible, though unclear: it reveals entirely new structural formations of the subject. So, too, slow motion not only presents familiar qualities of movement but reveals in them entirely unknown ones "which, far from looking like retarded rapid movements, give the effect of singularly gliding, floating, supernatural motions."[25] Evidently a different nature opens itself to the camera than opens to the naked eye—if only because an unconsciously penetrated space is substituted for a space consciously explored by man. Even if one has a general knowledge of the way people walk, one knows nothing of a person's posture during the fractional second of a stride. The act of reaching for a lighter or a spoon is familiar routine, yet we hardly know what really goes on between hand and metal, not to mention how this fluctuates with our moods. Here the camera intervenes with the resources of its lowerings and liftings, its interruptions and isolations, its extensions and accelerations, its enlargements and reductions. The camera introduces us to unconscious optics as does psychoanalysis to unconscious impulses.

XIV

One of the foremost tasks of art has always been the creation of a demand which could be fully satisfied only later.[26] The history of every art form shows critical epochs in which a certain art form aspires to effects which could be fully obtained only with a changed technical standard, that is to say, in a new art form. The extravagances and crudities of art which thus appear, particularly in the so-called decadent epochs, actually arise from the nucleus of its richest historical energies. In recent years, such barbarisms were abundant in dadaism. It is only now that its impulse becomes discernible: dadaism attempted to create by pictorial—and literary—means the effects which the public today seeks in the film.

Every fundamentally new, pioneering creation of demands will carry beyond its goal. Dadaism did so to the extent that it sacrificed the market values which are so characteristic of the film in favor of higher ambitions—though of course it was not conscious of such intentions as here described. The dadaists attached much less importance to the sales value of their work than to its uselessness for contemplative immersion. The studied degradation of their material was not the least of their means to achieve this uselessness. Their poems are "word salad" containing obscenities and every imaginable waste product of language. The same is true of their paintings, on which they mounted buttons and tickets. What they intended and achieved was a relentless destruction of the aura of their creations, which they branded as reproductions with the very means of production. Before a painting of Arp's or a poem by August Stramm it is impossible to take time for contemplation and evaluation as one would before a canvas of Derain's or a poem by Rilke. In the decline of middle-class society, contemplation became a school for asocial behavior; it was countered by distraction as a variant of social conduct.[27] Dadaistic activities actually assured a rather vehement distraction by making works of art the center of scandal. One requirement was foremost: to outrage the public.

From an alluring appearance or persuasive structure of sound the work of art of the dadaists became an instrument of ballistics. It hit the spectator like a bullet, it happened to him, thus acquiring a tactile quality. It promoted a demand for the film, the distracting element of which is also primarily tactile, being based on changes of place and focus which periodically assail the spectator. Let us compare the screen on which a film unfolds with the canvas of a painting. The painting invites the spectator to contemplation; before it the spectator can abandon himself to his associations. Before the movie frame he cannot do so. No sooner has his eye grasped a scene than it is already changed. It cannot be arrested. Duhamel, who detests the film and knows nothing of its significance, though something of its structure, notes this circumstance as follows: "I can no longer think what I want to think. My thoughts have been replaced by moving images."[28] The spectator's process of association in view of these images is indeed interrupted by their constant, sudden change. This constitutes the shock effect of the film, which, like all shocks, should be cushioned by heightened presence of mind.[29] By means of its technical structure, the film has taken the physical shock effect out of the wrappers in which dadaism had, as it were, kept it inside the moral shock effect.[30]

XV

The mass is a matrix from which all traditional behavior toward works of art issues today in a new form. Quantity has been transmuted into quality. The greatly increased mass of participants has produced a change in the mode of participation. The fact that the new mode of participation first appeared in a disreputable form must not confuse the spectator. Yet some people have launched spirited attacks against precisely this superficial aspect. Among these, Duhamel has expressed himself in the most radical manner. What he objects to most is the kind of participation which the movie elicits from the masses. Duhamel calls the movie "a pastime for helots, a diversion for uneducated, wretched, worn-out creatures who are consumed by their worries ..., a spectacle which requires no concentration and presupposes no intelligence ... which kindles no light in the heart and awakens no hope other than the ridiculous one of someday becoming a 'star' in Los Angeles."[31] Clearly, this is at bottom the same ancient lament that the masses seek distraction whereas art demands concentration from the spectator. That is a commonplace. The question remains whether it provides a platform for the analysis of the film. A closer look is needed here. Distraction and concentration form polar opposites which may be stated as follows: A man who concentrates before a work of art is absorbed by it. He enters into this work of art the way legend tells of the Chinese painter when he viewed his finished painting. In contrast, the distracted mass absorbs the work of art. This is most obvious with regard to buildings. Architecture has always represented the prototype of a work of art the reception of which is consummated by a collectivity in a state of distraction. The laws of its reception are most instructive.

Buildings have been man's companions since primeval times. Many art forms have developed and perished. Tragedy begins with the Greeks, is extinguished with them, and after centuries its "rules" only are revived. The epic poem, which had its origin in the youth of nations, expires in Europe at the end of the Renaissance. Panel painting is a creation of the Middle Ages, and nothing guarantees its uninterrupted existence. But the human need for shelter is lasting. Architecture has never been idle. Its history is more ancient than that of any other art, and its claim to being a living force has significance in every attempt to comprehend the relationship of the masses to art. Buildings are appropriated in a twofold manner: by use and by perception—or rather, by touch and sight. Such appropriation cannot be understood in terms of the attentive concentration of a tourist before a famous building. On the tactile side there is no counterpart to contemplation on the optical side. Tactile appropriation is accomplished not so much by attention as by habit. As regards architecture, habit determines to a large extent even optical reception. The latter, too, occurs much less through rapt attention than by noticing the object in incidental fashion. This mode of appropriation, developed with reference to architecture, in certain circumstances acquires canonical value. For the tasks which face the human apparatus of perception at the turning points of history cannot be solved by optical means, that is, by contemplation, alone. They are mastered gradually by habit, under the guidance of tactile appropriation.

The distracted person, too, can form habits. More, the ability to master certain tasks in a state of distraction proves that their solution has become a matter of habit. Distraction as provided by art presents a covert control of the extent to which new tasks have become soluble by apperception. Since, moreover, individuals are tempted to avoid such tasks, art will tackle the most difficult and most important ones where it is able to mobilize the masses. Today it does so in the film. Reception in a state of distraction, which is increasing noticeably in all fields of art and is symptomatic of profound changes in apperception, finds in the film its true means of exercise. The film with its shock effect meets this mode of reception halfway. The film makes the cult value recede into the background not only by putting the public in the position of the critic, but also by the fact that at the movies this position requires no attention. The public is an examiner, but an absent-minded one.

EPILOGUE

The growing proletarianization of modern man and the increasing formation of masses are two aspects of the same process. Fascism attempts
to organize the newly created proletarian masses without affecting the
property structure which the masses strive to eliminate. Fascism sees its
salvation in giving these masses not their right, but instead a chance to
express themselves.[32] The masses have a right to change property relations; fascism seeks to give them an expression while preserving property. The logical result of fascism is the introduction of aesthetics into
political life. The violation of the masses, whom fascism, with its *Führer*
cult, forces to their knees, has its counterpart in the violation of an apparatus which is pressed into the production of ritual values.

All efforts to render politics aesthetic culminate in one thing: war.
War and war only can set a goal for mass movements on the largest scale
while respecting the traditional property system. This is the political
formula for the situation. The technological formula may be stated as
follows: Only war makes it possible to mobilize all of today's technical
resources while maintaining the property system. It goes without saying
that the fascist apotheosis of war does not employ such arguments. Still,
Marinetti says in his manifesto on the Ethiopian colonial war: "For
twenty-seven years we Futurists have rebelled against the branding of
war as antiaesthetic. . . . Accordingly we state: . . . War is beautiful because it establishes man's dominion over the subjugated machinery by
means of gas masks, terrifying megaphones, flame throwers, and small
tanks. War is beautiful because it initiates the dreamt-of metalization of
the human body. War is beautiful because it enriches a flowering
meadow with the fiery orchids of machine guns. War is beautiful because it combines the gunfire, the cannonades, the cease-fire, the
scents, and the stench of putrefaction into a symphony. War is beautiful because it creates new architecture, like that of the big tanks, the
geometrical formation flights, the smoke spirals from burning villages,
and many others. . . . Poets and artists of Futurism! . . . remember these
principles of an aesthetics of war so that your struggle for a new literature and a new graphic art . . . may be illumined by them!"

This manifesto has the virtue of clarity. Its formulations deserve to be
accepted by dialecticians. To the latter, the aesthetics of today's war appears as follows: If the natural utilization of productive forces is im-
peded by the property system, the increase in technical devices, in
speed, and in the sources of energy will press for an unnatural utilization, and this is found in war. The destructiveness of war furnishes
proof that society has not been mature enough to incorporate technology as its organ, that technology has not been sufficiently developed to

cope with the elemental forces of society. The horrible features of imperialistic warfare are attributable to the discrepancy between the tremendous means of production and their inadequate utilization in the process of production—in other words, to unemployment and the lack of markets. Imperialistic war is a rebellion of technology which collects, in the form of "human material," the claims to which society has denied its natural material. Instead of draining rivers, society directs a human stream into a bed of trenches; instead of dropping seeds from airplanes, it drops incendiary bombs over cities; and through gas warfare the aura is abolished in a new way.

"*Fiat ars—pereat mundus,*" says fascism, and, as Marinetti admits, expects war to supply the artistic gratification of a sense perception that has been changed by technology. This is evidently the consummation of "*l'art pour l'art.*" Mankind, which in Homer's time was an object of contemplation for the Olympian gods, now is one for itself. Its self-alienation has reached such a degree that it can experience its own destruction as an aesthetic pleasure of the first order. This is the situation of politics which fascism is rendering aesthetic. Communism responds by politicizing art.

From *Illuminations*, Trans. Harry Zohn. New York: Schocken Books, 1969, pp. 217-251.

NOTES
1. Quoted from Paul Valéry, "The Conquest of Ubiquity," *Aesthetics*, trans. Ralph Manheim (New York: Pantheon Books, Bollingen Series, 1964), p. 225.
2. *Ibid.*, p. 226.
3. Of course, the history of a work of art encompasses more than this. The history of the *Mona Lisa*, for instance, encompasses the kind and number of its copies made in the seventeenth, eighteenth, and nineteenth centuries.
4. Precisely because authenticity is not reproducible, the intensive penetration of certain (mechanical) processes of reproduction was instrumental in differentiating and grading authenticity. To develop such differentiations was an important function of the trade in works of art. The invention of the woodcut may be said to have struck at the root of the quality of authenticity even before its late flowering. To be sure, at the time of its origin a medieval picture of the Madonna could not yet be said to be "authentic." It became "authentic" only during the succeeding centuries and perhaps most strikingly so during the last one.
5. The poorest provincial staging of *Faust* is superior to a Faust film in that, ideally, it competes with the first performance at Weimar. Before the screen it is unprofitable to remember traditional contents which might come to mind before the stage—for instance, that Goethe's friend Johann Heinrich Merck is hidden in Mephisto, and the like.
6. Abel Gance, "Le Temps de l'image est venu," *L'Art cinématographique* 2 (Paris, 1927), p. 94ff.
7. To satisfy the human interest of the masses may mean to have one's social function removed from the field of vision. Nothing guarantees that a portraitist of today,

when painting a famous surgeon at the breakfast table in the midst of his family, depicts his social function more precisely than a painter of the 17th century who portrayed his medical doctors as representing this profession, like Rembrandt in his *Anatomy Lesson.*

8. The definition of the aura as a "unique phenomenon of a distance however close it may be" represents nothing but the formulation of the cult value of the work of art in categories of space and time perception. Distance is the opposite of closeness. The essentially distant object is the unapproachable one. Unapproachability is indeed a major quality of the cult image. True to its nature, it remains "distant, however close it may be." The closeness which one may gain from its subject matter does not impair the distance which it retains in its appearance.

9. To the extent to which the cult value of the painting is secularized the ideas of its fundamental uniqueness lose distinctness. In the imagination of the beholder the uniqueness of the phenomena which hold sway in the cult image is more and more displaced by the empirical uniqueness of the creator or of his creative achievement. To be sure, never completely so; the concept of authenticity always transcends mere genuineness. (This is particularly apparent in the collector who always retains some traces of the fetishist and who, by owning the work of art, shares in its ritual power.) Nevertheless, the function of the concept of authenticity remains determinate in the evaluation of art; with the secularization of art, authenticity displaces the cult value of the work.

10. In the case of films, mechanical reproduction is not, as with literature and painting, an external condition for mass distribution. Mechanical reproduction is inherent in the very technique of film production. This technique not only permits in the most direct way but virtually causes mass distribution. It enforces distribution because the production of a film is so expensive that an individual who, for instance, might afford to buy a painting no longer can afford to buy a film. In 1927 it was calculated that a major film, in order to pay its way, had to reach an audience of nine million. With the sound film, to be sure, a setback in its international distribution occurred at first: audiences became limited by language barriers. This coincided with the fascist emphasis on national interests. It is more important to focus on this connection with fascism that on this setback, which was soon minimized by synchronization. The simultaneity of both phenomena is attributable to the Depression. The same disturbances which, on a larger scale, led to an attempt to maintain the existing property structure by sheer force led the endangered film capital to speed up the development of the sound film. The introduction of the sound film brought about a temporary relief, not only because it again brought the masses into the theaters but also because it merged new capital from the electrical industry with that of the film industry. Thus, viewed from the outside, the sound film promoted national interests, but seen from the inside it helped to internationalize film production even more than previously.

11. This polarity cannot come into its own in the aesthetics of Idealism. Its idea of beauty comprises these polar opposites without differentiating between them and consequently excludes their polarity. Yet in Hegel this polarity announces itself as clearly as possible within the limits of Idealism. We quote from his *Philosophy of History*: "Images were known of old. Piety at an early time required them for worship, but it could do without *beautiful* images. These might even be disturbing. In every beautiful painting there is also something nonspiritual, merely external, but its spirit speaks to man through its beauty.Worshipping, conversely, is concerned with the work as an object, for it is but a spiritless stupor of the soul. . . . Fine art has arisen . . . in the church . . ., although it has already gone beyond its principle as art." Likewise, the following passage from *The Philosophy of Fine Art* indicates that

Hegel sensed a problem here. "We are beyond the stage of reverence for works of art as divine and objects deserving our worship. The impression they produce is one of a more reflective kind, and the emotions they arouse require a higher test...." — G.W.F. Hegel, *The Philosophy of Fine Art*, trans., with notes, by F.P.B. Osmaston, Vol. 1 (London, 1920) p. 12.

The transition from the first kind of artistic reception to the second characterizes the history of artistic reception in general. Apart from that, a certain oscillation between these two polar modes of reception can be demonstrated for each work of art. Take the Sistine Madonna. Since Hubert Grimme's research it has been known that the Madonna originally was painted for the purpose of exhibition. Grimme's research was inspired by the question: What is the purpose of the molding in the foreground of the painting which the two cupids lean upon? How, Grimme asked further, did Raphael come to furnish the sky with two draperies? Research proved that the Madonna had been commissioned for the public lying-in-state of Pope Sixtus. The Popes lay in state in a certain side chapel of St. Peter's. On that occasion Raphael's picture had been fastened in a nichelike background of the chapel, supported by the coffin. In this picture Raphael portrays the Madonna approaching the papal coffin in clouds from the background of the niche, which was demarcated by green drapes. At the obsequies of Sixtus a pre-eminent exhibition value of Raphael's picture was taken advantage of. Some time later it was placed on the high altar in the church of the Black Friars at Piacenza. The reason for this exile is to be found in the Roman rites which forbid the use of paintings exhibited at obsequies as cult objects on the high altar. This regulation devalued Raphael's picture to some degree. In order to obtain an adequate price nevertheless, the Papal See resolved to add to the bargain the tacit toleration of the picture above the high altar. To avoid attention the picture was given to the monks of the far-off provincial town.

12. Bertolt Brecht, on a different level, engaged in analogous reflections: "If the concept of 'work of art' can no longer be applied to the thing that emerges once the work is transformed into a commodity, we have to eliminate this concept with cautious care but without fear, lest we liquidate the function of the very thing as well. For it has to go through this phase without mental reservation, and not as noncommittal deviation from the straight path; rather, what happens here with the work of art will change it fundamentally and erase its past to such an extent that should the old concept be taken up again—and it will, why not?—it will no longer stir any memory of the thing it once designated."

13. Abel Gance, "Le Temps de l'image est venu," pp. 100-101.

14. Séverin-Mars, quoted by Abel Gance, *ibid.*, p. 100.

15. Alexandre Armoux, *Cinéma pris* (1929), p. 28.

16. Franz Werfel, "Ein Sommernachstraum, Ein Film von Shakespeare und Reinhardt," *Neues Weiner Journal*, cited in *Lu* 15 (November 1935).

17. "The film ... provides—or could provide—useful insight into the details of human actions.... Character is never used as a source of motivation; the inner life of the persons never supplies the principal cause of the plot and seldom is its main result." (Bertolt Brecht, "Der Dreigroschenprozess," *Versuche*, p. 268.) The expansion of the field of the testable which mechanical equipment brings about for the actor corresponds to the extraordinary expansion of the field of the testable brought about for the individual through economic conditions. Thus, vocational aptitude tests become constantly more important. What matters in these tests are segmental performances of the individual. The film shot and the vocational aptitude test are taken before a committee of experts. The camera director in the studio occupies a place identical with that of the examiner during aptitude tests.

18. Luigi Pirandello, *Si Gira*, quoted by Léon Pierre-Quint, "Signification du cinéma,"

L'Art cinématographique 2 (Paris, 1927), pp. 14-15.

19. Rudolf Arnheim, *Film als Kunst* (Berlin, 1932), pp. 176ff. In this context certain seemingly unimportant details in which the film director deviates from stage practices gain in interest. Such is the attempt to let the actor play without make-up, as made among others by Dreyer in his *Jeanne d'Arc*. Dreyer spent months seeking the forty actors who constitute the Inquisitors' tribunal. The search for these actors resembled that for stage properties that are hard to come by. Dreyer made every effort to avoid resemblances of age, build, and physiognomy. If the actor thus becomes a stage property, this latter, on the other hand, frequently functions as actor. At least it is not unusual for the film to assign a role to the stage property. Instead of choosing at random from a great wealth of examples, let us concentrate on a particularly convincing one. A clock that is working will always be a disturbance on the stage. There it cannot be permitted its function of measuring time. Even in a naturalistic play, astronomical time would clash with theatrical time. Under these circumstances it is highly revealing that the film can, whenever appropriate, use time as measured by a clock. From this more than from many other touches it may clearly be recognized that under certain circumstances each and every prop in a film may assume important functions. From here it is but one step to Pudovkin's statement that "the playing of an actor which is connected with an object and is built around it ... is always one of the strongest methods of cinematic construction." (W. Pudovkin, *Filmregie und Filmmanuskript* (Berlin, 1928), p. 126). The film is the first art form capable of demonstrating how matter plays tricks on man. Hence, films can be an excellent means of materialistic representation.

20. The change noted here in the method of exhibition caused by mechanical reproduction applies to politics as well. The present crisis of the bourgeois democracies comprise a crisis of the conditions which determine the public presentation of the rulers. Democracies exhibit a member of government directly and personally before the nation's representatives. Parliament is his public. Since the innovations of camera and recording equipment make it possible for the orator to become audible and visible to an unlimited number of persons, the presentation of the man of politics before camera and recording equipment becomes paramount. Parliaments, as much as theaters, are deserted. Radio and film not only affect the function of the professional actor but likewise the function of those who also exhibit themselves before this mechanical equipment, those who govern. Though their tasks may be different, the change affects equally the actor and the ruler. The trend is toward establishing controllable and transferrable skills under certain social conditions. This results in a new selection, a selection before the equipment from which the star and the dictator emerge victorious.

21. The privileged character of the respective techniques is lost. Aldous Huxley writes: "Advances in technology have led ... to vulgarity. ... Process reproduction and the rotary press have made possible the indefinite multiplication of writing and pictures. Universal education and relatively high wages have created an enormous public who know how to read and can afford to buy reading and pictorial matter. A great industry has been called into existence in order to supply these commodities. Now, artistic talent is a very rare phenomenon; whence it follows ... that, at every epoch and in all countries, most art has been bad. But the proportion of trash in the total artistic output is greater now than at any other period. That it must be so is a matter of simple arithmetic. The population of Western Europe has a little more than doubled during the last century. But the amount of reading—and seeing—matter has increased, I should imagine, at least twenty and possibly fifty or even a hundred times. If there were n men of talent in a population of x millions, there will presumably be $2n$ men of talent among $2x$ millions. The situation may be summed

up thus. For every page of print and pictures published a century ago, twenty or perhaps even a hundred pages are published today. But for every man of talent then living, there are now only two men of talent. It may be of course that, thanks to universal education, many potential talents which in the past would have been stillborn are now enabled to realize themselves. Let us assume, then, that there are now three or even four men of talent to every one of earlier times. It still remains true to say that the consumption of reading—and seeing—matter has far outstripped the natural production of gifted writers and draughtsmen. It is the same with hearing-matter. Prosperity, the gramophone and the radio have created an audience of hearers who consume an amount of hearing-matter that has increased out of all proportion to the increase of population and the consequent natural increase of talented musicians. It follows from all this that in all the arts the output of trash is both absolutely and relatively greater than it was in the past; and that it must remain greater for just so long as the world continues to consume the present inordinate quantities of reading-matter, seeing-matter, and hearing-matter." —Aldous Huxley, *Beyond the Mexique Bay. A Traveller's Journal* (London, 1949), pp. 274 ff. First published in 1934. This mode of observation is obviously not progressive.

22. The boldness of the cameraman is indeed comparable to that of the surgeon. Luc Durtain lists among specific technical sleights of hand those "which are required in surgery in the case of certain difficult operations. I choose as an example a case from oto-rhino-laryngology; . . . the so-called endonasal perspective procedure; or I refer to the acrobatic tricks of larynx surgery which have to be performed following the reversed picture in the laryngoscope. I might also speak of ear surgery which suggests the precision work of watchmakers. What range of the most subtle muscular acrobatics is required from the man who wants to repair or save the human body! We have only to think of the couching of a cataract where there is virtually a debate of steel with nearly fluid tissue, or of the major abdominal operations (laparotomy)." Luc Durtain.

23. This mode of observation may seem crude, but as the great theoretician Leonardo has shown, crude modes of observation may at times be usefully adduced. Leonardo compares painting and music as follows: "Painting is superior to music because, unlike unfortunate music, it does not have to die as soon as it is born. . . . Music which is consumed in the very act of its birth is inferior to painting which the use of varnish has rendered eternal." (Trattato I, 29.)

24. Renaissance painting offers a revealing analogy to this situation. The incomparable development of this art and its significance rested not least on the integration of a number of new sciences, or at least of new scientific data. Renaissance painting made use of anatomy and perspective, of mathematics, meteorology, and chromatology. Valéry writes: "What could be further from us than the strange claim of a Leonardo to whom painting was a supreme goal and the ultimate demonstration of knowledge? Leonardo was convinced that painting demanded universal knowledge, and he did not even shrink from a theoretical analysis which to us is stunning because of its very depth and precision. . . ." —Paul Valéry, "Autour de Corot," *Pièces sur l'art* (Paris), p. 191.

25. Rudolf Arnheim, *Film als Kunst*, p. 138.

26. "The work of art," says André Breton, "is valuable only in so far as it is vibrated by the reflexes of the future." Indeed, every developed art form intersects three lines of development. Technology works toward a certain form of art. Before the advent of the film there were photo booklets with pictures which flitted by the onlooker upon pressure of the thumb, thus portraying a boxing bout or a tennis match. Then there were the slot machines in bazaars; their picture sequences were produced by the turning of a crank.

Secondly, the traditional art forms in certain phases of their development strenuously work toward effects which later are effortlessly attained by the new ones. Before the rise of the movie the dadaists' performances tried to create an audience reaction which Chaplin later evoked in a more natural way.

Thirdly, unspectacular social changes often promote a change in receptivity which will benefit the new art form. Before the movie had begun to create its public, pictures that were no longer immobile captivated an assembled audience in the so-called *Kaiserpanorama*. Here the public assembled before a screen into which stereoscopes were mounted, one to each beholder. By a mechanical process individual pictures appeared briefly before the stereoscopes, then made way for others. Edison still had to use similar devices in presenting the first movie strip before the film screen and projection were known. This strip was presented to a small public which stared into the apparatus in which the succession of pictures was reeling off. Incidentally, the institution of the *Kaiserpanorama* shows very clearly a dialectic of the development. Shortly before the movie turned the reception of pictures into a collective one, the individual viewing of pictures in these swiftly outmoded establishments came into play once more with an intensity comparable to that of the ancient priest beholding the statue of a divinity in the cella.

27. The theological archetype of this contemplation is the awareness of being alone with one's God. Such awareness, in the heyday of the bourgeoisie, went to strengthen the freedom to shake off clerical tutelage. During the decline of the bourgeoisie this awareness had to take into account the hidden tendency to withdraw from public affairs those forces which the individual draws upon in his communion with God.

28. Georges Duhamel, *Scènes de la vie future* (Paris, 1930), p. 52.

29. The film is the art form that is in keeping with the increased threat to his life which modern man has to face. Man's need to expose himself to shock effects is his adjustment to the dangers threatening him. The film corresponds to profound changes in the apperceptive apparatus—changes that are experienced on an individual scale by the man in the street in big-city traffic, on a historical scale by every present-day citizen.

30. As for dadaism, insights important for cubism and futurism are to be gained from the movie. Both appear as deficient attempts of art to accommodate the pervasion of reality by the apparatus. In contrast to the film, these schools did not try to use the apparatus as such for the artistic presentation of reality, but aimed at some sort of alloy in the joint presentation of reality and apparatus. In cubism, the premonition that this apparatus will be structurally based on optics plays a dominant part; in futurism, it is the premonition of the effects of this apparatus which are brought out by the rapid sequence of the film strip.

31. Duhamel, *Scènes de la vie future*, p. 58.

32. One technical feature is significant here, especially with regard to newsreels, the propagandist importance of which can hardly be overestimated. Mass reproduction is aided especially by the reproduction of masses. In big parades and monster rallies, in sports events, and in war, all of which nowadays are captured by camera and sound recording, the masses are brought face to face with themselves. This process, whose significance need not be stressed, is intimately connected with the development of the techniques of reproduction and photography. Mass movements are usually discerned more clearly by a camera than by the naked eye. A bird's-eye view best captures gatherings of hundreds of thousands. And even though such a view may be as accessible to the human eye as it is to the camera, the image received by the eye cannot be enlarged the way a negative is enlarged. This means that mass movements, including war, constitute a form of human behavior which particularly favors mechanical equipment.

The Radio as an Apparatus of Communication

Bertolt Brecht

IN OUR SOCIETY one can invent and perfect discoveries that still have to conquer their market and justify their existence; in other words discoveries that have not been called for. Thus there was a moment when technology was advanced enough to produce the radio and society was not yet advanced enough to accept it. The radio was then in its first phase of being a substitute: a substitute for theater, opera, concerts, lectures, café music, local newspapers, and so forth. This was the patient's period of halcyon youth. I am not sure if it is finished yet, but if so then this stripling who needed no certificate of competence to be born will have to start looking retrospectively for an object in life. Just as a man will begin asking at a certain age, when his first innocence has been lost, what he is supposed to be doing in the world.

As for the radio's object, I don't think it can consist merely in prettifying public life. Nor is radio in my view an adequate means of bringing back coziness to the home and making family life bearable again. But quite apart from the dubiousness of its functions, radio is one-sided when it should be two-. It is purely an apparatus for distribution, for mere sharing out. So here is a positive suggestion: change this apparatus over from distribution to communication. The radio would be the finest possible communication apparatus in public life, a vast network of pipes. That is to say, it would be if it knew how to receive as well as to transmit, how to let the listener speak as well as hear, how to bring him into a relationship instead of isolating him. On this principle the radio should step out of the supply business and organize its listeners as suppliers. Any attempt by the radio to give a truly public character to public occasions is a step in the right direction.

Whatever the radio sets out to do it must strive to combat that lack of consequences which makes such asses of almost all our public institutions. We have a literature without consequences, which not only itself sets out to lead nowhere, but does all it can to neutralize its readers by depicting each object and situation stripped of the consequences to which they lead. We have educational establishments without consequences, working frantically to hand on an education that leads nowhere and has come from nothing.

The slightest advance in this direction is bound to succeed far more spectacularly than any performance of a culinary kind. As for the technique that needs to be developed for all such operations, it must follow the prime objective of turning the audience not only into pupils but into teachers. It is the radio's formal task to give these educational operations an interesting turn, i.e. to ensure that these interests interest people. Such an attempt by the radio to put its instruction into an artistic form would link up with the efforts of modern artists to give art an instructive character. As an example or model of the exercises possible along these lines let me repeat the explanation of *Der Flug der Lindberghs* that I gave at the Baden-Baden music festival of 1929.

> "In obedience to the principle that the State shall be rich and man shall be poor, that the State shall be obliged to have many possibilities and man shall be allowed to have few possibilities, where music is concerned the State shall furnish whatever needs special apparatus and special abilities; the individual, however, shall furnish an exercise. Free-roaming feelings aroused by music, special thoughts such as may be entertained when listening to music, physical exhaustion such as easily arises just from listening to music, are all distractions from music. To avoid these distractions the individual shares in the music, thus obeying the principle that doing is better than feeling, by following the music with his eyes as printed, and contributing the parts and places reserved for him by singing them for himself or in conjunction with others (school class)."

Der Flug der Lindberghs is not intended to be of use to the present-day radio but to alter it. The increasing concentration of mechanical means and the increasingly specialized training—tendencies that should be accelerated—call for a kind of resistance by the listener, and for his mobilization and redrafting as a producer.

This exercise is an aid to discipline, which is the basis of freedom. The individual will reach spontaneously for a means to pleasure, but not for an object of instruction that offers him neither profit nor social advantages. Such exercises only serve the individual in so far as they serve the State, and they only serve a State that wishes to serve all men equally. Thus *Der Flug der Lindberghs* has no aesthetic and no revolutionary value independently of its application, and only the State can organize this. Its proper application, however, makes it so "revolutionary" that the present-day State has no interest in sponsoring such exercises.

This is an innovation, a suggestion that seems utopian and that I myself admit to be utopian. When I say that the radio or the theatre "could" do so-and-so, I am aware that these vast institutions cannot do all they "could," and not even all they want.

But it is not at all our job to renovate ideological institutions on the basis of the existing social order by means of innovations. Instead our innovations must force them to surrender that basis. So: For innovations, against renovation!

From *Brecht on Theatre*. Translated and edited by Jon Willett. New York: Hill and Wang, 1964. ["Der Rundfunk als Kommunikationsapparat" in *Blätter des Hessischen Landestheaters*, Darmstadt, No. 16, July 1932]

NOTE: There are one or two earlier notes on the radio by Brecht, including a set of "Suggestions for the Director of the Radio" published in the *Berliner Börsen-Courier* of 25 December 1927, which proposed the live broadcasting of law cases and Reichstag debates, as well as an increased proportion of interviews and discussion programs. He also suggested, apparently as a new idea, that composers should be invited to write for the radio.

The present essay was published in the program of the theatre that had first staged *Mann its Mann* in 1926, and is headed "From a report." It is not known whether, when, or to whom Brecht delivered this. —John Willett.

See also Bertolt Brecht, "Radio as an Means of Communication," Trans. Stuart Hood. *Screen* 20, No. 3/4 (Winter 1979/80): pp. 24-28. London: Society for Education in Film and Television. —Ed.

Ideology and Ideological State Apparatuses
(Notes Towards an Investigation)

Louis Althusser

*O*N THE REPRODUCTION OF THE CONDITIONS OF PRODUCTION[1]

I must now expose more fully something which was briefly glimpsed in my analysis when I spoke of the necessity to renew the means of production if production is to be possible. That was a passing hint. Now I shall consider it for itself.

As Marx said, every child knows that a social formation which did not reproduce the conditions of production at the same time as it produced would not last a year.[2] The ultimate condition of production is therefore the reproduction of the conditions of production. This may be "simple" (reproducing exactly the previous conditions of production) or "on an extended scale" (expanding them). Let us ignore this last distinction for the moment.

What, then, is *the reproduction of the conditions of production*?

Here we are entering a domain which is both very familiar (since *Capital* Volume Two) and uniquely ignored. The tenacious obviousness (ideological obviousnesses of an empiricist type) of the point of view of production alone, or even of that of mere productive practice (itself abstract in relation to the process of production) are so integrated into our everyday "consciousness" that it is extremely hard, not to say almost impossible, to raise oneself to the *point of view of reproduction*. Nevertheless, everything outside this point of view remains abstract (worse than one-sided: distorted)—even at the level of production, and, *a fortiori*, at that of mere practice.

Let us try and examine the matter methodically.

To simplify my exposition, and assuming that every social formation arises from a dominant mode of production, I can say that the process of production sets to work the existing productive forces in and under definite relations of production.

It follows that, in order to exist, every social formation must reproduce the conditions of its production at the same time as it produces, and in order to be able to produce. It must therefore reproduce:

1. the productive forces,
2. the existing relations of production.

Reproduction of the Means of Production

Everyone (including the bourgeois economists whose work is national accounting, or the modern "macro-economic" "theoreticians") now recognizes, because Marx compellingly proved it in *Capital* Volume Two, that no production is possible which does not allow for the reproduction of the material conditions of production: the reproduction of the means of production.

The average economist, who is no different in this than the average capitalist, knows that each year it is essential to foresee what is needed to replace what has been used up or worn out in production: raw material, fixed installations (buildings), instruments of production (machines), etc. I say the average economist = the average capitalist, for they both express the point of view of the firm, regarding it as sufficient simply to give a commentary on the terms of the firm's financial accounting practice.

But thanks to the genius of Quesnay who first posed this "glaring" problem, and to the genius of Marx who resolved it, we know that the reproduction of the material conditions of production cannot be thought at the level of the firm, because it does not exist at that level in its real conditions. What happens at the level of the firm is an effect, which only gives an idea of the necessity of reproduction, but absolutely fails to allow its conditions and mechanisms to be thought.

A moment's reflection is enough to be convinced of this: Mr. X, a capitalist who produces woolen yarn in his spinning-mill, has to "reproduce" his raw material, his machines, etc. But *he* does not produce them for his own production—other capitalists do: an Australian sheepfarmer, Mr. Y, a heavy engineer producing machine-tools, Mr. Z, etc., etc. And Mr. Y and Mr. Z, in order to produce those products which are the condition of the reproduction of Mr. X's conditions of production, also have to reproduce the conditions of their own production, and so on to infinity—the whole in proportions such that, on the national and even the world market, the demand for means of production (for reproduction) can be satisfied by the supply.

In order to think this mechanism, which leads to a kind of "endless chain," it is necessary to follow Marx's "global" procedure, and to study in particular the relations of the circulation of capital between Department I (production of means of production) and Department II (production of means of consumption), and the realization of surplus-value, in *Capital*, Volumes Two and Three.

We shall not go into the analysis of this question. It is enough to have mentioned the existence of the necessity of the reproduction of the material conditions of production.

Reproduction of Labor-Power

However, the reader will not have failed to note one thing. We have discussed the reproduction of the means of production — but not the reproduction of the productive forces. We have therefore ignored the reproduction of what distinguishes the productive forces from the means of production, i.e., the reproduction of labor power.

From the observation of what takes place in the firm, in particular from the examination of the financial accounting practice which predicts amortization and investment, we have been able to obtain an approximate idea of the existence of the material process of reproduction, but we are now entering a domain in which the observation of what happens in the firm is, if not totally blind, at least almost entirely so, and for good reason: the reproduction of labor power takes place essentially outside the firm.

How is the reproduction of labor power ensured?

It is ensured by giving labor power the material means with which to reproduce itself: by wages. Wages feature in the accounting of each enterprise, but as "wage capital,"[3] not at all as a condition of the material reproduction of labor power.

However, that is in fact how it "works," since wages represents only that part of the value produced by the expenditure of labor power which is indispensable for its reproduction: [namely] indispensable to the reconstitution of the labor power of the wage-earner (the wherewithal to pay for housing, food, and clothing, in short to enable the wage-earner to present himself again at the factory gate the next day— and every further day God grants him); and we should add: indispensable for raising and educating the children in whom the proletarian reproduces himself (in n models where n = 0, 1, 2, etc. ...) as labor power.

Remember that this quantity of value (wages) necessary for the reproduction of labor power is determined not by the needs of a "biological" Guaranteed Minimum Wage (*Salaire Minimum Interprofessionnel*

Garanti) alone, but by the needs of a historical minimum (Marx noted that English workers need beer while French proletarians need wine)—i.e. a historically variable minimum.

I should also like to point out that this minimum is doubly historical in that it is not defined by the historical needs of the working class "recognized" by the capitalist class, but by the historical needs imposed by the proletarian class struggle (a double class struggle: against the lengthening of the working day and against the reduction of wages).

However, it is not enough to ensure for labor power the material conditions of its reproduction if it is to be reproduced as labor power. I have said that the available labor power must be "competent," i.e. suitable to be set to work in the complex system of the process of production. The development of the productive forces and the type of unity historically constitutive of the productive forces at a given moment produce the result that the labor power has to be (diversely) skilled and therefore reproduced as such. Diversely: according to the requirements of the socio-technical division of labor, its different "jobs" and "posts."

How is this reproduction of the (diversified) skills of labor power provided for in a capitalist regime? Here, unlike social formations characterized by slavery or serfdom, this reproduction of the skills of labor power tends (this is a tendential law) decreasingly to be provided for "on the spot" (apprenticeship within production itself), but is achieved more and more outside production: by the capitalist education system, and by other instances and institutions.

What do children learn at school? They go varying distances in their studies, but at any rate they learn to read, to write, and to add—i.e. a number of techniques, and a number of other things as well, including elements (which may be rudimentary or on the contrary thoroughgoing) of "scientific" or "literary culture," which are directly useful in the different jobs in production (one instruction for manual workers, another for technicians, a third for engineers, a final one for higher management, etc.). Thus they learn "know-how."

But besides these techniques and knowledges, and in learning them, children at school also learn the "rules" of good behavior, i.e. the attitude that should be observed by every agent in the division of labor, according to the job he is "destined" for: rules of morality, civic and professional conscience, which actually means rule of respect for the socio-technical division of labor and ultimately the rules of the order established by class domination. They also learn to "speak proper French," to "handle" the workers correctly, i.e. actually (for the future capitalists and their servants) to "order them about" properly, i.e. (ideally) to "speak to them" in the right way, etc.

To put this more scientifically, I shall say that the reproduction of labor power requires not only a reproduction of its skills, but also, at the same time, a reproduction of its submission to the rules of the established order, i.e. a reproduction of submission to the ruling ideology for the workers, and a reproduction of the ability to manipulate the ruling ideology correctly for the agents of exploitation and repression, so that they, too, will provide for the domination of the ruling class "in words."

In other words, the school (but also other State institutions like the Church, or other apparatuses like the Army) teaches "know-how," but in forms which ensure *subjection to the ruling ideology* or the mastery of its "practice." All the agents of production, exploitation, and repression, not to speak of the "professionals of ideology" (Marx), must in one way or another be "steeped" in this ideology in order to perform their tasks "conscientiously"—the tasks of the exploited (the proletarians), of the exploiters (the capitalists), of the exploiters' auxiliaries (the managers), or of the high priests of the ruling ideology (its "functionaries"), etc.

The reproduction of labor power thus reveals as its *sine qua non* not only the reproduction of its "skills" but also the reproduction of its subjection to the ruling ideology or of the "practice" of that ideology, with the proviso that it is not enough to say "not only but also," for it is clear that *it is in the forms and under the forms of ideological subjection that provision is made for the reproduction of the skills of labor power.*

But this is to recognize the effective presence of a new reality: *ideology.*

Here I shall make two comments.

The first is to round off my analysis of reproduction.

I have just given a rapid survey of the forms of the reproduction of the productive forces, i.e. of the means of production on the one hand, and of labor power on the other.

But I have not yet approached the question of the *reproduction of the relations of production.* This is a *crucial question* for the Marxist theory of the mode of production. To let it pass would be a theoretical omission—worse, a serious political error.

I shall therefore discuss it. But in order to obtain the means to discuss it, I shall have to make another long detour.

The second comment is that in order to make this detour, I am obliged to re-raise my old question: what is a society?

INFRASTRUCTURE AND SUPERSTRUCTURE

On a number of occasions[4] I have insisted on the revolutionary character of the Marxist conception of the "social whole" insofar as it is distinct from the Hegelian "totality." I said (and this thesis only repeats famous propositions of historical materialism) that Marx conceived the structure of every society as constituted by "levels" or "instances" articulated by a specific determination: the *infrastructure*, or economic base (the "unity" of the productive forces and the relations of production) and the *superstructure*, which itself contains two "levels" or "instances": the politico-legal (law and the State) and ideology (the different ideologies, religious, ethical, legal, political, etc.).

Besides its theoretico-didactic interest (it reveals the difference between Marx and Hegel), this representation has the following crucial theoretical advantage: it makes it possible to inscribe in the theoretical apparatus of its essential concepts what I have called their *respective indices of effectivity*. What does this mean?

It is easy to see that this representation of the structure of every society as an edifice containing a base (infrastructure) on which are erected the two "floors" of the superstructure, is a metaphor, to be quite precise, a spatial metaphor: the metaphor of a topography (*topique*).[5] Like every metaphor, this metaphor suggests something, makes something visible. What? Precisely this: that the upper floors could not "stay up" (in the air) alone, if they did not rest precisely on their base.

Thus the object of the metaphor of the edifice is to represent above all the "determination in the last instance" by the economic base. The effect of this spatial metaphor is to endow the base with an index of effectivity known by the famous terms: the determination in the last instance of what happens in the upper "floors" (of the superstructure) by what happens in the economic base.

Given this index of effectivity "in the last instance," the "floors" of the superstructure are clearly endowed with different indices of effectivity. What kind of indices?

It is possible to say that the floors of the superstructure are not determinant in the last instance, but that they are determined by the effectivity of the base; that if they are determinant in their own (as yet undefined) ways, this is true only insofar as they are determined by the base.

Their index of effectivity (or determination), as determined by the determination in the last instance of the base, is thought by the Marxist tradition in two ways: (1) there is a "relative autonomy" of the superstructure with respect to the base; (2) there is a "reciprocal action" of the superstructure on the base.

We can therefore say that the great theoretical advantage of the Marxist topography, i.e. of the spatial metaphor of the edifice (base and superstructure) is simultaneously that it reveals that questions of determination (or of index of effectivity) are crucial; that it reveals that it is the base which in the last instance determines the whole edifice; and that, as a consequence, it obliges us to pose the theoretical problem of the types of "derivatory" effectivity peculiar to the superstructure, i.e. it obliges us to think what the Marxist tradition calls conjointly the relative autonomy of the superstructure and the reciprocal action of the superstructure on the base.

The greatest disadvantage of this representation of the structure of every society by the spatial metaphor of an edifice, is obviously the fact that it is metaphorical: i.e. it remains *descriptive*.

It now seems to me that it is possible and desirable to represent things differently. NB, I do not mean by this that I want to reject the classical metaphor, for that metaphor itself requires that we go beyond it. And I am not going beyond it in order to reject it as outworn. I simply want to attempt to think what it gives us in the form of a description.

I believe that it is possible and necessary to think what characterizes the essential of the existence and nature of the superstructure *on the basis of reproduction*. Once one takes the point of view of reproduction, many of the questions whose existence was indicated by the spatial metaphor of the edifice, but to which it could not give a conceptual answer, are immediately illuminated.

My basic thesis is that it is not possible to pose these questions (and therefore to answer them) *except from the point of view of reproduction*.

I shall give a short analysis of Law, the State and Ideology *from this point of view*. And I shall reveal what happens both from the point of view of practice and production on the one hand, and from that of reproduction on the other.

THE STATE

The Marxist tradition is strict, here: in the *Communist Manifesto* and the *Eighteenth Brumaire* (and in all the later classical texts, above all in Marx's writings on the Paris Commune and Lenin's on *State and Revolution*), the State is explicitly conceived as a repressive apparatus. The State is a "machine" of repression, which enables the ruling classes (in the nineteenth century the bourgeois class and the "class" of big landowners) to ensure their domination over the working class, thus enabling the former to subject the latter to the process of surplus-value extortion (i.e. to capitalist exploitation).

The State is thus first of all what the Marxist classics have called *the State apparatus*. This term means: not only the specialized apparatus (in the narrow sense) whose existence and necessity I have recognized in relation to the requirements of legal practice, i.e. the police, the courts, the prisons; but also the army, which (the proletariat has paid for this experience with its blood) intervenes directly as a supplementary repressive force in the last instance, when the police and its specialized auxiliary corps are "outrun by events"; and above this ensemble, the head of State, the government, and the administration.

Presented in this form, the Marxist-Leninist "theory" of the State has its finger on the essential point, and not for one moment can there be any question of rejecting the fact that this really is the essential point. The State apparatus, which defines the State as a force of repressive execution and intervention "in the interests of the ruling classes" in the class struggle conducted by the bourgeoisie and its allies against the proletariat, is quite certainly the State, and quite certainly defines its basic "function."

From Descriptive Theory to Theory as Such

Nevertheless, here too, as I pointed out with respect to the metaphor of the edifice (infrastructure and superstructure), this presentation of the nature of the State is still partly descriptive.

As I shall often have occasion to use this adjective (descriptive), a word of explanation is necessary in order to remove any ambiguity.

Whenever, in speaking of the metaphor of the edifice or of the Marxist "theory" of the State, I have said that these are descriptive conceptions or representations of their objects, I had no ulterior critical motives. On the contrary, I have every grounds to think that great scientific discoveries cannot help but pass through the phase of what I shall call *descriptive "theory."* This is the first phase of every theory, at least in the domain which concerns us (that of the science of social formations). As such, one might—and in my opinion one must—envisage this phase as a transitional one, necessary to the development of the theory. That it is transitional is inscribed in my expression: "descriptive theory," which reveals in its conjunction of terms the equivalent of a kind of "contradiction." In fact, the term theory "clashes" to some extent with the adjective "descriptive" which I have attached to it. This means quite precisely: (1) that the "descriptive theory" really is, without a shadow of a doubt, the irreversible beginning of the theory; but (2) that the "descriptive" form in which the theory is presented requires, precisely as an effect of this "contradiction," a development of the theory which goes beyond the form of "description."

Let me make this idea clearer by returning to our present object: the State.

When I say the Marxist "theory" of the State available to us is still partly "descriptive," that means first and foremost that this descriptive "theory" is without the shadow of a doubt precisely the beginning of the Marxist theory of the State, and that this beginning gives us the essential point, i.e. the decisive principle of every later development of the theory.

Indeed, I shall call the descriptive theory of the State correct, since it is perfectly possible to make the vast majority of the facts in the domain with which it is concerned correspond to the definition it gives of its object. Thus, the definition of the State as a class State, existing in the repressive State apparatus, casts a brilliant light on all the facts observable in the various orders of repression whatever their domains: from the massacres of June 1848 and of the Paris Commune, of Bloody Sunday, May 1905 in Petrograd, of the Resistance, of Charonne, etc., to the mere (and relatively anodyne) interventions of a "censorship" which has banned Diderot's *La Réligieuse* or a play by Gatti on Franco; it casts light on all the direct or indirect forms of exploitation and extermination of the masses of the people (imperialist wars); it casts light on that subtle everyday domination beneath which can be glimpsed, in the forms of political democracy, for example, what Lenin, following Marx, called the dictatorship of the bourgeoisie.

And yet the descriptive theory of the State represents a phase in the constitution of the theory which itself demands the "supersession" of this phase. For it is clear that if the definition in question really does give us the means to identify and recognize the facts of oppression by relating them to the State, conceived as the repressive State apparatus, this "interrelationship" gives rise to a very special kind of obviousness, about which I shall have something to say in a moment: "Yes, that's how it is, that's really true!"[6] And the accumulation of facts within the definition of the State may multiply examples, but it does not really advance the definition of the State, i.e. the scientific theory of the State. Every descriptive theory thus runs the risk of "blocking" the development of the theory, and yet that development is essential.

That is why I think that, in order to develop this descriptive theory into theory as such, i.e. in order to understand further the mechanisms of the State in its functioning, I think that it is indispensable to *add* something to the classical definition of the State as a State apparatus.

The Essentials of the Marxist Theory of the State

Let me first clarify one important point: the State (and its existence in its apparatus) has no meaning except as a function of *State power*. The whole of the political class struggle revolves around the State. By which I mean around the possession, i.e. the seizure and conservation of State power by a certain class or by an alliance between classes or class fractions. This first clarification obliges me to distinguish between State power (conservation of State power or seizure of State power), the objective of the political class struggle on the one hand, and the State apparatus on the other.

We know that the State apparatus may survive, as is proved by bourgeois "revolutions" in nineteenth-century France (1830, 1848), by *coups d'état* (2 December, May 1958), by collapses of the State (the fall of the Empire in 1870, of the Third Republic in 1940), or by the political rise of the petty bourgeoisie (1890-95 in France), etc., without the State apparatus being affected or modified: it may survive political events which affect the possession of State power.

Even after a social revolution like that of 1917, a large part of the State apparatus survived after the seizure of State power by the alliance of the proletariat and the small peasantry: Lenin repeated the fact again and again.

It is possible to describe the distinction between State power and State apparatus as part of the "Marxist theory" of the State, explicitly present since Marx's *Eighteenth Brumaire* and *Class Struggles in France*.

To summarize the "Marxist theory of the State" on this point, it can be said that the Marxist classics have always claimed that (1) the State is the repressive State apparatus, (2) State power and State apparatus must be distinguished, (3) the objective of the class struggle concerns State power, and in consequence the use of the State apparatus by the classes (or alliance of classes or of fractions of classes) holding State power as a function of their class objectives, and (4) the proletariat must seize the State power in order to destroy the existing bourgeois State apparatus and, in a first phase, replace it with a quite different, proletarian, State apparatus, then in later phases set in motion a radical process, that of the destruction of the State (the end of State power, the end of every State apparatus).

In this perspective, therefore, what I would propose to add to the "Marxist theory" of the State is already there in so many words. But it seems to me that even with this supplement, this theory is still in part descriptive, although it does not contain complex and differential elements whose functioning and action cannot be understood without recourse to further supplementary theoretical development.

The State Ideological Apparatuses

Thus, what has to be added to the "Marxist theory" of the State is something else.

Here we must advance cautiously in a terrain which, in fact, the Marxist classics entered long before us, but without having systematized in theoretical form the decisive advances implied by their experiences and procedures. Their experiences and procedures were indeed restricted in the main to the terrain of political practice.

In fact, i.e. in their political practice, the Marxist classics treated the State as a more complex reality than the definition of it given in the "Marxist theory of the State," even when it has been supplemented as I have just suggested. They recognized this complexity in their practice, but they did not express it in a corresponding theory.[7]

I should like to attempt a very schematic outline of this corresponding theory. To that end, I propose the following thesis.

In order to advance the theory of the State it is indispensable to take into account not only the distinction between *State power* and *State apparatus*, but also another reality which is clearly on the side of the (repressive) State apparatus, but must not be confused with it. I shall call this reality by its concept: *the ideological State apparatuses*.

What are the ideological State apparatuses (ISAs)?

They must not be confused with the (repressive) State apparatus. Remember that in Marxist theory, the State Apparatus (SA) contains: the Government, the Administration, the Army, the Police, the Courts, the Prisons, etc., which constitute what I shall in future call the Repressive State Apparatus. Repressive suggests that the State Apparatus in question "functions by violence"—at least ultimately (since repression, e.g. administrative repression, may take non-physical forms).

I shall call Ideological State Apparatuses a certain number of realities which present themselves to the immediate observer in the form of distinct and specialized institutions. I propose an empirical list of these which will obviously have to be examined in detail, tested, corrected, and reorganized. With all the reservations implied by this requirement, we can for the moment regard the following institutions as Ideological State Apparatuses (the order in which I have listed them has no particular significance):

— the religious ISA (the system of the different Churches),
— the educational ISA (the system of the different public and private "Schools"),
— the family ISA,[8]
— the legal ISA,[9]
—the political ISA (the political system, including the different

Parties),
— the trade-union ISA,
— the communications ISA (press, radio, and television, etc.),
— the cultural ISA (Literature, the Arts, sports, etc.).

I have said that the ISAs must not be confused with the (Repressive) State Apparatus. What constitutes the difference?

As a first moment, it is clear that while there is *one* (Repressive) State Apparatus, there is a *plurality* of Ideological State Apparatuses. Even presupposing that it exists, the unity that constitutes this plurality of ISAs as a body is not immediately visible.

As a second moment, it is clear that whereas the—unified—(Repressive) State Apparatus belongs entirely to the *public* domain, much of the larger part of the Ideological State Apparatuses (in their apparent dispersion) are part, on the contrary, of the *private* domain. Churches, Parties, Trade Unions, families, some schools, most newspapers, cultural ventures, etc., etc., are private.

We can ignore the first observation for the moment. But someone is bound to question the second, asking me by what right I regard as Ideological *State* Apparatuses, institutions which for the most part do not possess public status, but are quite simply *private* institutions. As a conscious Marxist, Gramsci already forstalled this objection in one sentence. The distinction between the public and the private is a distinction internal to bourgeois law, and valid in the (subordinate) domains in which bourgeois law exercises its "authority." The domain of the State escapes it because the latter is "above the law": the State, which is the State *of* the ruling class, is neither public nor private; on the contrary, it is the precondition for any distinction between public and private. The same thing can be said from the starting-point of our State Ideological Apparatuses. It is unimportant whether the institutions in which they are realized are "public" or "private." What matters is how they function. Private institutions can perfectly well "function" as Ideological State Apparatuses. A reasonably thorough analysis of any one of the ISAs proves it.

But now for what is essential. What distinguishes the ISAs from the (Repressive) State Apparatus is the following basic difference: the Repressive State Apparatus functions "by violence," whereas the Ideological State Apparatuses *function "by ideology."*

I can clarify matters by correcting this distinction. I shall say rather that every State Apparatus, whether Repressive or Ideological, "functions" both by violence and by ideology, but with one very important distinction which makes it imperative not to confuse the Ideological State Apparatuses with the (Repressive) State Apparatus.

This is the fact that the (Repressive) State Apparatus functions massively and predominantly *by repression* (including physical repression), while functioning secondarily by ideology. (There is no such thing as a purely repressive apparatus.) For example, the Army and the Police also function by ideology both to ensure their own cohesion and reproduction, and in the "values" they propound externally.

In the same way, but inversely, it is essential to say that for their part the Ideological State Apparatuses function massively and predominantly *by ideology*, but they also function secondarily by repression, even if ultimately, but only ultimately, this is very attenuated and concealed, even symbolic. (There is no such thing as a purely ideological apparatus). Thus Schools and Churches use suitable methods of punishment, expulsion, selection, etc., to "discipline" not only their shepherds, but also their flocks. The same is true of the Family.... The same is true of the cultural IS Apparatus (censorship, among other things), etc.

Is it necessary to add that this determination of the double "functioning" (predominantly, secondarily) by repression and by ideology, according to whether it is a matter of the (Repressive) State Apparatus or the Ideological State Apparatuses, makes it clear that very subtle explicit or tacit combinations may be woven from the interplay of the (Repressive) State Apparatus and the Ideological State Apparatuses? Everyday life provides us with innumerable examples of this, but they must be studied in detail if we are to go further than this mere observation.

Nevertheless, this remark leads us towards an understanding of what constitutes the unity of the apparently disparate body of the ISAs. If the ISAs "function" massively and predominantly by ideology, what unifies their diversity is precisely this functioning, insofar as the ideology by which they function is always in fact unified, despite its diversity and its contradictions, *beneath the ruling ideology*, which is the ideology of "the ruling class." Given the fact that the "ruling class" in principle holds State power (openly or more often by means of alliances between classes or class fractions), and therefore has at its disposal the (Repressive) State Apparatus, we can accept the fact that this same ruling class is active in the Ideological State Apparatuses insofar as it is ultimately the ruling ideology which is realized in the Ideological State Apparatuses, precisely in its contradictions. Of course, it is a quite different thing to act by laws and decrees in the (Repressive) State Apparatus and to "act" through the intermediary of the ruling ideology in the Ideological State Apparatuses. We must go into the details of this difference— but it cannot mask the reality of a profound identity. To my knowledge, *no class can hold State power over a long period without at the same time exercising its hegemony over and in the State Ideological Apparatuses.* I only need one example and proof of this: Lenin's anguished concern to revolutionize the educational Ideological State Apparatus (among others), simply to make it possible for the Soviet proletariat, who had seized State power, to secure the future of the dictatorship of the proletariat and the transition to socialism.[10]

This last comment puts us in a position to understand that the Ideological State Apparatuses may be not only the *stake*, but also the *site* of class struggle, and often of bitter forms of class struggle. The class (or class alliance) in power cannot lay down the law in the ISAs as easily as it can in the (repressive) State apparatus, not only because the former ruling classes are able to retain strong positions there for a long time, but also because the resistance of the exploited classes is able to find means and occasions to express itself there, either by the utilization of their contradictions, or by conquering combat positions in them in struggle.[11]

Let me run through my comments.

If the thesis I have proposed is well-founded, it leads me back to the classical Marxist theory of the State, while making it more precise in one point. I argue that it is necessary to distinguish between State power (and its possession by ...) on the one hand, and the State Apparatus on the other. But I add that the State Apparatus contains two bodies: the body of institutions which represent the Repressive State Apparatus on the one hand, and the body of institutions which represent the body of Ideological State Apparatuses on the other.

But if this is the case, the following question is bound to be asked, even in the very summary state of my suggestions: what exactly is the extent of the role of the Ideological State Apparatuses? What is their importance based on? In other words: to what does the "function" of these Ideological State Apparatuses, which do not function by repression but by ideology, correspond?

On the Reproduction of the Relations of Production

I can now answer the central question which I have left in suspense for many long pages: *how is the reproduction of the relations of production secured?*

In the topographical language (Infrastructure, Superstructure), I can say: for the most part, it is secured by the legal-political and ideological superstructure.

But as I have argued that it is essential to go beyond this still descriptive language, I shall say: for the most part,[12] it is secured by the exercise of State power in the State Apparatuses, on the one hand the (Repressive) State Apparatus, on the other the Ideological State Apparatuses.

What I have just said must also be taken into account, and it can be assembled in the form of the following three features:

1. All the State Apparatuses function both by repression and by ideology, with the difference that the (Repressive) State Apparatus functions massively and predominantly by repression, whereas the Ideological State Apparatuses function massively and predominantly by ideology.

2. Whereas the (Repressive) State Apparatus constitutes an organized whole whose different parts are centralized beneath a commanding unity, that of the politics of class struggle applied by the political representatives of the ruling classes in possession of State power, the Ideological State Apparatuses are multiple, distinct, "relatively autonomous" and capable of providing an objective field to contradictions which express, in forms which may be limited or extreme, the effects of the clashes between the capitalist class struggle and the proletarian class struggle, as well as their subordinate forms.

3. Whereas the unity of the (Repressive) State Apparatus is secured by its unified and centralized organization under the leadership of the representatives of the classes in power executing the politics of the class struggle of the classes in power, the unity of the different Ideological State Apparatuses is secured, usually in contradictory forms, by the ruling ideology, the ideology of the ruling class.

Taking these features into account, it is possible to represent the reproduction of the relations of production[13] in the following way, according to a kind of "division of labor."

The role of the repressive State apparatus, insofar as it is a repressive apparatus, consists essentially in securing by force (physical or otherwise) the political conditions of the reproduction of relations of production which are in the last resort *relations of exploitation*. Not only does the State apparatus contribute generously to its own reproduction (the capitalist State contains political dynasties, military dynasties, etc.), but also and above all, the State apparatus secures by repression (from the most brutal physical force, via mere administrative commands and interdictions, to open and tacit censorship) the political conditions for the action of the Ideological State Apparatuses.

In fact, it is the latter which largely secure the reproduction specifically of the relations of production, behind a "shield" provided by the repressive State apparatus. It is here that the role of the ruling ideology is heavily concentrated, the ideology of the ruling class, which holds State power. It is the intermediation of the ruling ideology that ensures a (sometimes teeth-gritting) "harmony" between the repressive State apparatus and the Ideological State Apparatuses, and between the different Ideological State Apparatuses.

We are thus led to envisage the following hypothesis, as a function precisely of the diversity of ideological State Apparatuses in their single, because shared, role of the reproduction of the relations of production.

Indeed we have listed a relatively large number of ideological State apparatuses in contemporary capitalist social formations: the educational apparatus, the religious apparatus, the family apparatus, the political apparatus, the trade-union apparatus, the communications apparatus, the "cultural" apparatus, etc.

But in the social formations of that mode of production characterized by "serfdom" (usually called the feudal mode of production), we observe that although there is a single repressive State apparatus which, since the earliest known Ancient States, let alone the Absolute Monarchies, has been formally very similar to the one we know today, the number of Ideological State Apparatuses is smaller and their individual types are different. For example, we observe that during the Middle Ages, the Church (the religious ideological State apparatus) accumulated a number of functions which have today devolved on to several distinct ideological State apparatuses, new ones in relation to the past I am invoking, in particular educational and cultural functions. Alongside the Church there was the family Ideological State Apparatus, which played a considerable part, incommensurable with its role in capitalist social formations. Despite appearances, the Church and the Family were not the only Ideological State Apparatuses. There was also a political Ideological State Apparatus (the Estates General, the *Parlement*, the different political factions and Leagues, the ancestors or the modern political parties, and the whole political system of the free Communes and then of the *Villes*). There was also a powerful "proto-trade-union" Ideological State Apparatus, if I may venture such an anachronistic term (the powerful merchants' and bankers' guilds and the journeymen's associations, etc.). Publishing and Communications, even, saw an indisputable development, as did the theater; initially both were integral parts of the Church, then they became more and more independent of it.

In the pre-capitalist historical period which I have examined extremely broadly, it is absolutely clear that *there was one dominant Ideological State Apparatus, the Church*, which concentrated within it not only religious functions, but also educational ones, and a large proportion of the functions of communications and "culture." It is no accident that all ideological struggle, from the sixteenth to the eighteenth century, starting with the first shocks of the Reformation, was *concentrated* in an anti-clerical and anti-religious struggle; rather this is a function precisely of the dominant position of the religious ideological State apparatus.

The foremost objective and achievement of the French Revolution was not just to transfer State power from the feudal aristocracy to the merchant-capitalist bourgeoisie, to break part of the former repressive State apparatus and replace it with a new one (e.g., the national popular Army)—but also to attack the number-one Ideological State Apparatus: the Church. Hence the civil constitution of the clergy, the confiscation of ecclesiastical wealth, and the creation of new ideological State apparatuses to replace the religious ideological State apparatus in its dominant role.

Naturally, these things did not happen automatically: witness the Concordat, the Restoration, and the long class struggle between the landed aristocracy and the industrial bourgeoisie throughout the nineteenth century for the establishment of bourgeois hegemony over the functions formerly fulfilled by the Church: above all by the Schools. It can be said that the bourgeoisie relied on the new political, parliamentary-democratic, ideological State apparatus, installed in the earliest years of the Revolution, then restored after long and violent struggles, for a few months in 1848 and for decades after the fall of the Second Empire, in order to conduct its struggle against the Church and wrest its ideological functions away from it, in other words, to ensure not only its own political hegemony, but also the ideological hegemony indispensable to the reproduction of capitalist relations of production.

That is why I believe that I am justified in advancing the following Thesis, however precarious it is. I believe that the ideological State apparatus which has been installed in the *dominant* position in mature capitalist social formations as a result of a violent political and ideological class struggle against the old dominant ideological State apparatus, is the *educational ideological apparatus*.

This thesis may seem paradoxical, given that for everyone, i.e. in the ideological representation that the bourgeoisie has tried to give itself and the classes it exploits, it really seems that the dominant ideological State apparatus in capitalist social formations is not the Schools, but the political ideological State apparatus, i.e. the regime of parliamentary democracy combining universal suffrage and party struggle.

However, history, even recent history, shows that the bourgeoisie has been and still is able to accommodate itself to political ideological State apparatuses other than parliamentary democracy: the First and Second Empires, Constitutional Monarchy (Louis XVIII and Charles X), Parliamentary Monarchy (Louis-Philippe), Presidential Democracy (de Gaulle), to mention only France. In England this is even clearer. The Revolution was particularly "successful" there from the bourgeois point of view, since unlike France, where the bourgeoisie, partly because of the stupidity of the petty aristocracy, had to agree to being carried to power by peasant and plebeian *"journées révolution-naires,"* something for which it had to pay a high price, the English bourgeoisie was able to "compromise" with the aristocracy and "share" State power and the use of the State apparatus with it for a long time (peace among all men of good will in the ruling classes!). In Germany it is even more striking, since it was behind a political ideological State apparatus in which the imperial Junkers (epitomized by Bismarck), their army and their police provided it with a shield and leading person-nel, that the imperialist bourgeoisie made its shattering entry into his-tory, before "traversing" the Weimar Republic and entrusting itself to Nazism.

Hence I believe I have good reasons for thinking that behind the scenes of its political Ideological State Apparatus, which occupies the front of the stage, what the bourgeoisie has installed as its number-one, i.e. as its dominant ideological State apparatus, is the educational ap-paratus, which has in fact replaced in its functions the previously domi-nant ideological State apparatus, the Church. One might even add: the School-Family couple has replaced the Church-Family couple.

Why is the educational apparatus in fact the dominant ideologi-cal State apparatus in capitalist social formations, and how does it function?

For the moment it must suffice to say:

1. All ideological State apparatuses, whatever they are, contribute to the same result: the reproduction of the relations of production, i.e. of capitalist relations of exploitation.

2. Each of them contributes towards this single result in the way proper to it. The political apparatus by subjecting individuals to the political State ideology, the "indirect" (parliamentary) or "direct" (plebiscitary or fascist) "democratic" ideology. The communications apparatus by cramming every "citizen" with daily doses of nationalism, chauvinism, liberalism, moralism, etc., by means of the press, the radio, and television. The same goes for the cultural apparatus (the role of sport in chauvinism is of the first importance), etc. The religious appa-ratus by recalling in sermons and the other great ceremonies of Birth, Marriage, and Death, that man is only ashes, unless he loves his neigh-bor to the extent of turning the other cheek to whoever strikes first. The family apparatus . . . but there is no need to go on.

3. This concert is dominated by a single score, occasionally disturbed by contradictions (those of the remnants of former ruling classes, those

of the proletarians and their organizations): the score of the Ideology of the current ruling class which integrates into its music the great themes of the Humanism of the Great Forefathers, who produced the Greek Miracle even before Christianity, and afterwards the Glory of Rome, the Eternal City, and the themes of Interest, particular and general, etc. nationalism, moralism, and economism.

4. Nevertheless, in this concern, one ideological State apparatus certainly has the dominant role, although hardly anyone lends an ear to its music: it is so silent! This is the School.

It takes children from every class at infant-school age, and then for years, the years in which the child is most "vulnerable," squeezed between the family State apparatus and the educational State apparatus, it drums into them, whether it uses new or old methods, a certain amount of "know-how" wrapped in the ruling ideology (French, arithmetic, natural history, the sciences, literature) or simply the ruling ideology in its pure state (ethics, civic instruction, philosophy). Somewhere around the age of sixteen, a huge mass of children are ejected "into production": these are the workers or small peasants. Another portion of scholastically adapted youth carries on: and, for better or worse, it goes somewhat further, until it falls by the wayside and fills the posts of small and middle technicians, white-collar workers, small and middle executives, petty bourgeois of all kinds. A last portion reaches the summit, either to fall into intellectual semi-employment, or to provide, as well as the "intellectuals of the collective laborer," the agents of exploitation (capitalists, managers), the agents of repression (soldiers, policemen, politicians, administrators, etc.) and the professional ideologists (priests of all sorts, most of whom are convinced "laymen").

Each mass ejected *en route* is practically provided with the ideology which suits the role it has to fulfill in class society: the role of the exploited (with a "highly-developed" "professional," "ethical," "civic," "national" and a-political consciousness); the role of the agent of exploitation (ability to give the workers orders and speak to them: "human relations"), of the agent of repression (ability to give orders and enforce obedience "without discussion," or ability to manipulate the demagogy of a political leader's rhetoric), or of the professional ideologist (ability to treat consciousness with the respect, i.e. with the contempt, blackmail, and demagogery they deserve, adapted to the accents of Morality, of Virtue, of "Transcendence," of the Nation, of France's World Role, etc.).

Of course, many of these contrasting Virtues (modesty, resignation, submissiveness on the one hand, cynicism, contempt, arrogance, confidence, self-importance, even smooth talk and cunning on the other) are also taught in the Family, in the Church, in the Army, in Good

Books, in films, and even in the football stadium. But no other ideological State apparatus has the obligatory (and not least, free) audience of the totality of the children in the capitalist social formation, eight hours a day for five or six days out of seven.

But it is by an apprenticeship in a variety of know-how wrapped up in the massive inculcation of the ideology of the ruling class that the *relations of production* in a capitalist socialist formation, i.e. the relations of exploited to exploiters and exploiters to exploited, are largely reproduced. The mechanisms which produce this vital result for the capitalist regime are naturally covered up and concealed by a universally reigning ideology of the School, universally reigning because it is one of the essential forms of the ruling bourgeois ideology: an ideology which represents the School as a neutral environment purged of ideology (because it is . . . lay), where teachers respectful of the "conscience" and "freedom" of the children who are entrusted to them (in complete confidence) by their "parents" (who are free, too, i.e. the owners of their children) open up for them the path to the freedom, morality, and responsibility of adults by their own example, by knowledge, literature, and their "liberating" virtues.

I ask the pardon of those teachers who, in dreadful conditions, attempt to turn the few weapons they can find in the history and learning they "teach" against the ideology, the system, and the practices in which they are trapped. They are a kind of hero. But they are rare and how many (the majority) do not even begin to suspect the "work" the system (which is bigger than they are and crushes them) forces them to do, or worse, put all their heart and ingenuity into performing it with the most advanced awareness (the famous new methods!). So little do they suspect it that their own devotion contributes to the maintenance and nourishment of this ideological representation of the School, which makes the School today as "natural," indispensable-useful, and even beneficial for our contemporaries as the Church was "natural," indispensable, and generous for our ancestors a few centuries ago.

In fact, the Church has been replaced today *in its role as the dominant Ideological State Apparatus* by the School. It is coupled with the Family just as the Church was once coupled with the Family. We can now claim that the unprecedentedly deep crisis which is now shaking the education system of so many States across the globe, often in conjunction with a crisis (already proclaimed in the *Communist Manifesto*) shaking the family system, takes on a political meaning, given that the School (and the School-Family couple) constitutes the dominant Ideological State Apparatus, the Apparatus playing a determinant part in the reproduction of the relations of production of a mode of production threatened in its existence by the world class struggle.

ON IDEOLOGY

When I put forward the concept of an Ideological State Apparatus, when I said that the ISAs "function by ideology," I invoked a reality which needs a little discussion: ideology.

It is well known that the expression "ideology" was invented by Cabanis, Destutt de Tracy, and their friends, who assigned to it as an object the (genetic) theory of ideas. When Marx took up the term fifty years later, he gave it a quite different meaning, even in his Early Works. Here, ideology is the system of the ideas and representations which dominate the mind of a man or a social group. The ideologico-political struggle conducted by Marx as early as his articles in the *Rheinische Zeitung* inevitably and quickly brought him face to face with this reality and forced him to take his earliest intuitions further.

However, here we come upon a rather astonishing paradox. Everything seems to lead Marx to formulate a theory of ideology. In fact, *The German Ideology* does offer us, after the *1844 Manuscripts*, an explicit theory of ideology, but ... it is not Marxist (we shall see why in a moment). As for *Capital*, although it does contain many hints towards a theory of ideologies (most visibly, the ideology of the vulgar economists), it does not contain that theory itself, which depends for the most part on a theory of ideology in general.

I should like to venture a first and very schematic outline of such a theory. The theses I am about to put forward are certainly not off the cuff, but they cannot be sustained and tested, i.e. confirmed or rejected, except by much thorough study and analysis.

Ideology has no History

One word first of all to expound the reason in principle which seems to me to found, or at least justify, the project of a theory of ideology *in general*, and not a theory of particular ideolog*ies*, which, whatever their form (religious, ethical, legal, political), always express *class positions*.

It is quite obvious that it is necessary to proceed towards a theory of ideolog*ies* in the two respects I have just suggested. It will then be clear that a theory of ideolog*ies* depends in the last resort on the history of social formations, and thus of the modes of production combined in social formations, and of the class struggles which develop in them. In this sense it is clear that there can be no question of a theory of ideolog*ies in general*, since ideolog*ies* (defined in the double respect suggested above: regional and class) have a history, whose determination in the last instance is clearly situated outside ideologies alone, although it involves them.

On the contrary, if I am able to put forward the project of a theory of ideology *in general,* and if this theory really is one of the elements on which theories of ideolog*ies* depend, that entails an apparently paradoxical proposition which I shall express in the following terms: *ideology has no history.*

As we know, this formulation appears in so many words in a passage from *The German Ideology.* Marx utters it with respect to metaphysics, which, he says, has no more history than ethics (meaning also the other forms of ideology).

In *The German Ideology,* this formulation appears in a plainly positivist context. Ideology is conceived as a pure illusion, a pure dream, i.e. as nothingness. All its reality is external to it. Ideology is thus thought as an imaginary construction whose status is exactly like the theoretical status of the dream among writers before Freud. For these writers, the dream was the purely imaginary, i.e. null, result of "day's residues," presented in an arbitrary arrangement and order, sometimes even "inverted," in other words, in "disorder." For them, the dream was the imaginary, it was empty, null, and arbitrarily "stuck together" (*bricolé*), once the eyes had closed, from the residues of the only full and positive reality, the reality of the day. This is exactly the status of philosophy and ideology (since in this book philosophy is ideology *par excellence*) in *The German Ideology.*

Ideology, then, is for Marx an imaginary assemblage (*bricolage*), a pure dream, empty and vain, constituted by the "day's residues" from the only full and positive reality, that of the concrete history of concrete material individuals materially producing their existence. It is on this basis that ideology has no history in *The German Ideology,* since its history is outside it, where the only existing history is, the history of concrete individuals, etc. In *The German Ideology,* the thesis that ideology has no history is therefore a purely negative thesis, since it means both:

1. ideology is nothing insofar as it is a pure dream (manufactured by who knows what power: if not by the alienation of the division of labor, but that, too, is a *negative* determination);

2. ideology has no history, which emphatically does not mean that there is no history in it (on the contrary, for it is merely the pale, empty, and inverted reflection of real history) but that it has no history *of its own.*

Now, while the thesis I wish to defend formally speaking adopts the terms of *The German Ideology* ("ideology has no history"), it is radically different from the positivist and historicist thesis of *The German Ideology.*

For on the one hand, I think it is possible to hold that ideolog*ies have* *a history of their own* (although it is determined in the last instance by the class struggle); and on the other, I think it is possible to hold that ideology *in general has no history*, not in a negative sense (its history is external to it), but in an absolutely positive sense.

This sense is a positive one if it is true that the peculiarity of ideology is that it is endowed with a structure and a functioning such as to make it a non-historical reality, i.e. an *omni-historical* reality, in the sense in which that structure and functioning are immutable, present in the same form throughout what we can call history, in the sense in which the *Communist Manifesto* defines history as the history of class struggles, i.e. the history of class societies.

To give a theoretical reference-point here, I might say that, to return to our example of the dream, in its Freudian conception this time, our proposition: ideology has no history, can and must (and in a way which has absolutely nothing arbitrary about it, but, quite the reverse, is theoretically necessary, for there is an organic link between the two propositions) be related directly to Freud's proposition that the *unconscious is eternal*, i.e. that it has no history.

If eternal means, not transcendent to all (temporal) history, but omnipresent, trans-historical and therefore immutable in form throughout the extent of history, I shall adopt Freud's expression word for word, and write *ideology is eternal*, exactly like the unconscious. And I add that I find this comparison theoretically justified by the fact that the eternity of the unconscious is not unrelated to the eternity of ideology in general.

That is why I believe I am justified, hypothetically at least, in proposing a theory of ideology *in general*, in the sense that Freud presented a theory of the unconscious *in general*.

To simplify the phrase, it is convenient, taking into account what has been said about ideologies, to use the plain term ideology to designate ideology in general, which I have just said has no history, or, what comes to the same thing, is eternal, i.e. omnipresent in its immutable form throughout history (= the history of social formulations containing social classes). For the moment I shall restrict myself to "class societies" and their history.

Ideology is a "Representation" of the Imaginary Relationship of Individuals to their Real Conditions of Existence

In order to approach my central thesis on the structure and functioning of ideology, I shall first present two theses, one negative, the other positive. The first concerns the object which is "represented" in the imaginary form of ideology, the second concerns the materiality of ideology.

THESIS I: Ideology represents the imaginary relationship of individuals to their real conditions of existence.

We commonly call religious ideology, ethical ideology, legal ideology, political ideology, etc., so many "world outlooks." Of course, assuming that we do not live one of these ideologies as the truth (e.g. "believe" in God, Duty, Justice, etc. . . .), we admit that the ideology we are discussing from a critical point of view, examining it as the ethnologist examines the myths of a "primitive society," that these "world outlooks" are largely imaginary, i.e. do not "correspond to reality."

However, while admitting that they do not correspond to reality, i.e. that they constitute an illusion, we admit that they do make allusion to reality, and that they need only be "interpreted" to discover the reality of the world behind their imaginary representation of that world (ideology = *illusion/allusion*).

There are different types of interpretation, the most famous of which are the *mechanistic* type, current in the eighteenth century (God is the imaginary representation of the real King), and the "*hermeneutic*" interpretation, inaugurated by the earliest Church Fathers, and revived by Feuerbach and the theologico-philosophical school which descends from him, e.g. the theologian Barth (to Feuerbach, for example, God is the essence of real Man). The essential point is that on condition that we interpret the imaginary transposition (and inversion) of ideology we arrive at the conclusion that in ideology "men represent their real conditions of existence to themselves in an imaginary form."

Unfortunately, this interpretation leaves one small problem unsettled: why do men "need" this imaginary transposition of their real conditions of existence in order to "represent to themselves" their real conditions of existence?

The first answer (that of the eighteenth century) proposes a simple solution: Priests or Despots are responsible. They "forged" the Beautiful Lies so that, in the belief that they were obeying God, men would in fact obey the Priests and Despots, who are usually in alliance in their imposture, the Priests acting in the interests of the Despots or *vice versa*, according to the political positions of the "theoreticians" concerned. There is therefore a cause for the imaginary transposition of the real conditions of existence: that cause is the existence of a small number of cynical men who base their domination and exploitation of the "people" on a falsified representation of the world which they have imagined in order to enslave other minds by dominating their imaginations.

The second answer (that of Feuerbach, taken over word for word by Marx in his Early Works) is more "profound," i.e. just as false. It, too, seeks and finds a cause for the imaginary transposition and distortion of men's real conditions of existence, in short, for the alienation in the imaginary of the representation of men's conditions of existence. This cause is no longer Priests or Despots, nor their active imagination and the passive imagination of their victims. This cause is the material alienation which reigns in the conditions of existence of men themselves. This is how, in *The Jewish Question* and elsewhere, Marx defends the Feuerbachian idea that men make themselves an alienated (= imaginary) representation of their conditions of existence because these conditions of existence are themselves alienating (in the *1844 Manuscripts*: because these conditions are dominated by the essence of alienated society—*"alienated labor"*).

All these interpretations thus take literally the thesis which they presuppose, and on which they depend, i.e. that what is reflected in the imaginary representation of the world found in an ideology is the conditions of existence of men, i.e. their real world.

Now I can return to a thesis which I have already advanced: it is not their real conditions of existence, their real world, that "men" "represent to themselves" in ideology, but above all it is their relation to those conditions of existence which is represented to them there. It is this relation which is at the center of every ideological, i.e. imaginary, representation of the real world. It is this relation that contains the "cause" which has to explain the imaginary distortion of the ideological representation of the real world. Or rather, to leave aside the language of causality it is necessary to advance the thesis that it is the *imaginary nature of this relation* which underlies all the imaginary distortion that we can observe (if we do not live in its truth) in all ideology.

To speak in a Marxist language, if it is true that the representation of the real conditions of existence of the individuals occupying the posts of agents of production, exploitation, repression, ideologization, and scientific practice, does in the last analysis arise from the relations of production, and from relations deriving from the relations of production, we can say the following: all ideology represents in its necessarily imaginary distortion not the existing relations of production (and the other relations that derive from them), but above all the (imaginary) relationship of individuals to the relations of production and the relations that derive from them. What is represented in ideology is therefore not the system of the real relations which govern the existence of individuals, but the imaginary relation of those individuals to the real relations in which they live.

If this is the case, the question of the "cause" of the imaginary distortion of the real relations in ideology disappears and must be replaced by a different question: why is the representation given to individuals of their (individual) relation to the social relations which govern their conditions of existence and their collective and individual life necessarily an imaginary relation? And what is the nature of this imaginariness? Posed in this way, the question explodes the solution by a "clique," [14] by a group of individuals (Priests or Despots) who are the authors of the great ideological mystification, just as it explodes the solution by the alienated character of the real world. We shall see why later in my exposition. For the moment I shall go no further.

THESIS II: Ideology has a material existence.

I have already touched on this thesis by saying that the "ideas" or "representations," etc., which seem to make up ideology do not have an ideal (*idéale* or *idéelle*) or spiritual existence, but a material existence. I even suggested that the ideal (*idéale, idéelle*) and spiritual existence of "ideas" arises exclusively in an ideology of the "idea" and of ideology, and let me add, in an ideology of what seems to have "founded" this conception since the emergence of the sciences, i.e. what the practicians of the sciences represent to themselves in their spontaneous ideology as "ideas," true or false. Of course, presented in affirmative form, this thesis is unproven. I simply ask that the reader be favorably disposed towards it, say, in the name of materialism. A long series of arguments would be necessary to prove it.

This hypothetical thesis of the not spiritual but material existence of "ideas" or other "representations" is indeed necessary if we are to advance in our analysis of the nature of ideology. Or rather, it is merely useful to us in order the better to reveal what every at all serious analysis of any ideology will immediately and empirically show to every observer, however critical.

While discussing the ideological State apparatuses and their practices, I said that each of them was the realization of an ideology (the unity of these different regional ideologies—religious, ethical, legal, political, aesthetic, etc.—being assured by their subjection to the ruling ideology). I now return to this thesis: an ideology always exists in an apparatus, and its practice, or practices. This existence is material.

Of course, the material existence of the ideology in an apparatus and its practices does not have the same modality as the material existence of a paving-stone or a rifle. But, at the risk of being taken for a Neo-Aristotelian (NB Marx had a very high regard for Aristotle), I shall say that "matter is discussed in many senses," or rather that it exists in different modalities, all rooted in the last instance in "physical" matter.

Having said this, let me move straight on and see what happens to the "individuals" who live in ideology, i.e. in a determinate (religious, ethical, etc.) representation of the world whose imaginary distortion depends on their imaginary relation to their conditions of existence, in other words, in the last instance, to the relations of production and to class relations (ideology = an imaginary relation to real relations). I shall say that this imaginary relation is itself endowed with a material existence.

Now I observe the following.

An individual believes in God, or Duty, or Justice, etc. This belief derives (for everyone, i.e. for all those who live in an ideological representation of ideology, which reduces ideology to ideas endowed by definition with a spiritual existence) from the ideas of the individual concerned, i.e. from him as a subject with a consciousness which contains the ideas of his belief. In this way, i.e. by means of the absolutely ideological "conceptual" device (*dispositif*) thus set up (a subject endowed with a consciousness in which he freely forms or freely recognizes ideas in which he believes), the (material) attitude of the subject concerned naturally follows.

The individual in question behaves in such and such a way, adopts such and such a practical attitude, and, what is more, participates in certain practices which are those of the ideological apparatus on which "depend" the ideas which he has in all consciousness freely chosen as a subject. If he believes in God, he goes to Church to attend Mass, kneels, prays, confesses, does penance (once it was material in the ordinary sense of the term) and naturally repents and so on. If he believes in Duty, he will have the corresponding attitudes, inscribed in ritual practices "according to the correct principles." If he believes in Justice, he will submit unconditionally to the rules of the Law, and may even protest when they are violated, sign petitions, take part in a demonstration, etc.

Throughout this schema we observe that the ideological representation of ideology is itself forced to recognize that every "subject" endowed with a "consciousness" and believing in the "ideas" that his "consciousness" inspires in him and freely accepts, must "*act* according to his ideas," must therefore inscribe his own ideas as a free subject in the actions of his material practice. If he does not do so, "that is wicked."

Indeed, if he does not do what he ought to do as a function of what he believes, it is because he does something else, which, still as a function of the same idealist scheme, implies that he has other ideas in his head as well as those he proclaims, and that he acts according to these other ideas, as a man who is either "inconsistent" ("no one is willingly evil") or cynical, or perverse.

In every case, the ideology of ideology thus recognizes, despite its imaginary distortion, that the "ideas" of a human subject exist in his actions, or ought to exist in his actions, and if that is not the case, it lends him other ideas corresponding to the actions (however perverse) that he does perform. This ideology talks of actions: I shall talk of actions inserted into *practices*. *And* I shall point out that these practices are governed by the *rituals* in which these practices are inscribed, within the *material existence of an ideological apparatus*, be it only a small part of that apparatus: a small mass in a small church, a funeral, a minor match at a sports club, a school day, a political party meeting, etc.

Besides, we are indebted to Pascal's defensive "dialectic" for the wonderful formula which will enable us to invert the order of the notional schema of ideology. Pascal says more or less: "Kneel down, move your lips in prayer, and you will believe." He thus scandalously inverts the order of things, bringing, like Christ, not peace but strife, and in addition something hardly Christian (for woe to him who brings scandal into the world!)—scandal itself. A fortunate scandal which makes him stick with Jansenist defiance to a language that directly names the reality.

I will be allowed to leave Pascal to the arguments of his ideological struggle with the religious ideological State apparatus of his day. And I shall be expected to use a more directly Marxist vocabulary, if that is possible, for we are advancing in still poorly explored domains.

I shall therefore say that, where only a single subject (such and such an individual) is concerned, the existence of the ideas of his belief is material in that *his ideas are his material actions inserted into material practices governed by material rituals which are themselves defined by the material ideological apparatus from which derive the ideas of that subject.* Naturally, the four inscriptions of the adjective "material" in my proposition must be affected by different modalities: the materialities of a displacement for going to mass, of kneeling down, of the gesture of the sign of the cross, or of the *mea culpa*, of a sentence, of a prayer, of an act of contrition, of a penitence, of a gaze, of a handshake, of an external verbal discourse or an "internal" verbal discourse (consciousness), are not one and the same materiality. I shall leave on one side the problem of a theory of the differences between the modalities of materiality.

It remains that in this inverted presentation of things, we are not dealing with an "inversion" at all, since it is clear that certain notions have purely and simply disappeared from our presentation, whereas others on the contrary survive, and new terms appear.

Disappeared: the term *ideas*.

Survive: the terms *subject, consciousness, belief, actions*.

Appear: the terms *practices, rituals, ideological apparatus*.

It is therefore not an inversion or overturning (except in the sense in which one might say a government or a glass is overturned), but a reshuffle (of a non-ministerial type), a rather strange reshuffle, since we obtain the following result.

Ideas have disappeared as such (insofar as they are endowed with an ideal or spiritual existence), to the precise extent that it has emerged that their existence is inscribed in the actions of practices governed by rituals defined in the last instance by an ideological apparatus. It therefore appears that the subject acts insofar as he is acted by the following system (set out in the order of its real determination): ideology existing in a material ideological apparatus, prescribing material practices governed by a material ritual, which practices exist in the material actions of a subject acting in all consciousness according to his belief.

But this very presentation reveals that we have retained the following notions: subject, consciousness, belief, actions. From this series I shall immediately extract the decisive central term on which everything else depends: the notion of the *subject*.

And I shall immediately set down two conjoint theses:

1. there is no practice except by and in an ideology;
2. there is no ideology except by the subject and for subjects.

I can now come to my central thesis.

Ideology Interpellates Individuals as Subjects

This thesis is simply a matter of making my last proposition explicit: there is no ideology except by the subject and for subjects. Meaning, there is no ideology except for concrete subjects, and this destination for ideology is only made possible by the subject: meaning, *by the category of the subject* and its functioning.

By this I mean that, even if it only appears under this name (the subject) with the rise of bourgeois ideology, above all with the rise of legal ideology,[15] the category of the subject (which may function under other names: e.g., as the soul in Plato, as God, etc.) is the constitutive category of all ideology, whatever its determination (regional or class) and whatever its historical date—since ideology has no history.

I say: the category of the subject is constitutive of all ideology, but at the same time and immediately I add that *the category of the subject is only constitutive of all ideology insofar as all ideology has the function (which defines it) of "constituting" concrete individuals as subjects*. In the interaction of this double constitution exists the functioning of all ideology, ideology being nothing but its functioning in the material forms of existence of that functioning.

In order to grasp what follows, it is essential to realize that both he who is writing these lines and the reader who reads them are themselves subjects, and therefore ideological subjects (a tautological proposition), i.e. that the author and the reader of these lines both live "spontaneously" or "naturally" in ideology in the sense in which I have said that "man is an ideological animal by nature."

That the author, insofar as he writes the lines of a discourse which claims to be scientific, is completely absent as a "subject" from "his" scientific discourse (for all scientific discourse is by definition a subjectless discourse, there is no "Subject of science" except in an ideology of science) is a different question which I shall leave on one side for the moment.

As St. Paul admirably put it, it is in the "Logos," meaning in ideology, that we "live, move and have our being." It follows that, for you and for me, the category of the subject is a primary "obviousness" (obviousnesses are always primary): it is clear that you and I are subjects (free, ethical, etc. . . .). Like all obviousnesses, including those that make a word "name a thing" or "have a meaning" (therefore including the obviousness of the "transparency" of language), the "obviousness" that you and I are subjects—and that that does not cause any problems—is an ideological effect, the elementary ideological effect.[16] It is indeed a peculiarity of ideology that it imposes (without appearing to do so, since these are "obviousnesses") obviousnesses as obviousnesses, which we cannot *fail to recognize* and before which we have the inevitable and natural reaction of crying out (aloud or in the "still, small voice of conscience"): "That's obvious! That's right! That's true!"

At work in this reaction is the ideological *recognition* function which is one of the two functions of ideology as such (its inverse being the function of *misrecognition—méconnaissance*).

To take a highly "concrete" example, we all have friends who, when they knock on our door and we ask, through the door, the question "Who's there?" answer (since "it's obvious") "It's me." And we recognize that "it is him," or "her." We open the door, and "it's true, it really was she who was there." To take another example, when we recognize somebody of our (previous) acquaintance (*(re)-connaissance*) in the street, we show him that we have recognized him (and have recognized that he has recognized us) by saying to him "Hello, my friend," and shaking his hand (a material ritual practice of ideological recognition in everyday life—in France, at least; elsewhere, there are other rituals).

In this preliminary remark and these concrete illustrations, I only wish to point out that you and I are *always already* subjects, and as such constantly practice the rituals of ideological recognition, which guarantee for us that we are indeed concrete, individual, distinguishable, and (naturally) irreplaceable subjects. The writing I am currently executing and the reading you are currently[17] performing are also in this respect rituals of ideological recognition, including the "obviousness" with which the "truth" or "error" of my reflections may impose itself on you.

But to recognize that we are subjects and that we function in the practical rituals of the most elementary everyday life (the handshake, the fact of calling you by your name, the fact of knowing, even if I do not know what it is, that you "have" a name of your own, which means that you are recognized as a unique subject, etc.)—this recognition only gives us the "consciousness" of our incessant (eternal) practice of ideological recognition—its consciousness, i.e. its *recognition*—but in no sense does it give us the (scientific) *knowledge* of the mechanism of this recognition. Now it is this knowledge that we have to reach, if you will, while speaking in ideology, and from within ideology we have to outline a discourse which tries to break with ideology, in order to dare to be the beginning of a scientific (i.e. subjectless) discourse on ideology.

Thus in order to represent why the category of the "subject" is constitutive of ideology, which only exists by constituting concrete subjects as subjects, I shall employ a special mode of exposition: "concrete" enough to be recognized, but abstract enough to be thinkable and thought, giving rise to a knowledge.

As a first formulation I shall say: *all ideology hails or interpellates concrete individuals as concrete subjects*, by the functioning of the category of the subject.

This is a proposition which entails that we distinguish for the moment between concrete individuals on the one hand and concrete subjects on the other, although at this level concrete subjects only exist insofar as they are supported by a concrete individual.

I shall then suggest that ideology "acts" or "functions" in such a way that it "recruits" subjects among the individuals (it recruits them all), or "transforms" the individuals into subjects (it transforms them all) by that very precise operation which I have called *interpellation* or hailing, and which can be imagined along the lines of the most commonplace everyday police (or other) hailing: "Hey, you there!" [18]

Assuming that the theoretical scene I have imagined takes place in the street, the hailed individual will turn round. By this mere 180-degree physical conversion, he becomes a *subject*. Why? Because he has recognized that the hail was "really" addressed to him, and that "it was *really him* who was hailed" (and not someone else). Experience shows that the practical telecommunication of hailings is such that they hardly ever miss their man: verbal call or whistle, the one hailed always recognizes that it is really him who is being hailed. And yet it is a strange phenomenon, and one which cannot be explained solely by "guilt feelings," despite the large numbers who "have something on their consciences."

Naturally for the convenience and clarity of my little theoretical theater I have had to present things in the form of a sequence, with a before and an after, and thus in the form of a temporal succession. There are individuals walking along. Somewhere (usually behind them) the hail rings out: "Hey, you there!" One individual (nine times out of ten it is the right one) turns round, believing/suspecting/knowing that it is for him, i.e. recognizing that "it really is he" who is meant by the hailing. But in reality these things happen without any succession. The existence of ideology and the hailing or interpellation of individuals as subjects are one and the same thing.

I might add: what thus seems to take place outside ideology (to be precise, in the street), in reality takes place in ideology. What really takes place in ideology seems therefore to take place outside it. That is why those who are in ideology believe themselves by definition outside ideology: one of the effects of ideology is the practical *denegation* of the ideological character of ideology by ideology: ideology never says, "I am ideological." It is necessary to be outside ideology, i.e. in scientific knowledge, to be able to say: I am in ideology (a quite exceptional case) or (the general case): I was in ideology. As is well known, the accusation of being in ideology only applies to others, never to oneself (unless one is really a Spinozist or a Marxist, which, in this matter, is to be exactly the same thing). Which amounts to saying that ideology *has no outside* (for itself), but at the same time *that it is nothing but outside* (for science and reality).

Spinoza explained this completely two centuries before Marx, who practiced it but without explaining it in detail. But let us leave this point, although it is heavy with consequences, consequences which are not just theoretical, but also directly political, since, for example, the whole theory of criticism and self-criticism, the golden rule of the Marxist-Leninist practice of the class struggle, depends on it.

Thus ideology hails or interpellates individuals as subjects. As ideology is eternal, I must now suppress the temporal form in which I have presented the functioning of ideology, and say: ideology has always-already interpellated individuals as subjects, which amounts to making it clear that individuals are always-already interpellated by ideology as subjects, which necessarily leads us to one last proposition: *individuals are always-already subjects.* Hence individuals are "abstract" with respect to the subjects which they always-already are. This proposition might seem paradoxical.

That an individual is always-already a subject, even before he is born, is nevertheless the plain reality, accessible to everyone and not a paradox at all. Freud shows that individuals are always "abstract" with respect to the subjects they always-already are, simply by noting the ideological ritual that surrounds the expectation of a "birth," that "happy event." Everyone knows how much and in what way an unborn child is expected. Which amounts to saying, very prosaically, if we agree to drop the "sentiments," i.e. the forms of family ideology (paternal/maternal/conjugal/fraternal) in which the unborn child is expected: it is certain in advance that it will bear its Father's Name, and will therefore have an identity and be irreplaceable. Before its birth, the child is therefore always-already a subject, appointed as a subject in and by the specific familial ideological configuration in which it is "expected" once it has been conceived. I hardly need add that this familial ideological configuration is, in its uniqueness, highly structured, and that it is in this implacable and more or less "pathological" (presupposing that any meaning can be assigned to that term) structure that the former subject-to-be will have to "find" "its" place, i.e. "become" the sexual subject (boy or girl) which it already is in advance. It is clear that this ideological constraint and pre-appointment, and all the rituals of rearing and then education in the family, have some relationship with what Freud studied in the forms of the pre-genital and genital "stages" of sexuality, i.e. in the "grip" of what Freud registered by its effects as being the unconsciousness. But let us leave this point, too, on one side.

Let me go one step further. What I shall now turn my attention to is the way the "actors" in this *mise en scène* of interpellation, and their respective roles, are reflected in the very structure of all ideology.

An Example: The Christian Religious Ideology

As the formal structure of all ideology is always the same, I shall restrict my analysis to a single example, one accessible to everyone, that of religious ideology, with the proviso that the same demonstration can be produced for ethical, legal, political, aesthetic ideology, etc.

Let us therefore consider the Christian religious ideology. I shall use a rhetorical figure and "make it speak," i.e. collect into a fictional discourse what it "says" not only in its two Testaments, its Theologians, Sermons, but also in its practices, its rituals, its ceremonies, and its sacraments. The Christian religious ideology says something like this:

It says: I address myself to you, a human individual called Peter (every individual is called by his name, in the passive sense, it is never he who provides his own name), in order to tell you that God exists and that you are answerable to Him. It adds: God addresses himself to you through my voice (Scripture having collected the Word of God, Tradition having transmitted it, Papal Infallibility fixing it for ever on "nice" points). It says: this is who you are: you are Peter! This is your origin, you were created by God for all eternity, although you were born in the 1920th year of Our Lord! This is your place in the world! This is what you must do! By these means, if you observe the "law of love" you will be saved, you, Peter, and will become part of the Glorious Body of Christ! Etc. . . .

Now this is quite a familiar and banal discourse, but at the same time quite a surprising one.

Surprising because if we consider that religious ideology is indeed addressed to individuals,[19] in order to "transform them into subjects," by interpellating the individual, Peter, in order to make him a subject, free to obey or disobey the appeal, i.e. God's commandments; if it calls these individuals by their names, thus recognizing that they are always-already interpellated as subjects with a personal identity (to the extent that Pascal's Christ says: "It is for you that I have shed this drop of my blood!"); if it interpellates them in such a way that the subject responds: "*Yes, it really is me!*" if it obtains from them the *recognition* that they really do occupy the place it designates for them as theirs in the world, a fixed residence: "It is really me, I am here, a worker, a boss or a soldier!" in this vale of tears; if it obtains from them the recognition of a destination (eternal life or damnation) according to the respect or contempt they show to "God's Commandments," Law becomes Love;—if everything does happen in this way (in the practices of the well-known rituals of baptism, confirmation, communion, confession, and extreme unction, etc. . . .), we should note that all this "procedure" to set up Christian religious subjects is dominated by a strange phenomenon: the fact that there can only be such a multitude of possible religious subjects on the absolute condition that there is a Unique, Absolute, *Other Subject*, i.e. God.

It is convenient to designate this new and remarkable Subject by writing Subject with a capital *S* to distinguish it from ordinary subjects, with a small *s*.

It then emerges that the interpellation of individuals as subjects presupposes the "existence" of a Unique and central Other Subject, in whose Name the religious ideology interpellates all individuals as subjects. All this is clearly[20] written in what is rightly called the Scriptures. "And it came to pass at that time that God the Lord (Yahweh) spoke to Moses in the cloud. And the Lord cried to Moses, 'Moses!' And Moses replied 'It is (really) I! I am Moses thy servant, speak and I shall listen!' And the Lord spoke to Moses and said to him, '*I am that I am.*'"

God thus defines himself as the Subject *par excellence*, he who is through himself and for himself ("I am that I am"), and he who interpellates his subject, the individual subjected to him by his very interpellation, i.e. the individual named Moses. And Moses, interpellated-called by his Name, having recognized that it "really" was he who was called by God, recognizes that he is a subject, a subject *of* God, a subject subjected to God, *a subject through the Subject and subjected to the Subject*. The proof: he obeys him, and makes his people obey God's Commandments.

God is thus the Subject, the Moses and the innumerable subjects of God's people, the Subject's interlocutors-interpellates: his *mirrors*, his *reflections*. Were not men made *in the image* of God? As all theological reflection proves, whereas He "could" perfectly well have done without men, God needs them, the Subject needs the subjects, just as men need God, the subjects need the Subject. Better: God needs men, the great Subject needs subjects, even in the terrible inversion of his image in them (when the subjects wallow in debauchery, i.e. sin).

Better: God duplicates himself and sends his Son to the Earth, as a mere subject "forsaken" by him (the long complaint of the Garden of Olives which ends in the Crucifixion), subject but Subject, man but God, to do what prepares the way for the final Redemption, the Resurrection of Christ. God thus needs to "make himself" a man, the Subject needs to become a subject, as if to show empirically, visibly to the eye, tangibly to the hands (see St. Thomas) of the subjects, that, if they are subjects, subjected to the Subject, that is solely in order that finally, on Judgment Day, they will re-enter the Lord's Bosom, like Christ, i.e. re-enter the Subject.[21]

Let us decipher into theoretical language this wonderful necessity for the duplication of *the Subject into subjects* and of *the Subject itself into a subject-Subject*.

We observe that the structure of all ideology, interpellating individuals as subjects in the name of a Unique and Absolute Subject is *speculary*, i.e. a mirror-structure, and *doubly* speculary: this mirror duplication is constitutive of ideology and ensures its functioning. Which means that all ideology is *centered*, that the Absolute Subject occupies the unique place of the Center, and interpellates around it the infinity of individuals into subjects in a double mirror-connection such that it *subjects* the subjects to the Subject, while giving them in the Subject in which each subject can contemplate its own image (present and future) the *guarantee* that this really concerns them and Him, and that since everything takes place in the Family (the Holy Family: the Family is in essence Holy), "God will *recognize* his own in it," i.e. those who have recognized God, and have recognized themselves in Him, will be saved.

Let me summarize what we have discovered about ideology in general.

The duplicate mirror-structure of ideology ensures simultaneously:

1. the interpellation of "individuals" as subjects;

2. their subjection to the Subject;

3. the mutual recognition of subjects and Subject, the subjects' recognition of each other, and finally the subject's recognition of himself;[22]

4. the absolute guarantee that everything really is so, and that on condition that the subjects recognize what they are and behave accordingly, everything will be all right: Amen— *"So be it."*

Result: caught in this quadruple system of interpellation as subjects, of subjection to the Subject, of universal recognition and of absolute guarantee, the subjects "work," they "work by themselves" in the vast majority of cases, with the exception of the "bad subjects" who on occasion provoke the intervention of one of the detachments of the (repressive) State apparatus. But the vast majority of (good) subjects work all right "all by themselves," i.e. by ideology (whose concrete forms are realized in the Ideological State Apparatuses). They are inserted into practices governed by the rituals of the ISAs. They "recognize" the existing state of affairs (*das Bestehende*), that "it really is true that it is so and not otherwise," and that they must be obedient to God, to their conscience, to the priest, to de Gaulle, to the boss, to the engineer, that thou shalt "love thy neighbor as thyself," etc. Their concrete, material behavior is simply the inscription in life of the admirable words of the prayer: *"Amen—So be it."*

Yes, the subjects "work by themselves." The whole mystery of this effect lies in the first two moments of the quadruple system I have just discussed, or, if you prefer, in the ambiguity of the term *subject*. In the ordinary use of the term, subject in fact means: (1) a free subjectivity, a center of initiatives, author of and responsible for its actions; (2) a subjected being, who submits to a higher authority, and is therefore stripped of all freedom except that of freely accepting his submission. This last note gives us the meaning of this ambiguity, which is merely a reflection of the effect which produces it: the individual *is interpellated as a (free) subject in order that he shall submit freely to the commandments of the Subject, i.e. in order that he shall (freely) accept his subjection, i.e. in order that he shall make the gestures and actions of his subjection "all by himself." There are no subjects except by and for their subjection.* That is why they "work all by themselves."

"So be it! . . ." This phrase which registers the effect to be obtained proves that it is not "naturally" so ("naturally": outside the prayer, i.e. outside the ideological intervention). This phrase proves that it *has* to be so if things are to be what they must be, and let us let the words slip: if the reproduction of the relations of production is to be assured, even in the process of production and circulation, every day, in the "consciousness," i.e. in the attitudes of the individual-subjects occupying

the posts which the socio-technical division of labor assigns to them in production, exploitation, repression, ideologization, scientific practice, etc. Indeed, what is really in question in this mechanism of the mirror recognition of the Subject and of the individuals interpellated as subjects, and of the guarantee given by the Subject to the subjects if they freely accept their subjection to the Subject's "commandments"? The reality in question in this mechanism, the reality which is necessarily *ignored (méconnue)* in the very forms of recognition (ideology = misrecognition/ignorance) is indeed, in the last resort, the reproduction of the relations of production and of the relations deriving from them.

January-April 1969

P.S. If these few schematic theses allow me to illuminate certain aspects of the functioning of the Superstructure and its mode of intervention in the Infrastructure, they are obviously *abstract* and necessarily leave several important problems unanswered, which should be mentioned:

1. The problem of the *total process* of the realization of the reproduction of the relations of production.

As an element of this process, the ISAs *contribute* to this reproduction. But the point of view of their contribution alone is still an abstract one.

It is only within the processes of production and circulation that this reproduction is *realized*. It is realized by the mechanisms of those processes, in which the training of the workers is "completed," their posts assigned them, etc. It is in the internal mechanisms of these processes that the effect of the different ideologies is felt (above all the effect of legal-ethical ideology).

But this point of view is still an abstract one. For in a class society the relations of production are relations of exploitation, and therefore relations between antagonistic classes. The reproduction of the relations of production, the ultimate aim of the ruling class, cannot therefore be a merely technical operation training and distributing individuals for the different posts in the "technical division" of labor. In fact there is no "technical division" of labor except in the ideology of the ruling class: every "technical" division, every "technical" organization of labor is the form and mask of a *social* (= class) division and organization of labor. The reproduction of the relations of production can therefore only be a class undertaking. It is realized through a class struggle which counterposes the ruling class and the exploited class.

The *total process* of the realization of the reproduction of the relations of production is therefore still abstract, insofar as it has not adopted the point of view of this class struggle. To adopt the point of view of reproduction is therefore, in the last instance, to adopt the point of view of the class struggle.

2. The problem of the class nature of the ideolog*ies* existing in a social formation.

The "mechanism" of ideology *in general* is one thing. We have seen that it can be reduced to a few principles expressed in a few words (as "poor" as those which, according to Marx, define production *in general*, or in Freud, define *the* unconscious *in general*). If there is any truth in it, this mechanism must be *abstract* with respect to every real ideological formation.

I have suggested that the ideologies were *realized* in institutions, in their rituals and their practices, in the ISAs. We have seen that on this basis they contribute to that form of class struggle, vital for the ruling class, the reproduction of the relations of production. But the point of view itself, however real, is still an abstract one.

In fact, the State and its Apparatuses only have meaning from the point of view of the class struggle, as an apparatus of class struggle ensuring class oppression and guaranteeing the conditions of exploitation and its reproduction. But there is no class struggle without antagonistic classes. Whoever says class struggle of the ruling class says resistance, revolt, and class struggle of the ruled class.

That is why the ISAs are not the realization of ideology *in general*, nor even the conflict-free realization of the ideology of the ruling class. The ideology of the ruling class does not become the ruling ideology by the grace of God, nor even by virtue of the seizure of State power alone. It is by the installation of the ISAs in which this ideology is realized and realizes itself that it becomes the ruling ideology. But this installation is not achieved all by itself; on the contrary, it is the stake in a very bitter and continuous class struggle: first against the former ruling classes and their positions in the old and new ISAs, then against the exploited class.

But this point of view of the class struggle in the ISAs is still an abstract one. In fact, the class struggle in the ISAs is indeed an aspect of the class struggle, sometimes an important and symptomatic one: e.g. the anti-religious struggle in the eighteenth century, or the "crisis" of the educational ISA in every capitalist country today. But the class struggles in the ISAs is only one aspect of a class struggle which goes beyond the ISAs. The ideology that a class in power makes the ruling ideology in its ISAs is indeed "realized" in those ISAs, but it goes beyond them, for it comes from elsewhere. Similarly, the ideology that a ruled class manages to defend in and against such ISAs goes beyond them, for it comes from elsewhere.

It is only from the point of view of the classes, i.e. of the class struggle, that it is possible to explain the ideolog*ies* existing in a social formation. Not only is it from this starting-point that it is possible to explain the realization of the ruling ideology in the ISAs and of the forms of class struggle for which the ISAs are the seat and the stake. But it is also and above all from this starting-point that it is possible to understand the provenance of the ideologies which are realized in the ISAs and confront one another there. For if it is true that the ISAs represent the *form* in which the ideology of the ruling class must *necessarily* be realized, and the form in which the ideology of the ruled class must *necessarily* be measured and confronted, ideologies are not "born" in the ISAs but from the social classes at grips in the class struggle: from their conditions of existence, their practices, their experience of the struggle, etc.

April 1970

From *Lenin and Philosophy*, Trans. Ben Brewster. New York: Monthly Review Press, 1971, pp. 127-186.

NOTES

1. This text is made up of two extracts from an ongoing study. The subtitle "Notes towards an Investigation" is the author's own. The ideas expounded should not be regarded as more than the introduction to a discussion.
2. Marx to Kugelmann, 11 July 1868, *Selected Correspondence* (Moscow, 1955), p. 209.
3. Marx gave it its scientific concept: *variable capital*.
4. In *For Marx* and *Reading Capital*, 1965 (English editions 1969 and 1970 respectively).
5. *Topography* from the Greek *topos*: place. A topography represents in a definite space the respective *sites* occupied by several realities: thus the economic is *at the bottom* (the base), the superstructure *above it*.
6. See below, [section entitled] *On Ideology*.
7. To my knowledge, Gramsci is the only one who went any distance in the road I am taking. He had the "remarkable" idea that the State could not be reduced to the (Repressive) State Apparatus, but included, as he put it, a certain number of institutions from *"civil society"*: the Church, the Schools, the trade unions, etc. Unfortunately, Gramsci did not systematize his institutions, which remained in the state of acute but fragmentary notes (cf. Gramsci, *Selections from the Prison Notebooks* (International Publishers, 1971), pp. 12, 259, 260-3; see also the letter to Tatiana Schucht, 7 September 1931, in *Lettre del Carcere* (Einaudi, 1968), p. 479.)
8. The family obviously has other "functions" than that of an ISA. It intervenes in the reproduction of labor power. In different modes of production it is the unit of production and/or the unit of consumption.
9. The "Law" belongs both to the (Repressive) State Apparatus and to the system of the ISAs.
10. In a pathetic text written in 1937, Krupskaya relates the history of Lenin's desperate

efforts and what she regards as his failure.

11. What I have said in these few brief words about the class struggle in the ISAs is obviously far from exhausting the question of the class struggle.

To approach this question, two principles must be borne in mind:

The first principle was formulated by Marx in the Preface to *A Contribution to the Critique of Political Economy*: "In considering such transformations [a social revolution] a distinction should always be made between the material transformation of the economic conditions of production, which can be determined with the precision of natural science, and the legal, political, religious, aesthetic or philosophic—in short, ideological forms in which men become conscious of this conflict and fight it out." The class struggle is thus expressed and exercised in ideological forms, thus also in the ideological forms of the ISAs. But the class struggle *extends far beyond* these forms, and it is because it extends beyond them that the struggle of the exploited classes may also be exercised in the forms of the ISAs, and thus turn the weapon of ideology against the classes in power.

This by virtue of the *second principle*: the class struggle extends beyond the ISAs because it is rooted elsewhere than in ideology, in the Infrastructure, in the relations of production, which are relations of exploitation and constitute the base for class relations.

12. For the most part. For the relations of production are first reproduced by the materiality of the processes of production and circulation. But it should not be forgotten that ideological relations are immediately present in these same processes.

13. *For that part* of reproduction to which the Repressive State Apparatus and the Ideological State Apparatus *contribute.*

14. I use this very modern term deliberately. For even in Communist circles, unfortunately, it is a commonplace to "explain" some political deviation (left or right opportunism) by the action of a "clique."

15. Which borrowed the legal category of "subject in law" to make an ideological notion: man is by nature a subject.

16. Linguists and those who appeal to linguistics for various purposes often run up against difficulties which arise because they ignore the action of the ideological effects in all discourses—including even scientific discourses.

17. NB: this double "currently" is one more proof of the fact that ideology is "eternal," since these two "currentlys" are separated by an indefinite interval; I am writing these lines on 6 April 1969, you may read them at any subsequent time.

18. Hailing as an everyday practice subject to a precise ritual takes a quite "special" form in the policeman's practice of "hailing" which concerns the hailing of "suspects."

19. Although we know that the individual is always already a subject, we go on using this term, convenient because of the contrasting effect it produces.

20. I am quoting in a combined way, not to the letter but "in spirit and truth."

21. The dogma of the Trinity is precisely the theory of the duplication of the Subject (the Father) into a subject (the Son) and of their mirror-connection (the Holy Spirit).

22. Hegel is (unknowingly) an admirable "theoretician" of ideology insofar as he is a "theoretician" of Universal Recognition who unfortunately ends up in the ideology of Absolute Knowledge. Feuerbach is an astonishing "theoretician" of the mirror connection, who unfortunately ends up in the ideology of the Human Essence. To find the material with which to construct a theory of the guarantee, we must turn to Spinoza.

Constituents of a Theory of the Media

Hans Magnus Enzensberger

If you should think this is Utopian, then I would ask you to consider why it is Utopian.

Bertolt Brecht: *Theory of Radio*

WITH THE DEVELOPMENT of the electronic media, the industry that shapes consciousness has become the pacemaker for the social and economic development of societies in the late industrial age. It infiltrates into all other sectors of production, takes over more and more directional and control functions, and determines the standard of the prevailing technology.

In lieu of normative definitions, here is an incomplete list of new developments which have emerged in the last twenty years: news satellites, color television, cable relay television, cassettes, videotape, videotape recorders, video-phones, stereophony, laser techniques, electrostatic reproduction processes, electronic high-speed printing, composing and learning machines, microfiches with electronic access, printing by radio, time-sharing computers, data banks. All these new forms of media are constantly forming new connections both with each other and with older media like printing, radio, film, television, telephone, teletype, radar, and so on. They are clearly coming together to form a universal system.

The general contradiction between productive forces and productive relationships emerges most sharply, however, when they are most advanced. By contrast, protracted structural crises, as in coal mining, can be solved merely by getting rid of a backlog, that is to say, essentially they can be solved within the terms of their own system, and a revolutionary strategy that relied on them would be shortsighted.

Monopoly capitalism develops the consciousness-shaping industry more quickly and more extensively than other sectors of production; it must at the same time fetter it. A socialist media theory has to work at this contradiction, demonstrate that it cannot be solved within the given productive relationships—rapidly increasing discrepancies, potential destructive forces. "Certain demands of a prognostic nature must be made" of any such theory (Benjamin).

A "critical" inventory of the status quo is not enough. There is danger of underestimating the growing conflicts in the media field, of neutralizing them, of interpreting them merely in terms of trade unionism or liberalism, on the lines of traditional labor struggles or as the clash of special interests (program heads/executive producers, publishers/authors, monopolies/medium-sized businesses, public corporations/private companies, etc.). An appreciation of this kind does not go far enough and remains bogged down in tactical arguments.

So far there is no Marxist theory of the media. There is therefore no strategy one can apply in this area. Uncertainty, alternations between fear and surrender, mark the attitude of the socialist Left to the new productive forces of the media industry. The ambivalence of this attitude merely mirrors the ambivalence of the media themselves without mastering it. It could only be overcome by releasing the emancipatory potential which is inherent in the new productive forces—a potential which capitalism must sabotage just as surely as Soviet revisionism, because it would endanger the rule of both systems.

The Mobilizing Power of the Media

2. The open secret of the electronic media, the decisive political factor, which has been waiting, suppressed or crippled, for its moment to come, is their mobilizing power.

When I say *mobilize* I mean *mobilize*. In a country which has had direct experience of fascism (and Stalinism) it is perhaps still necessary to explain, or to explain again, what that means—namely, to make men, more mobile than they are. As free as dancers, as aware as football players, as surprising as guerrillas. Anyone who thinks of the masses only as the object of politics cannot mobilize them. He wants to push them around. A parcel is not mobile; it can only be pushed to and fro. Marches, columns, parades, immobilize people. Propaganda, which does not release self-reliance but limits it, fits into the same pattern. It leads to depoliticization.

For the first time in history, the media are making possible mass participation in a social and socialized productive process, the practical means of which are in the hands of the masses themselves. Such a use of them would bring the communications media, which up to now have not deserved the name, into their own. In its present form, equipment like television or film does not serve communication but prevents it. It allows no reciprocal action between transmitter and receiver; technically speaking, it reduces feedback to the lowest point compatible with the system.

This state of affairs, however, cannot be justified technically. On the contrary. Electronic techniques recognize no contradiction in principle between transmitter and receiver. Every transistor radio is, by the nature of its construction, at the same time a potential transmitter; it can interact with other receivers by circuit reversal. The development from a mere distribution medium to a communications medium is technically not a problem. It is consciously prevented for understandable political reasons. The technical distinction between receivers and transmitters reflects the social division of labor into producers and consumers, which in the consciousness industry becomes of particular political importance. It is based, in the last analysis, on the basic contradiction between the ruling class and the ruled class—that is to say, between monopoly capital or monopolistic bureaucracy on the one hand and the dependent masses on the other.

This structural analogy can be worked out in detail. To the programs offered by the broadcasting cartels there correspond the politics offered by a power cartel consisting of parties constituted along authoritarian lines. In both cases marginal differences in their platforms reflect a competitive relationship which on essential questions is nonexistent. Minimal independent activity on the part of the voter/viewer is desired. As is the case with parliamentary elections under the two-party system, the feedback is reduced to indices. "Training in decision making" is reduced to the response to a single, three-point switching process: Program 1; Program 2; Switch off (abstention).

Radio must be changed from a means of distribution to a means of communication. Radio would be the most wonderful means of communication imaginable in public life, a huge linked system—that is to say, it would be such if it were capable not only of transmitting but of receiving, of allowing the listener not only to hear but to speak, and did not isolate him but brought him into contact. Unrealizable in this social system, realizable in another, these proposals, which are, after all, only the natural consequences of technical development, help towards the propagation and shaping of that *other* system.[1]

The Orwellian Fantasy

3. George Orwell's bogey of a monolithic consciousness industry derives from a view of the media which is undialectical and obsolete. The possibility of total control of such a system at a central point belongs not to the future but to the past. With the aid of systems theory, discipline which is part of bourgeois science—using, that is to say, categories which are immanent in the system—it can be demonstrated that a linked series of communications or, to use the technical term, switchable network, to the degree that it exceeds a certain critical size, can no longer be centrally controlled but only dealt with statistically. This basic "leakiness" of stochastic systems admittedly allows the calculation of probabilities based on sampling and extrapolations; but blanket supervision would demand a monitor that was bigger than the system itself. The monitoring of all telephone conversations, for instance, postulates an apparatus which would need to be n times more extensive and more complicated than that of the present telephone system. A censor's office, which carried out its work extensively, would of necessity become the largest branch of industry in its society.

But supervision on the basis of approximation can only offer inadequate instruments for the self-regulation of the whole system in accordance with the concepts of those who govern it. It postulates a high degree of internal stability. If this precarious balance is upset, then crisis measures based on statistical methods of control are useless. Interference can penetrate the leaky nexus of the media, spreading and multiplying there with the utmost speed, by resonance. The regime so threatened will in such cases, insofar as it is still capable of action, use force and adopt police or military methods.

A state of emergency is therefore the only alternative to leakage in the consciousness industry; but it cannot be maintained in the long run. Societies in the late industrial age rely on the free exchange of information; the "objective pressures" to which their controllers constantly appeal are thus turned against them. Every attempt to suppress the random factors, each diminution of the average flow and each distortion of the information structure must, in the long run, lead to an embolism.

The electronic media have not only built up the information network intensively, they have also spread it extensively. The radio wars of the fifties demonstrated that in the realm of communications, national sovereignty is condemned to wither away. The further development of satellites will deal it the *coup de grâce*. Quarantine regulations for information, such as were promulgated by fascism and Stalinism, are only possible today at the cost of deliberate industrial regression.

Example. The Soviet bureaucracy, that is to say the most widespread and complicated bureaucracy in the world, has to deny itself almost entirely an elementary piece of organizational equipment, the duplicating machine, because this instrument potentially makes everyone a printer. The political risk involved, the possibility of a leakage in the information network, is accepted only at the highest levels, at exposed switchpoints in political, military, and scientific areas. It is clear that Soviet society has to pay an immense price for the suppression of its own productive resources—clumsy procedures, misinformation, *faux frais*. The phenomenon incidentally has its analogue in the capitalist West, if in a diluted form. The technically most advanced electrostatic copying machine, which operates with ordinary paper—which cannot, that is to say, be supervised and is independent of suppliers—is the property of a monopoly (Xerox), on principle it is not sold but rented. The rates themselves ensure that it does not get into the wrong hands. The equipment crops up as if by magic where economic and political power are concentrated. Political control of the equipment goes hand in hand with maximization of profits for the manufacturer. Admittedly this control, as opposed to Soviet methods, is by no means "watertight" for the reasons indicated.

The problem of censorship thus enters a new historical stage. The struggle for the freedom of the press and freedom of ideas has, up till now, been mainly an argument within the bourgeoisie itself; for the masses, freedom to express opinions was a fiction since they were, from the beginning, barred from the means of production—above all from the press—and thus were unable to join in freedom of expression from the start. Today censorship is threatened by the productive forces of the consciousness industry which is already, to some extent, gaining the upper hand over the prevailing relations of production. Long before the latter are overthrown, the contradiction between what is possible and what actually exists will become acute.

Cultural Archaism in the Left Critique

4. The New Left of the sixties has reduced the development of the

media to a single concept—that of manipulation. This concept was originally extremely useful for heuristic purposes and has made possible a great many individual analytical investigations, but it now threatens to degenerate into a mere slogan which conceals more than it is able to illuminate, and therefore itself requires analysis.

The current theory of manipulation on the Left is essentially defensive; its effects can lead the movement into defeatism. Subjectively speaking, behind the tendency to go on the defensive lies a sense of impotence. Objectively, it corresponds to the absolutely correct view that the decisive means of production are in enemy hands. But to react to this state of affairs with moral indignation is naive. There is in general an undertone of lamentation when people speak of manipulation which points to idealistic expectations—as if the class enemy had ever stuck to the promises of fair play it occasionally utters. The liberal superstition that in political and social questions there is such a thing as pure, unmanipulated truth seems to enjoy remarkable currency among the socialist Left. It is the unspoken basic premise of the manipulation thesis.

This thesis provides no incentive to push ahead. A socialist perspective which does not go beyond attacking existing property relationships is limited. The expropriation of Springer is a desirable goal but it would be good to know to whom the media should be handed over. The Party? To judge by all experience of that solution, it is not a possible alternative. It is perhaps no accident that the Left has not yet produced an analysis of the pattern of manipulation in countries with socialist regimes.

The manipulation thesis also serves to exculpate oneself. To cast the enemy in the role of the devil is to conceal the weakness and lack of perspective in one's own agitation. If the latter leads to self-isolation instead of mobilizing the masses, then its failure is attributed holus-bolus to the overwhelming power of the media.

The theory of repressive tolerance has also permeated discussion of the media by the Left. This concept, which was formulated by its author with the utmost care, has also, when whittled away in an undialectical manner, become a vehicle for resignation. Admittedly, when an office-equipment firm can attempt to recruit sales staff with the picture of Che Guevara and the text *We would have hired him*, the temptation to withdraw is great. But fear of handling shit is a luxury a sewerman cannot necessarily afford.

The electronic media do away with cleanliness; they are by their nature "dirty." That is part of their productive power. In terms of structure, they are antisectarian—a further reason why the Left, insofar as it is not prepared to re-examine its traditions, has little idea what to do with them. The desire for a cleanly defined "line" and for the suppression of "deviations" is anachronistic and now serves only one's own need for security. It weakens one's own position by irrational purges, exclusions, and fragmentation, instead of strengthening it by rational discussion.

These resistances and fears are strengthened by a series of cultural factors which, for the most part, operate unconsciously, and which are to be explained by the social history of the participants in today's Left movement—namely their bourgeois class background. It often seems as if it were precisely because of their progressive potential that the media are felt to be an immense threatening power; because for the first time they present a basic challenge to bourgeois culture and thereby to the privileges of the bourgeois intelligentsia—a challenge far more radical than any self-doubt this social group can display. In the New Left's opposition to the media, old bourgeois fears such as the fear of "the masses" seem to be reappearing along with equally old bourgeois longings for pre-industrial times dressed up in progressive clothing.

At the very beginning of the student revolt, during the Free Speech Movement at Berkeley, the computer was a favorite target for aggression. Interest in the Third World is not always free from motives based on antagonism towards civilization which has its source in conservative culture critique. During the May events in Paris, the reversion to archaic forms of production was particularly characteristic. Instead of carrying out agitation among the workers with a modern offset press, the students printed their posters on the hand presses of the École des Beaux Arts. The political slogans were hand-painted; stencils would certainly have made it possible to produce them *en masse*, but it would have offended the creative imagination of the authors. The ability to make proper strategic use of the most advanced media was lacking. It was not the radio headquarters that were seized by the rebels, but the Odéon Theatre, steeped in tradition.

The obverse of this fear of contact with the media is the fascination they exert on left-wing movements in the great cities. On the one hand, the comrades take refuge in outdated forms of communication and esoteric arts and crafts instead of occupying themselves with the contradiction between the present constitution of the media and their revolutionary potential; on the other hand, they cannot escape from the consciousness industry's program or from its aesthetic. This leads, subjectively, to a split between a puritanical view of political action and the area of private "leisure"; objectively, it leads to a split between politically active groups and subcultural groups.

In Western Europe the socialist movement mainly addresses itself to a public of converts through newspapers and journals which are exclusive in terms of language, content, and form. These newssheets presuppose a structure of party members and sympathizers and a situation, where the media are concerned, that roughly corresponds to the historical situation in 1900; they are obviously fixated on the *Iskra* model. Presumably the people who produce them listen to the Rolling Stones, watch occupations and strikes on television, and go to the cinema to see a Western or a Godard; only in their capacity as producers do they make an exception, and, in their analyses, the whole media sector is reduced to the slogan of "manipulation." Every foray into this territory is regarded from the start with suspicion as a step towards integration. This suspicion is not unjustified; it can however also mask one's own ambivalence and insecurity. Fear of being swallowed up by the system is a sign of weakness; it presupposes that capitalism could overcome any contradiction—a conviction which can easily be refuted historically and is theoretically untenable.

If the socialist movement writes off the new productive forces of the consciousness industry and relegates work on the media to a subculture, then we have a vicious circle. For the Underground may be increasingly aware of the technical and aesthetic possibilities of the disc, of videotape, of the electronic camera, and so on, and is systematically exploring the terrain, but it has no political viewpoint of its own and therefore mostly falls a helpless victim to commercialism. The politically active groups then point to such cases with smug *Schaden-freude*. A process of unlearning is the result and both sides are the losers. Capitalism alone benefits from the Left's antagonism to the media, as it does from the depoliticization of the counterculture.

Democratic Manipulation

5. Manipulation—etymologically, "handling"—means technical treatment of a given material with a particular goal in mind. When the technical intervention is of immediate social relevance, then manipulation is a political act. In the case of the media industry, that is by definition the case.

Thus every use of the media presupposes manipulation. The most elementary processes in media production, from the choice of the medium itself to shooting, cutting, synchronization, dubbing, right up to distribution, are all operations carried out on the raw material. There is no such thing as unmanipulated writing, filming, or broadcasting. The question is therefore not whether the media are manipulated, but who manipulates them. A revolutionary plan should not require the manipulators to disappear; on the contrary, it must make everyone a manipulator.

All technical manipulations are potentially dangerous; the manipulation of the media cannot be countered, however, by old or new forms of censorship, but only by direct social control, that is to say, by the mass of the people, who will have become productive. To this end, the elimination of capitalistic property relationships is a necessary but by no means sufficient condition. There have been no historical examples up until now of the mass self-regulating learning process which is made possible by the electronic media. The Communists' fear of releasing this potential, of the mobilizing capabilities of the media, of the interaction of free producers, is one of the main reasons why even in the socialist countries, the old bourgeois culture, greatly disguised and distorted but structurally intact, continues to hold sway.

As a historical explanation, it may be pointed out that the consciousness industry in Russia at the time of the October Revolution was extraordinarily backward; their productive capacity has grown enormously since then, but the productive relationships have been artificially preserved, often by force. Then, as now, a primitively edited press, books, and theater were the key media in the Soviet Union. The development of radio, film, and television is politically arrested. Foreign stations like the BBC, the Voice of America, and the *Deutschland Welle*, therefore, not only find listeners, but are received with almost boundless faith. Archaic media like the handwritten pamphlet and poems orally transmitted play an important role.

6. The new media are egalitarian in structure. Anyone can take part in them by a simple switching process. The programs themselves are not material things and can be reproduced at will. In this sense the electronic media are entirely different from the older media like the book or the easel painting, the exclusive class character of which is obvious. Television programs for privileged groups are certainly technically conceivable—closed circuit television—but run counter to the structure. Potentially, the new media do away with all educational privileges and thereby with the cultural monopoly of the bourgeois intelligentsia. This is one of the reasons for the intelligentsia's resentment against the new industry. As for the "spirit" which they are endeavoring to defend against "depersonalization" and "mass culture," the sooner they abandon it the better.

Properties of the New Media

7. The new media are oriented towards action, not contemplation; to-

wards the present, not tradition. Their attitude to time is completely opposed to that of bourgeois culture, which aspires to possession, that is to extension in time, best of all, to eternity. The media produce no objects that can be hoarded and auctioned. They do away completely with "intellectual property" and liquidate the "heritage," that is to say, the class-specific handing-on of nonmaterial capital.

That does not mean to say that they have no history or that they contribute to the loss of historical consciousness. On the contrary, they make it possible for the first time to record historical material so that it can be reproduced at will. By making this material available for present-day purposes, they make it obvious to anyone using it that the writing of history is always manipulation. But the memory they hold in readiness is not the preserve of a scholarly caste. It is social. The banked information is accessible to anyone, and this accessibility is as instantaneous as its recording. It suffices to compare the model of a private library with that of a socialized data bank to recognize the structural difference between the two systems.

8. It is wrong to regard media equipment as mere means of consumption. It is always, in principle, also means of production and, indeed, since it is in the hands of the masses, socialized means of production. The contradiction between producers and consumers is not inherent in the electronic media; on the contrary, it has to be artificially reinforced by economic and administrative measures.

An early example of this is provided by the difference between telegraph and telephone. Whereas the former, to this day, has remained in the hands of a bureaucratic institution which can scan and file every text transmitted, the telephone is directly accessible to all users. With the aid of conference circuits, it can even make possible collective intervention in a discussion by physically remote groups.

On the other hand, those auditory and visual means of communication which rely on "wireless" are still subject to state control (legislation on wireless installations). In the face of technical developments, which long ago made local and international radio-telephony possible, and which constantly opened up new wavebands for television—in the UHF band alone, the dissemination of numerous programs in one locality is possible without interference, not to mention the possibilities offered by wired and satellite television—the prevailing laws for control of the air are anachronistic. They recall the time when the operation of a printing press was dependent on an imperial license. The socialist movements will take up the struggle for their own wavelengths and must, within the foreseeable future, build their own transmitters and relay stations.

9. One immediate consequence of the structural nature of the new media is that none of the regimes at present in power can release their potential. Only a free socialist society will be able to make them fully productive. A further characteristic of the most advanced media— probably the decisive one—confirms this thesis: their collective structure.

For the prospect that in future, with the aid of the media, anyone can become a producer, would remain apolitical and limited were this productive effort to find an outlet in individual tinkering. Work on the media is possible for an individual only insofar as it remains socially and therefore aesthetically irrelevant. The collection of transparencies from the last holiday trip provides a model of this.

That is naturally what the prevailing market mechanisms have aimed at. It has long been clear from apparatus like miniature and 8mm movie cameras, as well as the tape recorder, which are in actual fact already in the hands of the masses, that the individual, so long as he remains isolated, can become with their help at best an amateur but not a producer. Even so potent a means of production as the shortwave transmitter has been tamed in this way and reduced to a harmless and inconsequential hobby in the hands of scattered radio hams. The programs which the isolated amateur mounts are always only bad, outdated copies of what he in any case receives.

Private production for the media is no more than licensed cottage industry. Even when it is made public it remains pure compromise. To this end, the men who own the media have developed special programs which are usually called "Democratic Forum" or something of the kind. There, tucked away in the corner, "the reader (listener, viewer) has his say," which can naturally be cut short at any time. As in the case of public-opinion polling, he is only asked questions so that he may have a chance to confirm his own dependence. It is a control circuit where what is fed in has already made complete allowance for the feedback.

The concept of a license can also be used in another sense—in an economic one; the system attempts to make each participant into a concessionaire of the monopoly that develops his films or plays back his cassettes. The aim is to nip in the bud in this way that independence which video equipment, for instance, makes possible. Naturally, such tendencies go against the grain of the structure, and the new productive forces not only permit but indeed demand their reversal.

The poor, feeble, and frequently humiliating results of this licensed activity are often referred to with contempt by the professional media producers. On top of the damage suffered by the masses comes triumphant mockery because they clearly do not know how to use the media properly. The sort of thing that goes on in certain popular television shows is taken as proof that they are completely incapable of articulating on their own.

Not only does this run counter to the results of the latest psychological and pedagogical research, but it can easily be seen to be a reactionary protective formulation; the "gifted" people are quite simply defending their territories. Here we have a cultural analogue to the familiar political judgments concerning a working class which is presumed to be "stultified" and incapable of any kind of self-determination. Curiously, one may hear the view that the masses could never govern themselves out of the mouths of people who consider themselves socialists. In the best of cases, these are economists who cannot conceive of socialism as anything other than nationalization.

A Socialist Strategy

10. Any socialist strategy for the media must, on the contrary, strive to end the isolation of the individual participants from the social learning and production process. This is impossible unless those concerned organize themselves. This is the political core of the question of the media. It is over this point that socialist concepts part company with the neo-liberal and technocratic ones. Anyone who expects to be emancipated by technological hardware, or by a system of hardware however structured, is the victim of an obscure belief in progress. Anyone who imagines that freedom for the media will be established if only everyone is busy transmitting and receiving is the dupe of a liberalism which, decked out in contemporary colors, merely peddles the faded concepts of a preordained harmony of social interests.

In the face of such illusions, what must be firmly held on to is that the proper use of the media demands organization and makes it possible. Every production that deals with the interests of the producers postulates a collective method of production. It is itself already a form of self-organization of social needs. Tape recorders, ordinary cameras, and movie cameras are already extensively owned by wage-earners. The question is why these means of production do not turn up at factories, in schools, in the offices of the bureaucracy, in short, everywhere where there is social conflict. By producing aggressive forms of publicity which were their own, the masses could secure evidence of their daily experiences and draw effective lessons from them.

Naturally, bourgeois society defends itself against such prospects with a battery of legal measures. It bases itself on the law of trespass, on commercial and official secrecy. While its secret services penetrate everywhere and plug in to the most intimate conversations, it pleads a touching concern for confidentiality, and makes a sensitive display of worrying about the question of privacy when all that is private is the interest of the exploiters. Only a collective, organized effort can tear down these paper walls.

Communication networks which are constructed for such purposes can, over and above their primary function, provide politically interesting organizational models. In the socialist movements the dialectic of discipline and spontaneity, centralism and decentralization, authoritarian leadership and anti-authoritarian disintegration has long ago reached deadlock. Networklike communications models built on the principle of reversibility of circuits might give indications of how to overcome this situation: a mass newspaper, written and distributed by its readers, a video network of politically active groups.

More radically than any good intention, more lastingly than existential flight from one's own class, the media, once they have come into their own, destroy the private production methods of bourgeois intellectuals. Only in productive work and learning processes can their individualism be broken down in such a way that it is transformed from morally based (that is to say, as individual as ever) self-sacrifice to a new kind of political self-understanding and behavior.

11. An all-too-widely disseminated thesis maintains that present-day capitalism lives by the exploitation of unreal needs. That is at best a half-truth. The results obtained by popular American sociologists like Vance Packard are not un-useful but limited. What they have to say about the stimulation of needs through advertising and artificial obsolescence can in any case not be adequately explained by the hypnotic pull exerted on the wage-earners by mass consumption. The hypothesis of "consumer terror" corresponds to the prejudices of a middle class, which considers itself politically enlightened, against the allegedly integrated proletariat, which has become petty bourgeois and corrupt. The attractive power of mass consumption is based not on the dictates of false needs, but on the falsification and exploitation of quite real and legitimate ones without which the parasitic process of advertising would be redundant. A socialist movement ought not to denounce these needs, but take them seriously, investigate them, and make them politically productive.

That is also valid for the consciousness industry. The electronic media do not owe their irresistible power to any sleight-of-hand but to the elemental power of deep social needs which come through even in the present depraved form of these media.

Precisely because no one bothers about them, the interests of the masses have remained a relatively unknown field, at least insofar as they are historically new. They certainly extend far beyond those goals which the traditional working-class movement represented. Just as in the field of production, the industry which produces goods and the consciousness industry merge more and more, so too, subjectively, where needs are concerned, material and nonmaterial factors are closely interwoven. In the process old psycho-social themes are firmly embedded—social prestige, identification patterns—but powerful new themes emerge which are utopian in nature. From a materialistic point of view, neither the one nor the other must be suppressed.

Henri Lefèbvre has proposed the concept of the *spectacle*, the exhibition, the show, to fit the present form of mass consumption. Goods and shop windows, traffic and advertisements, stores and the world of communications, news and packaging, architecture and media production come together to form a totality, a permanent theater, which dominates not only the public city centers but also private interiors. The expression "beautiful living" makes the most commonplace objects of general use into props for this universal festival, in which the fetishistic nature of the commodities triumphs completely over their use value. The swindle these festivals perpetrate is, and remains, a swindle within the present social structure. But it is the harbinger of something else. Consumption as spectacle contains the promise that want will disappear. The deceptive, brutal, and obscene features of this festival derive from the fact that there can be no question of a real fulfillment of its promise. But so long as scarcity holds sway, use-value remains a decisive category which can only be abolished by trickery. Yet trickery on such a scale is only conceivable if it is based on mass need. This need—it is a utopian one—is there. It is the desire for a new ecology, for a breaking down of environmental barriers, for an aesthetic which is not limited to the sphere of "the artistic." These desires are not—or are not primarily—internalized rules of the game as played by the capitalist system. They have physiological roots and can no longer be suppressed. Consumption as spectacle is—in parody form—the anticipation of a utopian situation.

The promises of the media demonstrate the same ambivalence. They are an answer to the mass need for nonmaterial variety and mobility—which at present finds its material realization in private car ownership and tourism—and they exploit it. Other collective wishes, which capital often recognizes more quickly and evaluates more correctly than its opponents, but naturally only so as to trap them and rob them of their explosive force, are just as powerful, just as unequivocally emancipatory: the need to take part in the social process on a local, national, and international scale; the need for new forms of interaction, for release from ignorance and tutelage; the need for self-determination. "Be everywhere!" is one of the most successful slogans of the media industry. The readers' parliament of *Bild-Zeitung* (the Springer Press mass publication) was direct democracy used against the interests of the *demos*. "Open spaces" and "free time" are concepts which corral and neutralize the urgent wishes of the masses.

There is corresponding acceptance by the media of utopian stories: e.g., the story of the young Italo-American who hijacked a passenger plane to get home from California to Rome was taken up without protest even by the reactionary mass press and undoubtedly correctly understood by its readers. The identification is based on what has become a general need. Nobody can understand why such journeys should be reserved for politicians, functionaries, and businessmen. The role of the pop star could be analyzed from a similar angle; in it the authoritarian and emancipatory factors are mingled in an extraordinary way. It is perhaps not unimportant that beat music offers groups, not individuals, as identification models. In the productions of the Rolling Stones (and in the manner of their production) the utopian content is apparent. Events like the Woodstock Festival, the concerts in Hyde Park, on the Isle of Wight, and at Altamont, California, develop a mobilizing power which the political Left can only envy.

It is absolutely clear that, within the present social forms, the consciousness industry can satisfy none of the needs on which it lives and which it must fan, except in the illusory form of games. The point, however, is not to demolish its promises but to take them literally and to show that they can be met only through a cultural revolution. Socialists and socialist regimes which multiply the frustration of the masses by declaring their needs to be false, become the accomplices of the system they have undertaken to fight.

12. Summary

Repressive use of media	Emancipatory use of media
Centrally controlled program	Decentralized program
One transmitter, many receivers	Each receiver a potential transmitter
Immobilization of isolated individuals	Mobilization of the masses
Passive consumer behavior	Interaction of those involved, feedback
Depoliticization	A political learning process
Production by specialists	Collective production

| Control by property owners or bureaucracy | Social control by self-organization |

The Subversive Power of the New Media

13. As far as the objectively subversive potentialities of the electronic media are concerned, both sides in the international class struggle—except for the fatalistic adherents of the thesis of manipulation in the metropoles—are of one mind. Frantz Fanon was the first to draw attention to the fact that the transistor receiver was one of the most important weapons in the third world's fight for freedom. Albert Hertzog, ex-Minister of the South African Republic and the mouthpiece of the right wing of the ruling party, is of the opinion that "television will lead to the ruin of the white man in South Africa."[2] American imperialism has recognized the situation. It attempts to meet the "revolution of rising expectations" in Latin America—that is what its ideologues call it—by scattering its own transmitters all over the continent and into the remotest regions of the Amazon basin, and by distributing single-frequency transistors to the native population. The attacks of the Nixon Administration on the capitalist media in the USA reveal its understanding that their reporting, however one-sided and distorted, has become a decisive factor in mobilizing people against the war in Vietnam. Whereas only twenty-five years ago the French massacres in Madagascar, with almost 100,000 dead, became known only to the readers of *Le Monde* under the heading of "Other News" and therefore remained unnoticed and without sequel in the capital city, today the media drag colonial wars into the centers of imperialism.

The direct mobilizing potentialities of the media become still more clear when they are consciously used for subversive ends. Their presence is a factor that immensely increases the demonstrative nature of any political act. The student movements in the USA, in Japan, and in Western Europe soon recognized this and, to begin with, achieved considerable momentary success with the aid of the media. These effects have worn off. Naive trust in the magical power of reproduction cannot replace organizational work; only active and coherent groups can force the media to comply with the logic of their actions. That can be demonstrated from the example of the Tupamaros in Uruguay, whose revolutionary practice has implicit in it publicity for their actions. Thus the actors become authors. The abduction of the American ambassador in Rio de Janeiro was planned with a view to its impact on the media. It was a television production. The Arab guerrillas proceed in the same way. The first to experiment with these techniques internationally were the Cubans. Fidel appreciated the revolutionary potential of the media correctly from the first (Moncada, 1953). Today illegal political action demands at one and the same time maximum security and maximum publicity.

14. Revolutionary situations always bring with them discontinuous, spontaneous changes brought about by the masses in the existing aggregate of the media. How far the changes thus brought about take root and how permanent they are demonstrates the extent to which a cultural revolution is successful. The situation in the media is the most accurate and sensitive barometer for the rise of bureaucratic or Bonapartist anticyclones. So long as the cultural revolution has the initiative, the social imagination of the masses overcomes even technical backwardness and transforms the function of the old media so that their structures are exploded.

> With our work the Revolution has achieved a colossal labor of propaganda and enlightenment. We ripped up the traditional book into single pages, magnified these a hundred times, printed them in color and stuck them up as posters in the streets. . . . Our lack of printing equipment and the necessity for speed meant that, though the best work was hand-printed, the most rewarding was standardized, lapidary and adapted to the simplest mechanical form of reproduction. Thus State Decrees were printed as rolled-up illustrated leaflets, and Army Orders as illustrated pamphlets.[3]

In the twenties, the Russian film reached a standard that was far in advance of the available productive forces. Pudovkin's *Kinoglas* and Dziga Vertov's *Kinopravda* were no "newsreels" but political television magazine programs *avant l'écran*. The campaign against illiteracy in Cuba broke through the linear, exclusive, and isolating structure of the medium of the book. In the China of the Cultural Revolution, wall newspapers functioned like an electronic mass medium—at least in the big towns. The resistance of the Czechoslovak population to the Soviet invasion gave rise to spontaneous productivity on the part of the masses, which ignored the institutional barriers of the media. (Details to be supplied.) Such situations are exceptional. It is precisely their utopian nature, which reaches out beyond the existing productive forces (it follows that the productive relationships are not to be permanently overthrown), that makes them precarious, leads to reversals and defeats. They demonstrate all the more clearly what enormous political and cultural energies are hidden in the enchained masses and with what imagination they are able, at the moment of liberation, to realize all the opportunities offered by the new media.

The Media: An Empty Category of Marxist Theory

15. That the Marxist Left should argue theoretically and act practically from the standpoint of the most advanced productive forces in their society, that they should develop in depth all the liberating factors immanent in these forces and use them strategically, is no academic expectation but a political necessity. However, with a single great exception, that of Walter Benjamin (and in his footsteps, Brecht), Marxists have not understood the consciousness industry and have been aware only of its bourgeois-capitalist dark side and not of its socialist possibilities. An author like George Lukács is a perfect example of this theoretical and practical backwardness. Nor are the works of Horkheimer and Adorno free of a nostalgia which clings to early bourgeois media.

Their view of the cultural industry cannot be discussed here. Much more typical of Marxism between the two wars is the position of Lukács, which can be seen very clearly from an early essay in "Old Culture and New Culture."[4] "Anything that culture produces" can, according to Lukács, "have real cultural value only *if it is in itself* valuable, if the creation of each individual product is from the standpoint of its maker and a single, finite process. It must, moreover, be a process conditioned by the *human* potentialities and capabilities of the creator. The most typical example of such a process is the work of art, where the entire genesis of the work is exclusively the result of the artist's labor and each detail of the work that emerges is determined by the individual qualities of the artist. In highly developed mechanical industry, on the other hand, any connection between the product and the creator is abolished. *The human being serves the machine, he adapts to it.* Production becomes completely independent of the human potentialities and capabilities of the worker." These "forces which destroy culture" impair the work's "truth to the material," its "level," and deal the final blow to the "work as an end in itself." There is no more question of "the organic unity of the products of culture, its harmonious, joy-giving being." Capitalist culture must lack "the simple and natural harmony and beauty of the old culture—culture in the true, literal sense of the world." Fortunately things need not remain so. The "culture of proletarian society," although "in the context of such scientific research as is possible at this time" nothing more can be said about it, will certainly remedy these ills. Lukács asks himself "which are the cultural values which, in accordance with the nature of this context, *can be taken over from the old society* by the new *and further developed.*" Answer: Not the inhuman machines but "the idea of mankind as an end in itself, the basic idea of the new culture," for it is "the inheritance of the classical idealism of the nineteenth century." Quite right. "This is where the philistine concept of *art* turns up with all its deadly obtuseness—an idea to which all technical considerations are foreign and which feels that with the provocative appearance of the new technology its end has come." [5]

These nostalgic backward glances at the landscape of the last century, these reactionary ideals, are already the forerunners of socialist realism, which mercilessly galvanized and then buried those very "cultural values" which Lukács rode out to rescue. Unfortunately, in the process, the Soviet cultural revolution was thrown to the wolves; but this aesthete can in any case hardly have thought any more highly of it than did J.V. Stalin.

The inadequate understanding which Marxists have shown of the media and the questionable use they have made of them has produced a vacuum in Western industrialized countries into which a stream of non-Marxist hypothesis and practices has consequently flowed. From the Cabaret Voltaire to Andy Warhol's Factory, from the silent film comedians to the Beatles, from the first comic-strip artists to the present managers of the Underground, the apolitical have made much more radical progress in dealing with the media than any grouping of the Left. (Exception—Münzenberg.) Innocents have put themselves in the forefront of the new productive forces on the basis of mere institutions with which communism—to its detriment—has not wished to concern itself. Today this apolitical avant-garde has found its ventriloquist and prophet in Marshall McLuhan, an author who admittedly lacks any analytical categories for the understanding of social processes, but whose confused books serve as a quarry of undigested observations for the media industry. Certainly his little finger has experienced more of the productive power of the new media than all the ideological commissions of the CPSU and their endless resolutions and directives put together.

Incapable of any theoretical construction, McLuhan does not present his material as a concept but as the common denominator of a reactionary doctrine of salvation. He admittedly did not invent but was the first to formulate explicitly a mystique of the media which dissolves all political problems in smoke—the same smoke that gets in the eyes of his followers. It promises the salvation of man through the technology of television and indeed of television as it is practiced today. Now McLuhan's attempt to stand Marx on his head is not exactly new. He shares with his numerous predecessors the determination to suppress all problems of the economic base, their idealistic tendencies, and their belittling of the class struggle in the naive terms of a vague humanism. A new Rousseau—like all copies, only a pale version of the old—he preaches the gospel of the new primitive man who, naturally on a higher level, must return to prehistoric tribal existence in the "global village."

It is scarcely worthwhile to deal with such concepts. This charlatan's most famous saying—"the medium is the message"—perhaps deserves more attention. In spite of its provocative idiocy, it betrays more than its author knows. It reveals in the most accurate way the tautological nature of the mystique of the media. The one remarkable thing about the television set, according to him, is that it moves—a thesis which in view of the nature of American programs has, admittedly, something attractive about it.

The complementary mistake consists in the widespread illusion that media are neutral instruments by which any "messages" one pleases can be transmitted without regard for their structure or for the structure of the medium. In the East European countries the television newsreaders read fifteen-minute long conference communiqués and Central Committee resolutions which are not even suitable for printing in a newspaper, clearly under the delusion that they might fascinate a public of millions.

The sentence, "the medium is the message," transmits yet another message, however, and a much more important one. It tells us that the bourgeoisie does indeed have all possible means at its disposal to communicate something to us, but that it has nothing more to say. It is ideologically sterile. Its intention to hold on to the control of the means of production at any price, while being incapable of making the socially necessary use of them, is here expressed with complete frankness in the superstructure. It wants the media *as such* and *to no purpose.*

This wish has been shared for decades and given symbolical expression by an artistic avant-garde whose program logically admits only the alternative of negative signals and amorphous noise. Example: the already outdated "literature of silence," Warhol's films in which everything can happen at once or nothing at all, and John Cage's forty-five-minute-long *Lecture on Nothing* (1959).

The Achievement of Benjamin

16. The revolution in the conditions of production in the superstructure has made the traditional aesthetic theory unusable, completely un-

hinging its fundamental categories and destroying its "standards." The theory of knowledge on which it was based is outmoded. In the electronic media, a radically altered relationship between subject and object emerges with which the old critical concepts cannot deal. The idea of the self-sufficient work of art collapsed long ago. The long-drawn discussion over the death of art proceeds in a circle so long as it does not examine critically the aesthetic concept on which it is based, so long as it employs criteria which no longer correspond to the state of the productive forces. When constructing an aesthetic adapted to the changed situation, one must take as a starting point the work of the only Marxist theoretician who recognized the liberating potential of the new media. Thirty-five years ago, that is to say, at a time when the consciousness industry was relatively undeveloped, Walter Benjamin subjected this phenomenon to a penetrating dialectical-materialist analysis. His approach has not been matched by any theory since then, much less further developed.

One might generalize by saying: the technique of reproduction detaches the reproduced object from the domain of tradition. By making many reproductions it substitutes a plurality of copies for a unique existence. And in permitting the reproduction to meet the beholder or listener in his own particular situation, it reactivates the object reproduced. These two processes lead to a tremendous shattering of tradition which is the obverse of the contemporary crisis and renewal of mankind. Both processes are intimately connected with the contemporary mass movements. Their most powerful agent is the film. Its social significance, particularly in its most positive form, is inconceivable without its destructive, cathartic aspect, that is, the liquidation of the traditional value of the cultural heritage.

> For the first time in world history, mechanical reproduction emancipates the work of art from its parasitical dependence on ritual. To an ever greater degree the work of art reproduced becomes the work of art designed for reproducibility.... But the instant the criterion of authenticity ceases to be applicable to artistic production, the total function of art is reversed. Instead of being based on ritual, it begins to be based on another practice—politics.... Today, by the absolute emphasis on its exhibition value, the work of art becomes a creation with entirely new functions, among which the one we are conscious of, the artistic function, later may be recognized as incidental.[6]

The trends which Benjamin recognized in his day in the film and the true import of which he grasped theoretically, have become patent today with the rapid development of the consciousness industry. What used to be called art, has now, in the strict Hegelian sense, been dialectically surpassed by and in the media. The quarrel about the end of art is otiose so long as this end is not understood dialectically. Artistic productivity reveals itself to be the extreme marginal case of a much more widespread productivity, and it is socially important only insofar as it surrenders all pretensions to autonomy and recognizes itself to be a marginal case. Wherever the professional producers make a virtue out of the necessity of their specialist skills and even derive a privileged status from them, their experience and knowledge have become useless. This means that as far as an aesthetic theory is concerned, a radical change in perspectives is needed. Instead of looking at the productions of the new media from the point of view of the older modes of production we must, on the contrary, analyze the products of the traditional "artistic" media from the standpoint of modern conditions of production.

Earlier much futile thought had been devoted to the question of whether photography is an art. The primary question—whether the very invention of photography had not transformed the entire nature of art—was not raised. Soon the film theoreticians asked the same ill-considered question with regard to the film. But the difficulties which photography caused traditional aesthetics were mere child's play as compared to those raised by the film.[7]

The panic aroused by such a shift in perspectives is understandable. The process not only changes the old burdensome craft secrets in the superstructure into white elephants, it also conceals a genuinely destructive element. It is, in a word, risky. But the only chance for the aesthetic tradition lies in its dialectical supersession. In the same way, classical physics has survived as a marginal special case within the framework of a much more comprehensive theory.

This state of affairs can be identified in individual cases in all the traditional artistic disciplines. Their present-day developments remain incomprehensible so long as one attempts to deduce them from their own prehistory. On the other hand, their usefulness or otherwise can be judged as soon as one regards them as special cases in a general aesthetic of the media. Some indications of the possible critical approaches which stem from this will be made below, taking literature as an example.

The Supersession of Written Culture

17. Written literature has, historically speaking, played a dominant role for only a few centuries. Even today, the predominance of the book has an episodic air. An incomparably longer time preceded it in which literature was oral. Now it is being succeeded by the age of the electronic media, which tend once more to make people speak. At its period of fullest development, the book to some extent usurped the place of the more primitive but generally more accessible methods of production of the past; on the other hand, it was a stand-in for future methods which make it possible for everyone to become a producer.

The revolutionary role of the printed book has been described often enough and it would be absurd to deny it. From the point of view of its structure as a medium, written literature, like the bourgeoisie who produced it and whom it served, was progressive. (See the *Communist Manifesto*.) On the analogy of the economic development of capitalism, which was indispensable for the development of the industrial revolution, the nonmaterial productive forces could not have developed without their own capital accumulation. (We also owe the accumulation of *Das Kapital* and its teachings to the medium of the book.)

Nevertheless, almost everybody speaks better than he writes. (This also applies to authors.) Writing is a highly formalized technique which, in purely physiological terms, demands a peculiarly rigid bodily posture. To this there corresponds the high degree of social specialization that it demands. Professional writers have always tended to think in caste terms. The class character of their work is unquestionable, even in the age of universal compulsory education. The whole process is extraordinarily beset with taboos. Spelling mistakes, which are completely immaterial in terms of communication, are punished by the social disqualification of the writer. The rules that govern this technique have a normative power attributed to them for which there is no rational basis. Intimidation through the written word has remained a widespread and class-specific phenomenon even in advanced industrial societies.

These alienating factors cannot be eradicated from written literature. They are reinforced by the methods by which society transmits its writing techniques. While people learn to speak very early, and mostly in psychologically favorable conditions, learning to write forms an important part of authoritarian socialization by the school ("good writing" as a kind of breaking-in). This sets its stamp forever on written communication—on its tone, its syntax, and its whole style. (This also applies to the text on this page.)

The formalization of written language permits and encourages the repression of opposition. In speech, unresolved contradictions betray themselves by pauses, hesitations, slips of the tongue, repetitions, anacoluthons, quite apart from phrasing, mimicry, gesticulation, pace, and volume. The aesthetic of written literature scorns such involuntary factors as "mistakes." It demands, explicitly or implicitly, the smoothing out of contradictions, rationalization, regularization of the spoken form irrespective of content. Even as a child, the writer is urged to hide his unsolved problems behind a protective screen of correctness.

Structurally, the printed book is a medium that operates as a monologue, isolating producer and reader. Feedback and interaction are extremely limited, demand elaborate procedures, and only in the rarest cases lead to corrections. Once an edition has been printed it cannot be corrected; at best it can be pulped. The control circuit in the case of literary criticism is extremely cumbersome and elitist. It excludes the public on principle.

None of the characteristics that distinguish written and printed literature apply to the electronic media. Microphone and camera abolish the class character of the mode of production (not of the production itself). The normative rules become unimportant. Oral interviews, arguments, demonstrations, neither demand nor allow orthography or "good writing." The television screen exposes the aesthetic smoothing out of contradictions as camouflage. Admittedly, swarms of liars appear on it, but anyone can see from a long way off that they are peddling something. As at present constituted, radio, film, and television are burdened to excess with authoritarian characteristics, the characteristics of the monologue, which they have inherited from older methods of production—and that is no accident. These outworn elements in today's media aesthetics are demanded by the social relations. They do not follow from the structure of the media. On the contrary, they go against it, for the structure demands interaction.

It is extremely improbable, however, that writing as a special technique will disappear in the foreseeable future. That goes for the book as well, the practical advantages of which for many purposes remain obvious. It is admittedly less handy and it takes up more room than other storage systems, but up to now it offers simpler methods of access than, for example, the microfilm or the tape bank. It ought to be integrated into the system as a marginal case and thereby forfeit its aura of cult and ritual.

This can be deduced from technological developments. Electronics are noticeably taking over writing: teleprinters, reading machines, high-speed transmissions, automatic photographic and electronic composition, automatic writing devices, typesetters, electrostatic processes, ampex libraries, cassette encyclopedias, photocopiers and magnetic copiers, speedprinters.

The outstanding Russian media expert El Lissitsky, incidentally, demanded an "electro-library" as far back as 1923—a request which, given the technical conditions of the time, must have seemed ridiculous or at least incomprehensible. This is how far this man's imagination reached into the future:

I draw the following analogy:

Inventions in the field of verbal traffic	*Inventions in the field of general traffic*
Articulated language	Upright gait
Writing	The wheel
Gutenberg's printing press	Carts drawn by animal power
?	The automobile
?	The airplane

I have produced this analogy to prove that so long as the book remains a palpable object, i.e. so long as it is not replaced by auto-vocalizing and kino-vocalizing representations, we must look to the field of the manufacture of books for basic innovations in the near future.

There are signs at hand suggesting that this basic innovation is likely to come from the neighborhood of the collotype.[8]

Today, writing has in many cases already become a secondary technique, a means of transcribing orally recorded speech: tape-recorded proceedings, attempts at speech-pattern recognition, and the conversion of speech into writing.

18. The ineffectiveness of literary criticism when faced with so-called documentary literature is an indication of how far the critics' thinking has lagged behind the stage of the productive forces. It stems from the fact that the media have eliminated one of the most fundamental categories of aesthetics up to now—fiction. The fiction/nonfiction argument has been laid to rest just as was the nineteenth century's favorite dialectic of "art" and "life." In his day, Benjamin demonstrated that the "apparatus" (the concept of the medium was not yet available to him) abolishes authenticity. In the productions of the consciousness industry, the difference between the "geniune" original and the reproduction disappears—"that aspect of reality which is not dependent on the apparatus has now become its most artificial aspect." The process

of reproduction reacts on the object reproduced and alters it fundamentally. The efforts of this have not yet been adequately explained
epistemologically. The categorical uncertainties to which it gives rise
also affect the concept of the documentary. Strictly speaking, it has
shrunk to its legal dimensions. A document is something the "forg-
ing"—i.e. the reproduction—of which is punishable by imprisonment.
This definition naturally has no theoretical meaning. The reason is that
a reproduction, to the extent that its technical quality is good enough,
cannot be distinguished in any way from the original, irrespective of
whether it is a painting, a passport, or a bank note. The legal concept of
the documentary record is only pragmatically useful; it serves only to
protect economic interests.

The productions of the electronic media, by their nature, evade such
distinctions as those between documentary and feature films. They are
in every case explicitly determined by the given situation. The producer
can never pretend, like the traditional novelist, "to stand above things."
He is therefore partisan from the start. This fact finds formal expression in his techniques. Cutting, editing, dubbing—these are techniques
for conscious manipulation without which the use of the new media is
inconceivable. It is precisely in these work processes that their productive power reveals itself—and here it is completely immaterial whether
one is dealing with the production of a reportage or a play. The material, whether "documentary" or "fiction," is in each case only a prototype, a half-finished article, and the more closely one examines its
origins, the more blurred the difference becomes. (Develop more precisely. The reality in which a camera turns up is always faked, e.g. the
moon landing.)

The Desacralization of Art

19. The media also do away with the old category of works of art which
can only be considered as separate objects, not as independent of their
material infrastructure. The media do not produce such objects. They
create programs. Their production is in the nature of a process. That
does not mean only (or not primarily) that there is no foreseeable end to
the program—a fact which, in view of what we are at present presented
with, admittedly makes a certain hostility to the media understandable.
It means, above all, that the media program is open to its own consequences without structural limitations. (This is not an empirical description but a demand. A demand which admittedly is not made of the
medium from without; it is a consequence of its nature, from which the
much-vaunted open form can be derived—and not as a modification of

it—from an old aesthetic.) The programs of the consciousness industry must subsume into themselves their own results, the reactions and the corrections which they call forth, otherwise they are already out-of-date. They are therefore to be thought of not as means of consumption but as means of their own production.

20. It is characteristic of artistic avant-gardes that they have, so to speak, a presentiment of the potentiality of media which still lie in the future. "It has always been one of the most important tasks of art to give rise to a demand, the time for the complete satisfaction of which has not yet come. The history of every art form has critical periods when that form strives towards effects which can only be easily achieved if the technical norm is changed, that is to say, in a new art form. The artistic extravagances and crudities which arise in this way, for instance in the so-called decadent period, really stem from art's richest historical source of power. Dadaism in the end teemed with such barbarisms. We can only now recognize the nature of its striving. Dadaism was attempting to achieve those effects which the public today seeks in film with the means of painting (or of literature)."[9] This is where the prognostic value of otherwise inessential productions, such as happenings, flux, and mixed-media shows, is to be found. There are writers who in their work show an awareness of the fact that media with the characteristics of the monologue today have only a residual use-value. Many of them admittedly draw fairly shortsighted conclusions from this glimpse of the truth. For example, they offer the user the opportunity to arrange the material provided by arbitrary permutations. Every reader as it were should write his own book. When carried to extremes, such attempts to produce interaction, even when it goes against the structure of the medium employed, are nothing more than invitations to freewheel. Mere noise permits of no articulated interactions. Short cuts, of the kind that concept art peddles, are based on the banal and false conclusion that the development of the productive forces renders all work superfluous. With the same justification, one could leave a computer to its own devices on the assumption that a random generator will organize material production by itself. Fortunately, cybernetics experts are not given to such childish games.

21. For the old-fashioned "artist"—let us call him the author—it follows from these reflections that he must see it as his goal to make himself redundant as a specialist in much the same way as a teacher of literacy only fulfills his task when he is no longer necessary. Like every learning process, this process too is reciprocal. The specialist will learn as much or more from the nonspecialists as the other way round. Only then can he contrive to make himself dispensable.

Meanwhile, his social usefulness can best be measured by the degree to which he is capable of using the liberating factors in the media and bringing them to fruition. The tactical contradictions in which he must become involved in the process can neither be denied nor covered up in any way. But strategically his role is clear. The author has to work as the agent of the masses. He can lose himself in them only when they themselves become authors, the authors of history.

22. "Pessimism of the intelligence, optimism of the will" (Antonio Gramsci).

From *The Consciousness Industry*. Trans. Stuart Hood. New York: the Seabury Press, 1974, pp. 95-128.

NOTES

1. Bertolt Brecht, *Theory of Radio* (1932), *Gesammelte Werke*, Band VIII, pp. 129 ff, 134.
2. *Der Spiegel*, Oct. 20, 1969.
3. El Lissitsky, "The Future of the Book," *New Left Review* 41, p. 42.
4. *Kommunismus, Zeitschrift der Kommunistischen Internationale für die Länder Südosteuropas*, 1920, pp. 1538-49.
5. Walter Benjamin, "Kleine Geschichte der Photographie" in *Das Kunstwerk im Zeitalter seiner technischen Reproduzierbarkeit* (Frankfurt: 1963), p. 69.
6. Walter Benjamin, "The Work of Art in the Age of Mechanical Reproduction," *Illuminations* (New York: 1969), pp. 221-25. [pp. 33-34 in this volume.]
7. Ibid., p. 227. [p. 35 in this volume.]
8. Lissitsky, "The Future of the Book," p. 40.
9. Benjamin, "The Work of Art in the Age of Mechanical Reproduction," p. 237 [p. 43 in this volume.]

Requiem for the Media

Jean Baudrillard

*I*NTROIT

There is no theory of the media. The "media revolution" has remained
empirical and mystical, as much in the work of McLuhan as with his opponents. McLuhan has said, with his usual Canadian-Texan brutalness,
that Marx, the spiritual contemporary of the steam engine and railroads, was already obsolete in his lifetime with the appearance of the
telegraph.[1] In his candid fashion, he is saying that Marx, in his
materialist analysis of production, had virtually circumscribed productive forces as a privileged domain from which language, signs, and communication in general found themselves excluded. In fact, Marx does
not even provide for a genuine theory of railroads as "media," as modes
of communication: they hardly enter into consideration. And he certainly established no theory of technical evolution in general, except
from the point of view of production—primary, material, infrastruc-
tural production as the almost exclusive determinant of social relations.
Dedicated to an intermediate ideality and a blind social practice, the
"mode of communication" has had the leisure for an entire century of
"making revolution" without changing the theory of the mode of production one iota in the process.

Having admitted this much, and on condition (which is already a revolution by comparison to orthodox Marxism) that the exchange of
signs is not treated as a marginal, superstructural dimension in relation
to those beings whom the only "true" theory (materialist) defines as
"producers of their real life" (i.e., of goods destined to satisfy their
needs), it is possible to imagine two perspectives:

1. One retains the general form of Marxist analysis (dialectical con-

tradiction between forces and relations of production), but admits that the classical definition of productive forces is too restricted, so one expands the analysis in terms of productive forces to the whole murky field of signification and communication. This involves setting loose in all their originality the contradictions born from this theoretical and practical extension of the field of political economy. Such a hypothesis is the point of departure for Enzensberger: "Monopoly capitalism develops the consciousness-shaping industry more quickly and more extensively than other sectors of production; it must at the same time fetter it. A socialist media theory has to work at this contradiction."[2] But this hypothesis does little more than signal the virtual extension of the commodity form to all the domains of social life (and tardily, at that). It recognizes the existence, here and now, of a classical communication theory, a bourgeois political economy of signs and of their production (just as there existed one of material production as early as the 18th century). It is a class-bound theoretical discipline.[3] It has not been answered by any fundamental critique that could be seen as the logical extension of Marx's. Since the entire domain was related to the superstructure, this *critique of the political economy of the sign* was rendered unthinkable. Thus, at best, Enzensberger's hypothesis can do little more than try to vitiate the immense retardation of classical Marxist theory. It is only radical in the eyes of official Marxism, which is totally submerged into the dominant models, and would risk its own survival if it went even that far. *The radical alternative lies elsewhere.*

2. The production of meaning, messages, and signs poses a crucial problem to revolutionary theory. Instead of reinterpreting it in terms of classical forces of production—that is, instead of merely generalizing an analysis that is considered final and stamped with the seal of approval by the "spokesmen of the revolution"—the alternative is to thoroughly disrupt the latter in the light of the eruption of this new problem into the theoretical field (an approach no self-respecting Marxist would take, even under the guise of a hypothesis).

In other words: perhaps the Marxist theory of production is irredeemably partial, and cannot be generalized. Or again: the theory of production (the dialectical chaining of contradictions linked to the development of productive forces) is strictly homogeneous with its object—*material* production—and is non-transferable, as a postulate or theoretical framework, to contents that were never given for it in the first place.[4] The dialectical form is adequate to certain contents, those of material production: it exhausts them of meaning, but unlike an archetype, it does not exceed the definition of this object. The dialectic lies in ashes because it offered itself as a system of interpreting the *separated* order of material production.

All in all, this point of view is quite logical. It accords a global coherence to Marxist analysis—an internal homogeneity that prevents certain elements from being retained and others from being excluded, according to a technique of *bricolage* of which the Althusserians are the most subtle artificers. On the other hand, we credit Marxism with a maximum coherence. And so we demand that this coherence be breached, for it is incapable of responding to a social process that far exceeds material production.[5]

Enzensberger: A "Socialist" Strategy

In the absence of a theory and a positive strategy, argues Enzensberger, the Left remains disarmed. It is content to denounce mass-media culture as an ideological manipulation. The Left dreams of a media takeover, sometimes as a *means* of nudging the revolutionary *prise de conscience* of the masses, sometimes as a *consequence* of radical change in social structures. But this is a contradictory velleity, reflecting quite straightforwardly the impossibility of integrating the media into a theory of infra- and superstructure. The media (and the entire domain of signs and communication, it should be added) remain a social mystery for the Left, according to Enzensberger, because the Left has failed to conceive of them as a new and gigantic potential of productive forces. The Left is divided between fascination and practice before this sorcery to which it also falls victim, but which it reproves morally and intellectually (here is that Left intellectual speaking through Enzensberger himself, making his autocritique). This ambivalence only reflects the ambivalence of the media themselves, without going beyond it or reducing it.[6] With a bold stroke of Marxist sociology, Enzensberger imputes this "phobia" of intellectuals and Left movements to their bourgeois or petty bourgeois origins: they defend themselves instinctively from mass culture because it snaps their cultural privilege.[7] True or false, perhaps it would be more valuable to ask, with respect to this mesmerized distrust, this tactical disarray and the Left intelligentsia's refusal to get involved with the media, precisely how much are Marxist preconceptions themselves to blame? The nostalgic idealism of the infrastructure? The theoretical allergy to everything that isn't "material" production and "productive labor"? "Revolutionary" doctrine has never come to terms with the exchange of signs other than as pragmatically functional use: information, broadcasting, and propaganda. The contemporary new look of left-wing public relations, and the whole modernist party subculture, are hardly designed to transform this tendency. They demonstrate quite sufficiently how bourgeois ideology can be generated independently of "social origin."

All of this, Enzensberger continues, results in a political schizophrenia of the Left. On one side, a whole (subversive) revolutionary faction abandons itself to apolitical exploration of new media (subculture, underground); on the other, militant political groups still live essentially through archaic modes of communication, refusing to "play the game," or to exploit the immense possibilities of the electronic media. Thus, he reproaches the students of May '68 for having regressed to artisanal means (referring to the hand presses of the Ecole des Beaux Arts) for spreading their slogans and for having occupied the Odéon, "steeped in tradition," instead of the ORTF.[8,9]

Enzensberger attempts to develop an optimistic and offensive position. The media are monopolized by the dominant classes, which *divert* them to their own advantage. But the structure of the media remains "fundamentally egalitarian," and it is up to the revolutionary praxis to disengage this potentiality inscribed in the media, but perverted by the capitalist order. Let us say the word: to liberate the media, to return them to their social vocation of open communication and unlimited democratic exchange, their true socialist destiny.

Clearly what we have here is an extension of the same schema assigned, since time immemorial, from Marx to Marcuse, to productive forces and technology: they are the promise of human fulfillment, but capitalism freezes or confiscates them. They are liberatory, but it is necessary to liberate them.[10] The media, as we can see, do not escape this fantastic logic of inscribing the revolution *inter alia* onto things. To set the media back to the logic of productive forces no longer qualifies as a critical act, for it only locks them more firmly into the revolutionary metaphysic.

As usual, this position bogs down in contradictions. Through their own (capitalist) development, the media assure that socialization is pushed to more and more advanced stages. Even though it is technically quite imaginable, there is no closed-circuit television for the happy few who could afford it, "because this would go against the grain of the structure" of the medium.[11] "For the first time in history, the media make possible the participation of the masses in a collective process that is social and socialized, participation in which the practical means are in the hands of the masses themselves."[12] But the "socialist movements must fight and will fight for their own wavelengths."[13] Why fight (above all for wavelengths), if the media realize themselves in socialism? If such is their structural vocation?

The existing order, says Enzensberger following Brecht (*Theory of Radio*, 1932), reduces the media to a simple "medium of distribution."[14] So they must be revamped into a true medium of communication (always the same dream haunts the Marxist imaginary: strip objects of their exchange value in order to restore their use value); and this transformation, he adds, "is not technically a problem." But:

1. It is false that in the present order the media are "purely and simply means of distribution." Once again, that is to treat them as the relay of an ideology that would find its determinations elsewhere (in the mode of material production); in other words, the media as marketing and merchandizing of the dominant ideology. It is from this perspective that the relation media producer-transmitter *versus* irresponsible, receptive masses is assimilated to that of capitalist versus salaried worker. But it is not as vehicles of content, but in their form and very operation, that media induce a social relation; and this is not an exploitative relation: it involves the abstraction, separation, and abolition of exchange itself. The media are not *co-efficients*, but *effectors* of ideology. Not only is their destiny far from revolutionary; the media are not even, somewhere else or potentially, neutral or non-ideological (the phantasm of their technical status or of their social use value). Reciprocally, ideology does not exist in some place apart, as the discourse of the dominant class, *before* it is channeled through the media. The same applies to the sphere of commodities: nowhere do the latter possess ontological status independently of the form they take in the operation of the exchange value system. Nor is ideology some Imaginary floating in the wake of exchange value: it is the very operation of the exchange value itself. After the *Requiem* for the dialectic, it is necessary to toll the *Requiem* of the infra- and superstructure.

2. It follows that when Brecht and Enzensberger assert that the transformation of the media into a true medium of communication is not technically a problem ("it is nothing more," says Brecht, "than the natural consequence of their technical development"), it is necessary to understand (but, contrarily, and without playing on words) that in effect it is quite correctly *not a technical problem*, since media ideology functions at the level of *form*, at the level of the separation it establishes, which is a *social* division.

Speech Without Response

The mass media are anti-mediatory and intransitive. They fabricate non-communication—this is what characterizes them, if one agrees to define communication as an exchange, as a reciprocal space of a speech and a response, and thus of a *responsibility* (not a psychological or moral responsibility, but a personal, mutual correlation in exchange). We must understand communication as something other than the simple transmission-reception of a message, whether or not the latter is considered reversible through feedback. Now, the totality of the existing architecture of the media founds itself on this latter definition: *they are what always prevents response*, making all processes of exchange impossible (except in the various forms of response *simulation*, themselves integrated in the transmission process, thus leaving the unilateral nature of the communication intact). This is the real abstraction of the media. And the system of social control and power is rooted in it.

To understand the term *response* properly, we must take it in an emphatic sense, by referring to an equivalent in "primitive" societies: power belongs to the one who can give and *cannot be repaid*. To give, and to do it in such a way that one is unable to repay, is to disrupt the exchange to your profit and to institute a monopoly. The social process is thus thrown out of equilibrium, whereas repaying disrupts this power relationship and institutes (or reinstitutes), on the basis of an antagonistic reciprocity, the circuit of symbolic exchange. The same goes for the media: they speak, or something is spoken there, but in such a way as *to exclude any response anywhere*. This is why the only revolution in this domain—indeed, the revolution everywhere: the revolution *tout court*—lies in restoring this possibility of response. But such a simple possibility presupposes an upheaval in the entire existing structure of the media.

No other theory or strategy is possible. All vague impulses to democratize content, subvert it, restore the "transparency of the code," control the information process, contrive a reversibility of circuits, or take power over media are hopeless—unless the monopoly of speech is broken; and one cannot break the monopoly of speech if one's goal is simply to distribute it equally to everyone. Speech must be able to exchange, give, and repay itself[15] as is occasionally the case with looks and smiles. It cannot simply be interrupted, congealed, stockpiled, and redistributed in some corner of the social process.[16]

For the time being, we live in the era of non-response—of irresponsibility. "Minimal autonomous activity on the part of the spectator and voter," says Enzensberger. The mass medium *par excellence*, and the most beautiful of them all, is the electoral system: its crowning achievement is the referendum, where the response is implied in the question itself, as in the polls. It is a speech that answers itself via the simulated detour of a response, and here as well, the absolutization of speech under the formal guise of exchange is *the* definition of power. Roland Barthes has made note of the same non-reciprocity in literature: "Our literature is characterized by the pitiless divorce which the literary institution maintains between the producer of the text and its user, between its owner and customer, between its author and its reader. This reader is thereby plunged into a kind of idleness—he is intransitive; he is, in short, *serious*: instead of functioning himself, instead of gaining access to the magic of the signifier, to the pleasure of writing, he is left with no more than the poor freedom either to accept or reject the text: reading is nothing more than a *referendum*." [17]

Today, the status of the *consumer* defines this banishment. The generalized order of consumption is nothing other than that sphere where it is no longer permitted to give, to reimburse, or to exchange, but only to take and to make use of (appropriation, individualized use value). In this case, consumption goods also constitute a mass medium: they answer to the general state of affairs we have described. Their specific function is of little import: the consumption of products and messages is the abstract social relation that they establish, the ban raised against all forms of response and reciprocity.

Thus, it is far from true that, as Enzensberger affirms, "for the first time in history, the media make possible a mass participation in a productive social process;" nor that "the practical means of this participation are in the hands of the masses themselves." As if owning a TV set or a camera inaugurated a new possibility of relationship and exchange. Strictly speaking, such cases are no more significant than the possession of a refrigerator or a toaster. There is no *response* to a functional object: its function is already there, an integrated speech to which it has already responded, leaving no room for play, or reciprocal *putting in play* (unless one destroys the object, or turns its function inside out). [18] So the functionalized object, like all messages functionalized by the media, like the operation of a referendum, controls rupture, the emergence of meaning, and censorship. As an extreme case, authority would provide every citizen with a TV set without preoccupying itself with programming (assuming an authority that was not also obsessed by content and convinced of the ideological force of media "persuasion," and thus of the need to control the message). It is useless to fantasize about the state projection of police control through TV (as Enzensberger has remarked of Orwell's *1984*): TV, by virtue of its mere presence, is a social control in itself. There is no need to imagine it as a state periscope spying on everyone's private life—the situation as it stands is more efficient than that: it is the *certainty that people are no longer speaking to each other*, that they are definitively isolated in the fact of a speech without response.

From this perspective, McLuhan, whom Enzensberger scorns as a kind of ventriloquist, is much closer to a theory when he declares that "the medium is the message" (save that, in his total blindness to the social forms discussed here, he exalts the media and their global message with a delirious tribal optimism). *The medium is the message* is not a critical proposition. But in its paradoxical form, it has analytic value, [19] whereas the ingenuity of Enzensberger with regard to the "structural properties of the media" such that "no power can permit the liberation of their potentiality" turns out to be mysticism, although it wants to be revolutionary. The mystique of the socialist predestination of the media is opposite but complementary to the Orwellian myth of their terrorist manipulation by authority. Even God would approve of socialism: Christians say it all the time.

Subversive Strategy and "Symbolic Action"

It could be objected that the media did, after all, play a significant role in the events of May '68 in France, by spontaneously playing up the revolutionary movement. During at least one moment of the action, they were turned against the power structure. It is through this breach and on the possibility of this reversal that the subversive strategy of the American Yippies (e.g., Hoffman, Rubin) is founded, and on which a theory of "symbolic action" is elaborated in the world revolutionary movements: co-opt the media through their power to chain react; use their power to generalize information instantaneously. The assumption here of course is that the impact of the media is reversible, a variable in the class struggle that one must learn to appropriate. But this position should be questioned, for it is perhaps another rather large strategic illusion.

May '68 will serve well enough as an example. Everything would lead us to believe in the subversive impact of the media during this period. Suburban radio stations and newspapers spread the student action everywhere. If the students were the detonators, the media were the resonators. Furthermore, the authorities quite openly accused the media of "playing the revolutionary game." But this sort of argument has been constructed in the absence of analysis. I would say to the contrary that the media have never discharged their responsibilities with more efficiency, and that, indeed, in their function of *habitual* social control, they were right on top of the action. This is because, beneath the disarray of their routine content, they preserved their form; and this form, regardless of the context, is what inexorably connects them with the system of power. By broadcasting the events in the *abstract universality* of public opinion, they imposed a sudden and inordinate development on the movement of events; and through this forced and anticipated extension, they deprived the original movement of its own rhythm and of its meaning. In a word: they short-circuited it.

In the sphere of traditional politics (left- or right-wing),[20] where sanctified models and a kind of canonical speech are exchanged, the media are able to transmit without distorting the meanings intended. They are homogeneous with this kind of speech, as they are with the circulation of the commodity. But transgression and subversion never get "on the air" without being subtly negated as they are: transformed into models, neutralized into signs, they are eviscerated of their meaning.[21] There is no model of transgression, prototypical or serial. Hence, there is no better way to reduce it than to administer it a mortal dose of publicity. Originally, this process might have left one impressed with the possibility of "spectacular" results. In fact, it was tantamount to dismantling the movement by depriving it of its own momentum. The act of rupture was transformed into a bureaucratic model at a distance— and such, in fact, is the ordinary labor of the media.[22]

All of this can be read from the derivation and distortion of the term "symbolic" itself. The action of March 22 at Nanterre was symbolic because it was transgressive: at a given time in a given place, an act of radical rupture was invented—or, to resume the analysis proposed above, a particular response was invented there, where the institutions of administrative and pedagogical power were engaged in a private *oratoria* and functioned precisely to interdict any answer. The fact of mass media diffusion and contagion had nothing to do with the symbolic quality of the action. However, today it is precisely this interpretation, stressing the impact of disclosure, which suffices to define symbolic action. At the extreme, the subversive act is no longer produced *except as a function of its reproducibility.*[23] It is no longer created, it is produced directly as a *model*, like a gesture. The symbolic has slipped from the order of the very production of meaning to that of its *re*production, which is always the order of power. The symbolic becomes its own coefficient, pure and simple, and transgression is turned into exchange value.

Rationalist critical thought (i.e., Benjamin, Brecht, Enzensberger) sees this as a sign of decisive progress. The media simply actualize and reinforce the "demonstrative nature of no matter which political act" (Enzensberger). This evidently conforms with the *didactic* conception of the revolution and further with the "dialectic of coming to consciousness," etc. This tradition has yet to renounce the bourgeois Enlightenment. It has inherited all its ideas about the democratic (here revolutionary) virtues of spreading light (broadcasting). The pedagogical illusion of this position overlooks that—in aiming its own political acts at the media, and awaiting the moment to assume the media's mantle of power—the media themselves are in deliberate pursuit of the political act, in order to depoliticize it.

An interesting fact might be cited here as support: the contemporary eruption of tabloid trivia and natural disaster in the political sphere (which converges with Benjamin's notion of the graduation of the art object to the political stage by virtue of its reproducibility). There is a tidal wave in Pakistan, a black title fight in the U.S.; a youth is shot by a bistro owner, etc. These sorts of events, once minor and apolitical, suddenly find themselves invested with a power of diffusion that lends them a social and "historic" aura. New forms of political action have crystallized around this conflictualization of incidents that were hitherto consigned to the social columns. There is no doubt that, to a large extent, the new meanings thay have taken on are largely the doing of the media. Such *faits divers* are like undeliberated "symbolic actions," but they take part in the same process of political signification. Doubtless, their reception is ambiguous and mixed; and if, thanks to the media, the political re-emerges under the category of *faits divers*, thanks to the same media the category of *faits divers* has totally invaded politics. Furthermore, it has changed status with the extension of the mass media: from a parallel category (descended from almanacs and popular chronicles), it has evolved into a total system of mythological interpretation, a closed system of models of signification from which no event escapes. Mass mediatization: that is its quintessence. It is no ensemble of techniques for broadcasting messages; it is the *imposition of models*. McLuhan's formula is worth re-examining here: "The medium is the message" operates a transfer of meaning onto the medium itself qua technological structure. Again we are confronted with technological idealism. In fact, the essential Medium is the Model. What is mediatized is not what comes off the daily press, out of the tube, or on the radio: it is what is reinterpreted by the sign form, articulated into models, and administered by the code (just as the commodity is not what is produced industrially, but what is mediatized by the exchange value system of abstraction). At best, what can occur under the aegis of the media is a formal surpassing of the categories of *faits divers* and politics, and of their traditional separation, but only the better to assign them together to the same general code. It is strange that no one has tried to measure the strategic import of this forced socialization as a system of social control. Once again, the first great historical example of this was the electoral system. And it has never lacked revolutionaries (formerly among the greatest, today the least significant) who believed they could "do it" within the system. The general strike itself, this insurrectional myth of so many generations, has become a schematic reducing agent. That of May '68, to which the media significantly contributed by exporting the strike to all corners of France, was in appearance the culminating point of the crisis. In fact, it was the moment of its decompression, of its asphyxiation by extension, and of its defeat. To be sure, millions of workers went on strike. But no one knew what to do with this "mediatized" strike, transmitted and received as a model of action (whether via the media or the unions). Reduced to a single meaning, it neutralized the local, transversal, spontaneous forms of action (though not all). The Grenelle accords[24] hardly betrayed this tendency. They sanctioned *this passage to the generality of political action, which puts an end to the singularity of revolutionary action*. Today it has become (in the form of the calculated extension of the strike) the absolute weapon of the unions against wildcat strikes.

So far the electoral system and the general strike are also media, after a fashion. Playing on extensive formal socialization, they are the subtlest and stealthiest institutions of filtration, dismantling and censorship. They are neither exceptions, nor miracles.

The real revolutionary media during May were the walls and their speech, the silk-screen posters and the hand-painted notices, the street where speech began and was exchanged—everything that was an *immediate* inscription, given and returned, spoken and answered, mobile in the same space and time, reciprocal and antagonistic. The street is, in this sense, the alternative and subversive form of the mass media, since it isn't, like the latter, an objectified support for answerless messages, a transmission system at a distance. It is the frayed space of the symbolic exchange of speech—ephemeral, mortal: a speech that is not reflected on the Platonic screen of the media. Institutionalized by reproduction, reduced to a spectacle, this speech is expiring.

It is a strategic illusion to have any faith in the critical reversal of the media. A comparable speech can emerge only from the destruction of the media such as they are—through their deconstruction as systems of non-communication. Their liquidation does not follow from this, any more than the radical critique of discourse implies the negation of language as signifying material. But it certainly does imply the liquidation of the existing functional and technical structure of the media—of their operational form, so to speak—which *in toto* reflects their social form. At the limit, to be sure, it is the very concept of medium that disappears—and must disappear: speech exchanged dissolves the idea and function of the medium, and of the intermediary, as does symbolic land reciprocal exchange. It can involve a technical apparatus (sound, image, waves, energy, etc.) as well as the corporeal one (gestures, language, sexuality), but in this case, it no longer acts as a *medium*, as an autonomous system administered by the code. Reciprocity comes into being through the destruction of mediums per se. "People meet their neighbors for the first time while watching their apartment houses burn down."[25]

The Theoretical Model of Communication

Let us summarize the various hypotheses:
1. McLuhan (for memory's sake): The media make—indeed, they are—the revolution, independently of their content, by virtue of their technological structure alone. After the phonetic alphabet and the printed book comes the radio and the cinema. After radio, television. We live, here and now, in the age of instantaneous, global communication.
2. The media are controlled by power. The imperative is to strip them of it, whether by taking the media over, or reversing them by outbidding the spectacle with subversive content. Here, the media are envisioned as pure message. Their form is never called into question (any more than it is, in fact, by McLuhan, who views the medium only in its aspect as medium).
3. Enzensberger: the present form of the media induces a certain type of social relation (assimilative to that of the capitalist mode of production). But the media contain, by virtue of their structure and development, an immanent socialist and democratic mode of communication, an immanent rationality and universality of information. It suffices to liberate this potential.

We are only interested in Enzensberger's hypothesis (enlightened Marxist) and that of the radical American Left (leftists of the spectacle). The practice of the official Left, Marxist or otherwise, which is confounded with that of the bourgeoisie, will be left out of account here. We have analyzed these positions as *strategic illusions*. The cause of this failure is that both share with the dominant ideology the implicit reference to the same *communication theory*. The theory is accepted practically everywhere, strengthened by received evidence and a (highly scientific) formalization by one discipline, the semio-linguistics of communication, supported on one side by structural linguistics, by information theory on the other, swallowed whole by the universities and by mass culture in general (the mass mediators are its connoisseurs). The entire conceptual infrastructure of this theory is ideologically connected with dominant practice, as was and still is that of classical political economy. It *is* the equivalent of this political economy in the field of communications. And I think that if revolutionary practice has bogged down in this strategic illusion *vis-à-vis* the media, it is because critical analyses have been superficial and fallen short of radically identifying the ideological matrix that communication theory embraces.

Formalized most notably by Roman Jakobsen, its underlying unity is based on the following sequence:

TRANSMITTER–MESSAGE—RECEIVER
(ENCODER—MESSAGE—DECODER)

The message itself is structured by the code and determined by the context. A specific function corresponds to each of these "concepts": the referential, poetic, phatic, etc.[26] Each communication process is thus vectorized into a single meaning, from the transmitter to the receiver: the latter can become transmitter in its turn, and the same schema is reproduced. Thus communication can always be reduced to this simple unity in which the two polar terms are mutually exclusive. This structure is given as objective and scientific, since it follows the methodological rule of decomposing its object into simple elements. In fact, it is satisfied with an emperical given, an abstraction from lived experience and reality: that is, the ideological categories that express a certain type of social relation, namely, in which one speaks and the other doesn't, where one has the choice of the code, and the other only liberty to acquiesce or abstain. This structure is based on the same arbitrariness as that of signification (i.e., the arbitrariness of the sign): two terms are artificially isolated and artificially reunited by an objectified content called a message. There is neither reciprocal relation nor simultaneous mutual presence of the two terms,[27] since each determines itself in its relation to the message or code, the "intermedium" that maintains both in a respective situation (it is the code that holds both in "respect"), at a distance from one another, a distance that seals the full and autonomized "value" of the message (in fact, its exchange value). This "scientific" construction is rooted in a *simulation model* of communication. It excludes, from its inception, the reciprocity and antagonism of interlocutors, and the ambivalence of their exchange. What really circulates is information, a semantic content that is assumed to be legible and univocal. The agency of the code guarantees this univocality, and by the same token the respective positions of encoder and decoder. So far so good: the formula has a formal coherence that assures it as the only *possible* schema of communication. But as soon as one posits ambivalent relations, it all collapses. There is no code for ambivalence; and without a code, no more encoder, no more decoder: the extras flee the stage. Even a message becomes impossible, since it would, after all, have to be defined as "emitted" and "received." It is as if the entire formalization exists only to avert this catastrophe. And therein resides its "scientific" status. What it underpins, in fact, is the terrorism of the code. In this guiding schema, the code becomes the only agency that speaks, that exchanges itself and reproduces through the dissociation of the two terms and the univocality (or equivocality, or multivocality—it hardly matters: through the non-ambivalence) of the message. (Likewise, in the process of economic exchange, it is no longer people who exchange; the system of exchange value reproduces itself through them). So, this basic communication formula succeeds in giving us, as a reduced model, a perfect epitome of social exchange *such as it is*—such as, at any rate, the abstraction of the code, the forced rationality and terrorism of separation regulate it. So much for scientific objectivity.

The schema of separation and closure already operates, as we have noted, at the level of the sign, in linguistic theory. Each sign is divided into a signifier, and a signified, which are mutually appointed, but held in "respective" position: and from the depths of its arbitrary isolation, each sign "communicates" with all the others through a code called a language. Even here, a scientific injunction is invoked against the immanent possibility of the terms exchanging amongst each other symbolically, beyond the signifier-signified distinction—in poetic language, for example. In the latter, as in symbolic exchange, the terms *respond* to each other beyond the code. It is this response that we have marked out during the entire essay as ultimately deconstructive of all codes, of all control and power, which always base themselves on the separation of terms and their abstract articulation.

Thus the theory of signification serves as a nuclear model for communication theory, and the arbitrariness of the sign (that theoretical schema for the repression of meaning) takes on its political and ideological scope in the arbitrariness of the theoretical schema of communication and information. As we have seen, all of this is echoed, not only in the dominant social practice (characterized by the virtual monopoly of the transmission pole and the irresponsibility of the receiving pole, the discrimination between the terms of the exchange and the *diktat* of the code), but also in all the velleities of revolutionary media practice. For example, it is clear that those who aim to subvert media content only reinforce the autonomy of the message as a separated notion, and thus the abstract bipolarity of the term(inal)s of communication.

The Cybernetic Illusion

Sensible of the non-reciprocity of the existing process, Enzensberger believes the situation can be mitigated by insisting that the same revolution intervene at the level of the media that once disoriented the exact sciences and the epistemological subject-object relation, which has been engaged in continuous "dialectical" interreaction ever since. The media would have to take into account all the consequences of interreaction, whose effect is to breach monopoly and permit everyone's integration in an open process. "The programs of the consciousness industry must subsume into themselves their own results, the reactions and the corrections that they call forth.... They are therefore to be thought of not as means of consumption but as means of their own production."[28] Now, this seductive perspective leaves the separated agency of the code and the message intact while it attempts, instead, to break down the discrimination of the two poles of communication toward a more supple structure of the role exchange and feedback ("reversibility of circuits"). "In its present form, equipment like television or film does not serve communication but prevents it. It allows no reciprocal action between transmitter and receiver; technically speaking, it reduces feedback to the lowest point compatible with the system."[29] Again, we fail to get beyond the categories of receiver and transmitter, whatever may be the effort to mobilize them through "switching." *Reversibility* has nothing to do with reciprocity. Doubtless it is for this deeper reason that cybernetic systems today understand perfectly well how to put this complex regulation and feedback to work without affecting the abstraction of the process as a whole or allowing any real "responsibility" in exchange. This is indeed the system's surest line of defense, since it thus integrates the contingency of any such response in advance.

As Enzensberger has demonstrated in his critique of the Orwellian myth, it no longer makes sense to conceive a megasystem of centralized control (a monitoring system for the telephone network would have to exceed it *n* times in size and complexity; hence, it is practically excluded). But it is a little naive to assume that the fact of media extension thus eliminates censorship. Even over the long haul, the impracticality of police megasystems simply means that present systems will integrate these otherwise useless metasystems of control by means of feedback and autoregulation. They know how to introduce what negates them *as supplementary variables*. Their very operation is censorship: megasystems are hardly required. Hence they do not cease to be totalitarian: in a way, they realize the ideal one might refer to as decentralized totalitarianism.

On a more practical level, the media are quite aware how to set up formal "reversibility" of circuits (letters to the editor, phone-in programs, polls, etc.), without conceding any response or abandoning in any way the discrimination of roles.[30] This is the social and political form of feedback. Thus, Enzensberger's "dialectization" of communication is oddly related to cybernetic regulation. Ultimately, he is the victim, though in a more subtle fashion, of the ideological model we have been discussing.

From the same perspective, Enzensberger would break down the unilateral character of communication, which translates simultaneously into the monopoly of specialists and professionals and that of the class enemy over the media, by proposing, as a revolutionary solution, that *everyone become a manipulator*, in the sense of active operator, producer, etc., in brief, move from receiver status to that of producer-transmitter. Here is a sort of critical reversal of the ideological concept of manipulation. But again, because this "revolution" at bottom conserves the category of transmitter, which it is content to generalize as separated, transforming everyone into his own transmitter, it fails to place the mass media system in check. We know the results of such phenomena as mass ownership of walkie-talkies, or everyone making their own cinema: a kind of personalized amateurism, the equivalent of Sunday tinkering on the periphery of the system.[31]

Of course, this isn't at all what Enzensberger has in mind. He is thinking of a press edited, distributed, and worked by its own readers (as is the underground press, in part), of video systems at the disposal of political groups, and so on.

This would be the only way to unfreeze a blocked situation: "In the socialist movements the dialectic of discipline and spontaneity, centralism and decentralism, authoritarian leadership and antiauthoritarian disintegration has long ago reached a deadlock. Networklike communications models built on the principle of reversibility of circuits might give new indications of how to overcome this situation."[32] Thus it is a question of reconstituting a dialectical practice. But can the problem continue to be posed in dialectical terms? Isn't it the dialectic itself which has reached the moment of deadlock?

The examples Enzensberger gives are interesting precisely in that they go beyond a "dialectic" of transmitter and receiver. In effect, an immediate communication process is rediscovered, one not filtered through bureaucratic models—an original form of exchange, in fact, because there are *neither transmitters, nor receivers*, but only people responding to each other. The problem of spontaneity and organization is not overcome dialectically here: its terms are *transgressed*.

There is the essential difference: the other hypotheses allow the dichotomized categories to subsist. In the first case (media on the private scale), transmitter and receiver are simply reunited in a single individual: manipulation is, after a fashion, "interiorized."[33] In the other case (the "dialectic of circuits"), transmitter and receiver are simultaneously on both sides: manipulation becomes reciprocal (hermaphroditic grouping). The system can play these two variations as easily as it can the classic bureaucratic model. It can play on all their possible combinations. The only essential is that these two ideological categories be safe, and with them the fundamental structure of the political economy of communication.

To repeat, in the symbolic exchange relation, there is a simultaneous response. There is not transmitter or receiver on both sides of a message: nor, for that matter, is there any longer any "message," any corpus of information to decode univocally under the aegis of a code. The symbolic consists precisely in breaching the univocality of the "message," in restoring the ambivalence of meaning and in demolishing in the same stroke the agency of the code.

All of this should be helpful in assessing Umberto Eco's hypothesis.[34] To summarize his position: changing the contents of the message serves no purpose; it is necessary to modify the reading codes, to impose other interpretive codes. The receiver (who in fact isn't really one) intervenes here at the most essential level—he opposes his own code to that of the transmitter, he invents a true response by escaping the trap of controlled communication. But what does this "subversive" reading actually amount to? Is it still a reading, that is, a deciphering, a disengaging of a univocal meaning? And what is this code that opposes? Is it a unique minicode (an ideolect, but thus without interest)? Or is it yet another controlling schema of interpretation, rising from the ashes of the previous one? Whatever the case, it is only a question of textual variation. One example can illustrate Eco's perspective: the graffiti reversal of advertising after May '68. Graffiti is transgressive, not because it substitutes another content, another discourse, but simply because it responds, there, on the spot, and breaches the fundamental role of non-response enunciated by all the media. Does it oppose one code to another? I don't think so: it simply smashes the code. It doesn't lend itself to deciphering as a text rivaling commercial discourse; it presents itself as a transgression. So, for example, the witticism, which is a transgressive reversal of discourse, does not act on the basis of another code as such; it works through the instantaneous deconstruction of the dominant discursive code. It volatilizes the category of the code, and that of the message.

This, then, is the key to the problem: by trying to preserve (even as one "dialectically transcends" them) *any separated instances of the structural communication grid*, one obviates the possibility of fundamental change, and condemns oneself to fragile manipulatory practices that would be dangerous to adopt as a "revolutionary strategy." What is strategic in this sense is only what radically checkmates the dominant form.

From *For a Critique of the Political Economy of the Sign*, Trans. Charles Levin. St. Louis, Mo.: Telos Press, 1981. pp. 164-84.

NOTES
  1. Marshall McLuhan, *War and Peace in the Global Village* (New York: 1968), p. 5.
  2. Hans Magnus Enzensberger, "Constituents of a Theory of the Media," *The Con-*

sciousness Industry (New York: Seabury Press, 1974), pp.95-128. [see pp. 96-123 in this volume].

3. This political economy of the sign is structural linguistics (together with semiology, to be sure, and all its derivatives, of which communication theory will be discussed below). It is apparent that within the general ideological framework, structural linguistics is the contemporary master discipline, inspiring anthropology, the human sciences, etc., just as, in its time, did political economy, whose postulates profoundly informed all of psychology, sociology, and the "moral and political" sciences.

4. In this case, the expression "consciousness industry" which Enzensberger uses to characterize the existing media is a dangerous metaphor. Unfortunately, it underlies his entire analytic hypothesis, which is to extend the Marxist analysis of the capitalist mode of production to the media, to the point of discovering a structural analogy between the following relations:

dominant class/dominated class
producer-entrepreneur/consumer
transmitter-broadcaster/receiver

5. In fact, Marxist analysis can be questioned at two very different levels of radicality: either as a system for interpreting the separated order of *material* production, or else as that of the separated order of *production* (in general). In the first case, the hypothesis of the non-relevance of the dialectic outside its field of "origin" must be logically pushed further: if "dialectical" contradictions between the productive forces and the relations of production largely vanish in the field of language, signs, and ideology, *perhaps they were never really operative in the field of material production either*, since a certain capitalist development of productive forces has been able to absorb—not all conflict, to be sure—but revolutionary antagonisms at the level of social relations. Wherein lies the validity of these concepts, then, aside from a purely conceptual coherence?

In the second case, the concept of production must be interrogated at its very root (and not in its diverse contents), along with the separated form which it establishes and the representational and rationalizing schema it imposes. Undoubtedly it is here, at the extreme, that the real work needs to be done. [See Baudrillard's *Mirror of Production*, Trans. Mark Poster (St. Louis: Telos Press, 1975). —*Trans.*]

6. Enzensberger, "Constituents of a Theory of the Media," p. 96.

7. This genre of reductive determinism may be found in the works of Bourdieu and in the phraseology of the Communist Party. It is theoretically worthless. It turns the *mechanism* of democratization into a revolutionary value per se. That intellectuals may find mass culture repugnant hardly suffices to make it a revolutionary alternative. Aristocrats used to make sour faces at bourgeois culture, but no one ever said the latter was anything more than a class culture.

8. Most of the above references are to Enzensberger, "Constituents of a Theory of the Media," pp. 102-103.

9. French radio-TV headquarters. The ORTF is a highly centralized state-run monoploy.

10. Thus we find authority, the state, and other institutions either devoid or full up with revolutionary content, depending on whether they are still in the grip of capital or the people have taken them over. Their form is rarely questioned.

11. Enzensberger, "Constituents of a Theory of the Media," pp. 105, 108.

12. *Ibid.*, p. 97.

13. *Ibid.*, p. 107.

14. *Ibid.*, pp. 97-98.

15. It is not a question of "dialogue," which is only the functional adjustment of two abstract speeches without response, where the "interlocutors" are never mutually present, but only their stylized discourses.

16. The occupation of the ORTF changed nothing in itself, even if subversive "contents" were "broadcast." If only those involved had scuttled the ORTF as such, for its entire technical and functional structure reflects the monopolistic use of speech.

17. Roland Barthes, *S/Z* (New York: 1974), p. 4.

18. Multifunctionality evidently changes nothing on this score. Multifunctionality, multidisciplinarity—polyvalence in all its forms—are just the system's response to its own obsession with centrality and standardization (uni-equivalence). It is the system's reaction to its own pathology, glossing over the underlying logic.

19. Enzensberger (pp. 118-19) interprets it this way: "The medium is the message" is a bourgeois proposition. It signifies that the bourgeoisie has nothing left to say. Having no further message to transmit, it plays the card of medium for medium's sake. —If the bourgeoisie has nothing left to say, "socialism" would do better to keep quiet.

20. This left-right distinction is just about meaningless from the point of view of the media. We should give credit where credit is due and grant them the honor of having contributed largely to its elimination. The distinction is interconnected with an order characterized by the *transcendence* of politics. But let us not mistake ourselves, here: the media only help to liquidate this transcendence of politics in order to substitute their own transcendence, abstracted from the mass media form, which is thoroughly integrated and no longer even offers a conflictive structure (left-right). Mass media transcendence is thus reductive of the traditional transcendence of politics, but it is even more reductive of the new transversality of politics.

21. This form of so-called "disclosure" or "propagation" can be analyzed readily in the fields of science or art. Generalized reproducibility obliterates the processes of work and meaning so as to leave nothing but modelized contents (cf. Raoul Ergmann, "Le miroir en miettes," *Diogene*, no. 68, 1969; Baudouin Jurdant, "La vulgarisation scientifique," *Communications*, no. 14).

22. It should be pointed out that this labor is always accompanied by one of selection and reinterpretation at the level of the membership group (Lazarsfeld's *two-step flow of communication*). This accounts for the highly relative impact of media contents, and the many kinds of resistance they provoke. (However we should ask ourselves whether these resistances are not aimed at the abstraction of the medium itself, rather than its contents: Lazarsfeld's double articulation would lead us to this conclusion, since the second articulation belongs to the network of *personal* relations, opposed to the generality of media messages.) Still, this "second" reading, where the membership group opposes its own code to the transmitter's (cf. my discussion of Umberto Eco's thesis towards the end of this article) certainly doesn't neutralize or "reduce" the dominant ideological contents of the media in the same way as it does the critical or subversive contents. To the extent that the dominant ideological contents (cultural models, value systems, imposed without alternative or response; bureaucratic contents) are homogeneous with the general form of the mass media (non-reciprocity, irresponsibility), and are integrated with this form in reduplicating it, they are, so to speak, overdetermined, and have greater impact. They "go over" better than subversive *contents*. But this is not the essence of the problem. It is more important to recognize that the *form* of transgression never "comes off" more or less well on the media: it is radically denied by the mass media form.

23. Thus, for Walter Benjamin, the reproduced work becomes more and more the work "designed" *for reproducibility*. In this way, according to him, the work of art graduates from ritual to politics. "Exhibition value" revolutionizes the work of art and its functions. Walter Benjamin, "The Work of Art in the Age of Mechanical Reproduction," *Illuminations* (New York: Schocken Books, 1969) [see pp. 27-52 in this volume].

24. The Grenelle accords were worked out between Georges Séguy of the CGT and Georges Pompidou during the May '68 general strike. Although the monetary concessions involved were fairly broad, they missed the point, and were massively rejected by workers. —*Trans.*

25. Jerry Rubin, *Do It* (New York: Simon and Schuster), p. 234.

26. See Roman Jakobsen, "Closing Statement: Linguistics and Poetics," in T.A. Sebeok, ed., *Style in Language* (Cambridge, Mass.: M.I.T. Press, 1960), pp. 350-377.

27. These two terms are so faintly present to each other that it has proven necessary to create a "contact" category to reconstitute the totality theoretically!

28. Enzensberger, "Constituents of a Theory of the Media," pp. 119, 127.

29. *Ibid.*, p. 97.

30. Once again Enzensberger, who analyses and denounces these control circuits, nevertheless links up with idealism: "Naturally [!] such tendencies go against the grain of the structure, and the new productive forces not only permit, but indeed demand [!] their reversal." (*Ibid.*, p. 108.) Feedback and interaction are the very logic of cybernetics. Underestimating the ability of the system to integrate its own revolutionary innovations is as delusory as underestimating the capacity of capitalism to develop the productive forces.

31. Evoking the possibility of an open free press, Enzensberger points to the Xerox monopoly and their exorbitant rental rates. But if everyone had his own Xerox—or even his own wavelength—the problem would remain. The real monopoly is never that of technical means, but of speech.

32. Enzensberger, "Constituents of a Theory of the Media," p. 110.

33. This is why the *individual* amateur cameraman remains within the separated abstraction of *mass* communication: through this internal dissociation of the two agencies (instances), the entire code and all of the dominant models sweep in, and seize his activity from behind.

34. Umberto Eco, *La Struttura assente* (Milan: Bompiani, 1968).

VIDEO AND
TELEVISION

Video: The Distinctive Features of the Medium

David Antin

VIDEO ART. The name is equivocal. A good name. It leaves open all the questions and asks them anyway. Is this an art form, a new genre? An anthology of valued activity conducted in a particular arena defined by display on a cathode ray tube? The kind of video made by a special class of people—artists—whose works are exhibited primarily in what is called "the art world"—ARTISTS' VIDEO? An inspection of the names in the catalogue gives the easy and not quite sufficient answer that it is this last we are considering, ARTISTS' VIDEO. But is this a class apart? Artists have been making video pieces for scarcely ten years—if we disregard one or two flimsy studio jobs and Nam June Paik's 1963 kamikaze TV modifications—and video has been a fact of gallery life for barely five years. Yet we've already had group exhibitions, panels, symposia, magazine issues devoted to this phenomenon, for the very good reasons that more and more artists are using video and some of the best work being done in the art world is being done with video. Which is why a discourse has already arisen to greet it. Actually two discourses: one, a kind of enthusiastic welcoming prose peppered with fragments of communication theory and McLuhanesque media talk; the other, a rather nervous attempt to locate the "unique properties of the medium." Discourse 1 could be called "cyberscat" and Discourse 2, because it engages the issues that pass for "formalism" in the art world, could be called "the formalist rap." Though there is no necessary relation between them, the two discourses occasionally occur together as they do in the words of Frank Gillette, which offer a convenient sample:

D1: The emergence of relationships between the culture you're in and the parameters that allow you expression are fed back through a technology. It's the state of the art technology within a particular culture that gives shape to ideas.

D2: What I'm consciously involved in is devising a way that is structurally intrinsic to television. For example, what makes it *not* film? Part of it is that you look *into* the source of light, with film you look *with* the source of light. In television, the source of light and the source of information are one.[1]

Though it is not entirely clear what "high class" technology has to do with the rather pleasantly shabby technical state of contemporary video art, or what the significance is to human beings of the light source in two adjacent representational media, statements of this type are characteristic, and similar quotes could be multiplied endlessly. And if these concerns seem somewhat gratuitous or insufficient with respect to the work at hand, they often share a kind of aptness of detail, even though it is rarely clear what the detail explains of the larger pattern of activity in which these artists are involved. In fact, what seems most typical of both types of discourse is a certain anxiety, which may be seen most clearly in a recent piece by Hollis Frampton:

Moreover it is doubly important that we try to say what video art is at present because we posit for it a privileged future. Since the birth of video art from the Jovian backside (I dare not say brow) of the Other Thing called television, I for one have felt a more and more pressing need for precise definitions of what film art *is*, since I extend to film, as well, the hope of a privileged future.[2]

It would be so much more convenient to develop the refined discussion of the possible differences between film and video, if we could only forget the Other Thing—television. Yet television haunts all exhibitions of video art, though when actually present it is only minimally represented, with perhaps a few commercials or "the golden performances" of Ernie Kovacs (a television "artist"); otherwise its presence is manifest mainly in quotes, allusion, parody, and protest, as in Telethon's *TV History*, Douglas Davis's installation piece with the TV set forced to face the wall, or Richard Serra's *Television Delivers People*. No doubt, in time there will be an *auteur* theory of television, which will do for Milton Berle and Sid Caesar what Sarris and Farber and *Cahiers du Cinéma* have done for John Ford and Nicholas Ray and Howard Hawkes. But the politics of the art world is, for good reasons, rather hostile to Pop, and that kind of admiring discussion will have to wait; even *Cahiers du Cinéma* has abandoned Hitchcock and Nicholas Ray for Dziga Vertov and the European avant-garde on sociopolitical, aesthetic grounds. But it's unwise to despise an enemy, especially a more powerful, older enemy, who happens also to be your frightful parent. So it is with television that we have to begin to consider video, because if anything has defined the formal and technical properties of the video medium, it is the television industry.

The history of television in the United States is well known. Commercial television is essentially a post-World War phenomenon, and its use was, logically enough, patterned on commercial radio, since control of the new medium was in the hands of the powerful radio networks, which constitute essentially a government-protected, private monopoly. This situation determined many of the fundamental communication characteristics of the new medium. The most basic of these is the social relation between "sending" and "receiving," which is profoundly unequal and asymmetrical. Since the main potential broadcasters, the powerful radio networks, were already deeply involved with the electronics industry through complex ownership affiliation, and since they also constituted the single largest potential customer for the electronic components of television, the components were developed entirely for their convenience and profit. While this may not seem surprising, the result was that the facts of "picture-taking" and "transmission" were made enormously expensive. Cameras and transmission systems were designed and priced out of the reach of anything but corporate ownership. Moreover, government regulations set standards on "picture quality" and the transmission signal, which effectively ensured that "taking" and "transmission" control would remain in the hands of the industry into which the federal government had already assigned the airwaves channel by channel. The receivers alone were priced within the range of individual ownership. This fundamental ordering—establishing the relations between the taker-sender and the receiver—had, of course, been worked out for commercial radio.

Only ham transmission—also hemmed in severely by government regulation—and special uses like ship-to-shore, pilot-to-control tower, and police-band radio deal in the otherwise merely potential equalities of wireless telephony. That this was not technically inevitable, but merely an outcome of the social situation and the marketing strategies of the industry, is obvious. There is nothing necessarily more complex or expensive in the camera than there is in the receiver. It is merely that the great expense of receiver technology was defrayed by the mass production of the sets, whose multiplication multiplied the dollar exchange value of transmission time sold by the transmitter to his advertisers. So the broadcasters underwrote receiver development, because every set bought delivers its viewers as salable goods in an exchange that pays for the "expensive" technology.

For television also there is a special-use domain—educational, industrial, and now artistic—where the relation between the camera and receiver may be more or less equalized, but this is because transmission is not an issue and the distribution of the images is severely restricted. The economic fact remains—transmission is more expensive than reception. This ensures a power hierarchy—transmission dominates reception. And it follows from this asymmetry of power relations that the taker-transmitter dominates whatever communication takes place.

This is clearer when you consider the manners of telephony. A would-be transmitter asks for permission to transmit, rings the home of a potential receiver. It's like ringing a doorbell. Or a would-be receiver rings the home of a possible transmitter, asks him/her to transmit. This formal set of relations has become even more refined with the introduction of the *Answerphone* and the answering service, which mediates between the ring—an anonymous invitation to communicate—and the response, requiring the caller to identify himself and leaving the receiver with a choice of whether or not to respond. In telephony manners are everything. While in commercial television manners are nothing. If you have a receiver you merely plug in to the possibility of a signal, which may or may not be there and which you cannot modify except in the trivial manner of switching to nearly identical transmission or in a decisive but final manner by switching off. Choice is in the hands of the sender.

Now while this asymmetry is not inherent in the technology, it has become so normative for the medium that it forms the all-pervasive and invisible background of all video. This may not be so dramatically manifested in most artwork video, but that's because most artworks have very equivocal relations to the notion of communication and are, like industry, producer-dominated. Yet it has a formidable effect on all attempts at interactive video, which operates primarily in reaction to this norm. In this sense the social structure of the medium is a matrix that defines the formal properties of the medium—since it limits the possibilities of a video communication genre—and these limits then become the target against which any number of artists have aimed their works. What else could Ira Schneider have had in mind about the 1969 piece, *Wipe Cycle*, he devised with Frank Gillette:

> The most important thing was the notion of information presentation, and the notion of the integration of the audience into the information. One sees oneself exiting from the elevator. If one

stands there for 8 seconds, one sees oneself entering the gallery from the elevator again. Now at the same time one is apt to be seeing oneself standing there watching *Wipe Cycle*. You can watch yourself live watching yourself 8 seconds ago, watching yourself 16 seconds ago, *eventually feeling free enough to interact with this matrix, realizing one's own potential as an actor.*[3] [my italics].

What is attempted is the conversion (liberation) of an audience (receiver) into an actor (transmitter), which Schneider and Gillette must have hoped to accomplish by neutralizing as much as possible the acts of "taking" and electronic transmission. If they failed to accomplish this, they were hardly alone in their failure, which seems to have been the fate of just about every interactive artwork employing significantly technological means. Apparently, the social and economic distribution of technological resources in this culture has a nearly determining effect on the semiotics of technological resources. More concretely, an expensive video camera and transmission system switched on and ready for use don't lose their peculiar prestigious properties just because an artist may make them available under special circumstances for casual use to an otherwise passive public. In fact, this kind of interactive video situation almost invariably begins by intimidating an unprepared audience which has already been indoctrinated about the amount of preparedness (professionalism) the video camera deserves, regardless of the trivial nature of television professionalism, which is not measured by competence (as in the elegant relation of ends to means) but by the amount of money notably expended on this preparation. Yet while the most fundamental property of television is its social organization, this is manifested most clearly in its money metric, which applies to every aspect of the medium, determining the tempo of its representations and the style of the performances, as well as the visual syntax of its editing. The money metric has also played a determining role in neutralizing what is usually considered the most markedly distinctive feature of the medium: the capacity for instantaneous transmission.

In principle, television seemed to combine the photographic reproduction capacities of the camera, the motion capabilities of film, and the instantaneous transmission properties of the telephone. But just as the photographic reproduction capacity of the camera is essentially equivocal and mainly significant as mythology, so is the fabled instantaneity of television essentially a rumor that combines with photographic duplicity to produce a quasi-recording medium, the main feature of which is unlikeliness in relation to any notion of reality. The history of the industry is very instructive with respect to this remarkable outcome.

In the beginning television made widespread use of live broadcasting both for transmitting instant news of events that were elapsing in real time and for more or less well-rehearsed studio performances, and some of the most interesting events recorded by media were the result of the unpredictability of instantaneous transmission. Spokesmen for the industry never failed to call attention to this feature of instantaneity, and as late as 1968 a standard handbook for television direction and production by Stasheff and Bretz asserted:

> Perhaps the most distinctive function of television is its ability to show distant events at the moment when they are taking place. The Kefauver hearings, with a close-up of the hands of gangster Frank Costello; the Army-McCarthy hearings; the complete coverage of the orbital shots; the presidential nominating conventions; the Great Debates of 1960; the live transmissions from Europe and Japan via satellite—this is television doing what no other medium can do.[4]

Yet the same handbook casually points out a few pages later that between 1947 and 1957, kine-recordings, films taken directly from the TV screen, were in constant and heavy use, especially for delayed broadcast of East Coast programs on the West Coast, in spite of the much poorer image quality of the kines, and that by 1961 virtually all television dramatic programs were being produced on film. There were, apparently, from the industry's standpoint, great inconveniences in instantaneous transmission. The most obvious of these was that at the same instant of time the life cycles of New York and Los Angeles are separated by three full hours, and since the day for the industry is metrically divided into prime and nonprime viewing time, in accordance with whether more or fewer viewers may be sold to the advertisers, the money value of instantaneous transmission is inversely related in a complicated way to the temporal distance of transmission. But this is only the most obvious manner in which the money metric worked to eliminate instantaneity. A more basic conflict exists between the structure of the industry and the possibility of instantaneity and unpredictability.

Any series of events that is unfolding for the first time, or in a new way, or with unanticipated intensity or duration threatens to overrun or elude the framing conventions of the recording artists (the cameramen and directors). This element of surprise is always in conflict with the image of smoothness, which has the semiotic function of marking the producer's competence by emphasizing his mastery and control, his grasp of events. The signs of unpredictability and surprise are discontinuities and ragged edges that mark the boundaries of that competence by puncturing or lacerating that grasp. The image of smoothness depends always upon the appearance of the unimpeded forward course of the producer's intention, of facility, which means that there must be no doubt in the viewer's mind that what is transmitted is what the transmitter wants to transmit. And the only ways to achieve this were through (a) repeated preparation of the events, (b) very careful selection of highly predictable events, or (c) deletion of unexpected and undesirable aspects of events, which meant editing a recorded version of these events. Videotape came in 1956, and at the beginning Ampex was taping the Douglas Edwards newscasts and, not much later, the stage presentations of *Playhouse 90*. Once again, according to Stasheff and Bretz:

> ... by 1957 a new TV revolution was under way. Undistinguishable from live TV on the home receiver, video tape quickly replaced the kine-recording done by the TV networks. Not only did the stations put out a better picture, but the savings were tremendous ... Live production, video-tape recording of live production, kine-recording, and film began to assume complementary roles in the pattern of TV production. Video-tape recording by 1961 became so commonplace that the true live production—reaching the home at the moment of its origination—was a rarity limited largely to sports and special events. *The live production on video tape, though delayed in reaching the home by a few hours or a few days, was generally accepted as actual live television by the average viewer.*[5] [my italics].

Yet this did not place television in the same position as film, which from its origins appeared to be situated squarely in the domain of illusion. Film, after all, has made very few and very insubstantial claims to facticity. Amet's bathtub battle of Santiago Bay may have convinced Spanish military historians of its authenticity, but that was back in 1897 before the movie palaces together with the moviemakers dispelled any illusion of potential facticity. Flaherty looks as clearly fictional as Méliès now. But a genre that is marked "fictional" doesn't raise issues of truth and falsehood, and television never ceases to raise these issues. The social uses of television continually force the issue of "truth" to the center of attention. A President goes on television to declare his "honesty," a minister announces his "intentions," the evening news reports "what is being done to curb the inflation." The medium maintains a continual assertion that it can and does provide an adequate representation of reality, while everyone's experience continually denies it. Moreover, the industry exhibits a persistent positive tropism toward the appearance of the spontaneous and unrehearsed event in its perpetually recurring panel shows and quiz programs and in the apparently casual format of its late-evening news shows. According to Stasheff and Bretz:

> ... the television audience will not only accept, but even enjoy, a production error or even a comedian who blows his lines and admits it or who asks his straight man to feed him a cue once again so that he can make another try at getting the gag to come out right. This leniency on the part of the audience is caused by the increased feeling of spontaneity and immediacy which minor crises create. The audience loves to admire the adroitness with which the performer "pulls himself out of a jam."[6]

The industry wishes, or feels obligated, to maintain the illusion of immediacy, which it defines rather precisely as "the *feeling* that what one sees on the TV screen is living and actual reality, at that very moment taking place."[7] The perfection of videotape made possible the careful manipulation and selective presentation of desirable "errors" and "minor crises" as marks of spontaneity, which become as equivocal in their implications as the drips and blots of third-generation Abstract Expressionists. It's not that you couldn't see the Los Angeles police department's tactical assault squad in real time, in full living color, in your own living room, leveling a small section of the city in search of three or four suspected criminals, but that what you would see couldn't be certainly discriminated from a carefully edited videotape screened three hours later. So what television provides video with is a tradition not of falseness, which would be a kind of guarantee of at least a certain negative reliability, but of a profoundly menacing equivocation and mannerism, determining a species of unlikeness.

At first glance artists' video seems to be defined by the total absence of any of the features that define television. But this apparent lack of relation is in fact a very definite and predictable inverse relation. If we temporarily ignore the subfamily of installation pieces, which are actually quite diverse among themselves but nevertheless constitute a single genre, the most striking contrast between video pieces and television is in relation to time. It may not be quite hip to say so without qualification, but it is a commonplace to describe artists' videotapes as "boring" or "long," even when one feels that this in no way invalidates or dishonors the tapes in question (viz. Bruce Boice's comment that Lynda Benglis's video is "boring, interesting, and funny;"[8] or Richard Serra's own videotape, *Prisoner's Dilemma*, where one character advises another that he may have to spend two hours in the basement of the Castelli Gallery, which is "twice as long as the average boring videotape"). This perceived quality of being boring or long has little to do with the actual length of the tapes. It has much more to do with the attitude of just about all the artists using video to the task at hand. John Baldessari has a tape called *Some Words I Mispronounce*. He turns to a blackboard and writes:

1.	poor	4.	Beelzebub
2.	cask	5.	bough
3.	bade	6.	sword

As soon as he completes the "d" of "sword" the tape is over. Running time is under a minute. It feels amazingly short. But it is longer than most commercials.

Robert Morris's *Exchange*, a series of verbal meditations on exchanges of information, collaborations, and interferences with a woman, accompanied by a variety of images taped and retaped from other tapes and photographs for the most part as indefinite and suggestive as the discourse, goes on till it arrives at a single distinct and comic story of not getting to see the Gattamelata, after which the tape trails off in a more or less leisurely fashion. Running time is forty-three minutes. Television has many programs that are much longer. The two artists' tapes are very different. Baldessari's is a routine, explicitly defined from the outset and carried out deadpan to its swift conclusion. *Exchange* is a typical member of what is by now a well-defined genre of artist narrative, essentially an extended voiceover in a carefully framed literary style that seeks its end intuitively in the exhaustion of its mild narrative energy. But they both have the same attitude toward time. The work ends whenever its intention is accomplished. The time is inherent time, the time required for the task at hand. The work is "boring," as Les Levine remarked, "if you demand that it be something else. If you demand that it be itself then it is not boring."[9] Which is not to say that the videotapes may not be uninteresting. Whether they are interesting or not is largely a matter of judging the value of the task at hand, and this could hardly be the issue for people who can look with equanimity at what hangs on the wall in the most distinguished galleries. For whatever we think of the videotapes of Morris, or Sonnier, or Serra, these are certainly not inferior to whatever else they put in the gallery. Levine is right. Videotapes are boring if you demand that they be something else. But they're not judged boring by comparison with paintings or sculpture, they're judged boring in comparison with television, which for the last twenty years has set the standard of video time.

But the time standard of television is based firmly on the social and economic nature of the industry itself, and has nothing whatever to do with the absolute technical and phenomenological possibilities of visual representation by cathode ray tube. For television, time has an absolute existence independent of any imagery that may or may not be transmitted over its well-defended airwaves and cables. It is television's only solid, a tangible commodity that is precisely divisible into further and further subdivisible homogeneous units, the smallest quantum of which is measured by the smallest segment that could be purchased by a potential advertiser, which is itself defined by the minimum particle required to isolate a salable product from among a variable number of equivalent alternatives. The smallest salable piece turns out to be the ten-second spot, and all television is assembled from it.

But the social conventions of television dictate a code of behavior according to which the transmitter must assume two apparently different roles in transmission. In one he must appear to address the viewer on the station's behalf as entertainer; in the other on the sponsor's behalf as salesman. The rules of the game, which are legally codified, prescribe a sharp demarcation between the roles, and the industry makes a great show of marking off the boundaries between its two types of performances—the programs and the commercials. At their extremes of hard-sell and soft-show, one might suppose that the stylistic features of the two roles would be sufficient to distinguish them, but the extremes are rare, the social function of the roles are not so distinct, and the stylistic features seldom provide sufficient separation. Since the industry's most tangible presentation is metrically divisible time, the industry seems to mark the separation emphatically by assigning the two roles different time signatures. The commercial is built on a scale of the minute out of multiple 10-second units. It comes in four common sizes— 10, 30, 60 and 120 seconds—of which the 30-second slot is by far the commonest. The program is built on the scale of the hour out of truncated and hinged 15-minute units that are also commonly assembled in four sizes—15, 30, and 60 and 120 minutes—of which the half-hour program is the commonest, though the hour length is usual for important programs, two hours quite frequent for specials and feature films, and fifteen minutes not entirely a rarity for commentary. Television inherited the split roles and the two time signatures from radio, as well as the habit of alternating them in regularly recurrent intervals, which creates the arbitrary-appearing, mechanical segmentation of both media's presentations. But television carried this mechanical segmentation to a new extreme and presented it in such a novel way—through a special combination of its own peculiar technology and production conventions—that television time, in spite of structural similarity with radio time, has an entirely different appearance from it, bearing the relationship to it of an electronically driven, digital counter to a spring-driven, hand-wound alarm clock.

Television achieved its extreme segmentation of transmission time mainly through the intense development of multiple sponsorship. Old radio programs from the 1930s and 1940s tended to have a single sponsor. *The Lone Ranger* was sponsored for years by Silvercup Bread, *Ma Perkins* by Oxydol, *Uncle Don* by Ovaltine, and these sponsors would reappear regularly at the beginning, middle, and end of each program with pretty much the same commercial pitch. This pattern continued by and large into the early days of television with *Hallmark Theater, The Kraft Playhouse*, and so on. But current television practice is generally quite different. A half-hour program might have something like six minutes of commercial fitted to it in three two-minute blocks at the beginning, middle, and end of the program. But these six minutes of commercial time might promote the commodities of twelve different sponsors, or twelve different commodities of some smaller number of sponsoring agencies. The commodities could be nearly anything—a car, a cruise, a furniture polish, a breakfast food, a funeral service, a scent for men, a cure for smoking, an ice show, an X-rated movie, or a politician. In principle they could apply to nearly any aspect of human life and be presented in any order, with strategies of advocacy more various than the commodities themselves. In practice the range of commodity and styles of advocacy are somewhat more limited, but the fact remains that in half an hour you might see a succession of four complete, distinct, and unrelated thirty-second presentations, followed by a twelve-minute half of a presentation, followed by a one-minute presentation, one thirty-second presentation, and two ten-second presentations, followed by the second and concluding half presentation (twelve minutes long) followed by yet another four unrelated thirty-second presentations. But since this would lead to bunching of two two-minute commercials into a four-minute package of commercial at the end of every hour, and since viewers are supposed to want mainly to look at the programs—or because program-makers are rather possessive about their own commercials and want complete credit for them—the program-makers have recently developed the habit of presenting a small segment of their own program as a kind of prologue before the opening commercial, to separate it from the tail end of the preceding program, while the program-makers of the preceding program may attempt to tag onto the end of their own program a small epilogue at the end of their last commercial, to affix it more securely to their own program. Meanwhile the station may itself interject a small commercial promoting itself or its future presentations. All of these additional segments—prologues, epilogues, station promotions, and coming attractions—usually last no more than two minutes, and are scaled to commercial time, and are in their functional nature promotions for either immediately succeeding or eventually succeeding transmissions. This means that you may see upward of fourteen distinct segments of presentations in any half-hour, all but two of which will be scaled to commercial time. Since commercial time is the most common signature, we could expect it to dominate the tempo of television, especially since the commercial segments constitute the only example of integral (complete and uninterrupted) presentation in the medium. And it does, but not in the way one would generally suppose.

It is very easy to exaggerate the apparent differences between commercial time and program time by concentrating on the dramatic program. Television has many programs that share a mechanically segmented structure with the packet of commercials. The most extreme cases are the news programs, contests, and the so-called talk shows. What is called news on television is a chain of successive, distinct, and structurally unrelated narrations called stories. These average from thirty seconds to two minutes in length, are usually presented in successions of three or four in a row, and are bracketed between packets of commercials from one to two minutes long. The "full" story is built very much like a common commercial. It will usually have a ten- to thirty-second introduction narrated by an actor seen in a chest shot, followed by a segment of film footage about one minute in length. There are alternate forms, but all of them are built on exactly the same type of segmentation. The narrating actor may merely narrate (read off) the event from the same chest shot seen against a background of one or two slides plausibly related to the event. The only continuity for the six- or seven-minute packet of programming called news consists of an abstract categorial designation (e.g., national) and the recurrent shots of the newsmen, actors who project some well-defined character considered appropriate for this part of the show, such as informed concern, alert aggressiveness, world-weary moralism, or genial confidence. This tends to be more obvious in the packets designated as sports and weather, where what passes for information consists of bits so small, numerous, and unrelated that they come down to mere lists. These may be held together respectively by more obvious character actors like a suave ex-jock and a soft-touch comic.

Similarly, contest shows consist of structurally identical, separate events joined edge to edge and connected mainly by the continuous presence of the leading actor (the host). Television has also—through selection of the events themselves and manner of representation—managed to present most of its sports programs as sequences of nearly identical unrelated events. Baseball gets reduced to a succession of pitches, hits, and catches, football to a succession of runs, passes, and tackles, while the ensemble of events that may be unfolding lies outside the system of representation. If we count together all the programs that are constructed out of these linearly successive, distinct segments of commercial scale, the contrast between commercial and program becomes much less sharp.

Moreover, a close inspection of both will show that there are really no stylistic distinctions between commercials and programs, because just about every genre of program appears also as a commercial. Dramas, comedies, documentaries, science talks, lists, all show up in thirty- and sixty-second forms. Even their distinctive integralness can be exaggerated, because often there is a clean partition between the programmatic parts of the commercial—its dramatic or imagistic material—and the details of the pitch that specify the name of the product and where you can get it. This separation is so common that it is possible to watch three thirty-second commercials in succession with some pleasure and find it difficult to remember the name or even the nature of the commodity promoted. This is not a functional defect in the commercial, the main function of which is to produce a kind of praise poetry that will elevate to a mild prominence one member out of the general family of commodities that television promotes as a whole tribe all of its transmitting day. Poems in praise of particular princes are addressed to an audience already familiar with the tribe, and commercials are constructed to particularize an already existing interest. Nobody unconcerned with body odors will care which deodorant checks them best. It takes the whole television day to encode the positive images of smoothness, cleanliness, or blandness upon which the massive marketing of deodorants and soaps depends. There is no fundamental distinction between commercial and program, there is only a difference in focus and conciseness, which gives the thirty-second commercial its appearance of much greater elegance and style. Both commercials and programs are assembled out of the same syntax: the linear succession of logically independent units of nearly equal duration. But this mechanically divisible, metrical presentation had none of the percussive or disjunctive properties of radio presentation. This is because of the conventions of camerawork and editing that television has developed to soften the shock of its basically mechanical procedures.

It is probably fair to say that the entire technology, from the shape of the monitor screen to the design of camera mounts, was worked out to soften the tick of its metronome. Almost every instrument of television technique and technology seems to have the effect of a shock absorber. As in film, the television presentation is assembled out of separate shots. But these shots are very limited in type and duration. Because of the poor resolution of the television image (525 bits of information presented on photosensitive phosphors) and the normal screen size, the bread-and-butter shots of television are almost all sub-forms of what film would consider a close-up. Common shot names illustrate this—knee shot, thigh shot, waist shot, bust shot, head shot, tight head shot. Or else they count the number of people in the frame—two shot, four shot, etc. Probably primarily for this reason shot durations are very limited in range—usually from two to ten seconds—and very predictable in function and type. The two- to three-second shot is almost always a reaction shot or a transition detail in a narrative, so it will usually be a head shot or detail of some activity. Distant shots of moving cars, or whatever, will usually run seven to ten seconds, like action in general. Shots of a second and under are very rare and only used for special occasions, but distinct shots over twenty seconds are practically nonexistent. "Distinct" because television's camera conventions include a cameraman who is trained to act like an antiaircraft gunner, constantly making minute adjustments of the camera—loosening up a bit here, tightening up there, gently panning and trucking in a nearly imperceptible manner to keep the target on some imaginary pair of cross hairs. These endless, silken adjustments, encouraged and sometimes specifically called for by the director and usually built into the cameraman's training, tend to blur the edges of what the film director would normally consider a shot. To this we can add the widespread use of fade-ins and fade-outs and dissolves to effect temporal and spatial transitions, and the directors' regular habit of cutting on movement to cushion the switch from one camera to another. This whole arsenal of techniques has a single function—to soften all shocks of transition. Naturally the different apparent functions of various genres of program or commercial will alter the degree of softening, so a news program will maintain a sense of urgency through its use of cuts, soft though they may be, while the soap opera constantly melts together its various close shots with liquid adjustment and blends scene to scene in recurrent dissolves and fades. This ceaseless softening combines with the regular segmentation to transform the metronomic tick-tock of the transmission into the silent succession of numbers on a digital clock.

Because of the television industry's special aesthetic of time and the electronics industry's primary adaptation of the technology to the needs and desires of television, the appearance of an art-world video had to wait for the electronics industry to attempt to expand the market for its technology into special institutional and consumer domains. The basic tool kit of artists' video is the portapak with its small, mobile camera and ½-inch black and white videotape recorder that can accommodate nothing larger than thirty-minute tapes. Combined with a small monitor and perhaps an additional microphone, the whole operation costs something in the vicinity of $2,000—a bit less than a cheap car and a bit more than a good stereo system. This is the fundamental unit, but it allows no editing whatever. The most minimal editing—edge-to-edge assembling of tapes into units larger than thirty minutes—requires access to at least another videotape recorder with a built-in editing facility, which means the investment of at least another $1,200. This is a primitive editing capacity, but increases the unit cost by 50% to about $3,000. Yet precision editing and smoothness are still out of the question. Unlike film, where editing is a scissors-and-paste job anyone can do with very little equipment, and where you can sit in a small room and shave pieces of film down to the half-frame with no great difficulty, video pictures have to be edited electronically by assembling image sequences from some source or sources in the desired order on the tape of a second machine. The images are electronically marked off from each other by an electronic signal recurring (in the U.S.) thirty times a second. If you want to place one sequence of images right after another that you've already recorded onto the second tape, you have to join the front edge of the first new frame to the final edge of the other, which means that motors of both machines have to be synchronized to the 30th of a second and that there must be a way of reading off each frame edge to assure that the two recorded sequences are in phase with each other. Half-inch equipment is not designed to do this, and the alignment of frame edge with frame edge is a matter of accident.

Alignment of a particular frame edge with a particular frame edge is out of the question. If the frame edges don't come together, the tape is marked by a characteristic momentary breakup or instability of the image. You may or may not mind this, but it's the distinctive mark of this type of editing. Since this is absolutely unlike television editing, it carries its special mark of homemade or cheap or unfinicky or direct or honest. But the dominance of television aesthetics over anything seen on a TV screen makes this rather casual punctuation mark very emphatic and loaded with either positive or negative value. An installation with synchronized, multiple cameras, with capabilities for switching through cutting, fading, and dissolving, and some few special effects like black and white reversal, will cost somewhere in the $10,000 range, provided you stick to black and white and ½-inch equipment. This is only a minor increase in editing control and a cost increase of one order of magnitude. If you want reliably smooth edits that will allow you to join predictably an edge to an edge, without specifying which edge, you will need access to an installation whose cost begins at around $100,000. One major art gallery has a reduced form of such a facility that permits this sort of editing, which costs about half that. Again we have an increase of control that is nearly minimal and a cost increase of another order of magnitude. Some artists have solved this problem by obtaining occasional access to institutions possessing this kind of installation, but usually this takes complete editing control out of the hands of most artists. There are also ways of adapting the one-inch system to precisionist frame-for-frame capacity, but that requires the investment of several thousand dollars more. A rule of thumb might specify that each increase in editing capacity represents an order of magnitude increase in cost. Color is still another special problem. Though it is hardly necessary, and possibly a great drawback in the sensible use of video for most artists' purposes (viz., Sonnier's pointless color work), it is by now television's common form and has certain normative marks associated with it. To use black and white is a marked move, regardless of what the mark may be construed to mean. So, many artists will seek color for mere neutrality. But it comes at a price. There are bargain-basement color systems, wonderfully cheesy in appearance, but the most common system is the ¾-inch cassette ensemble, which together with camera, videotape recorder, and monitor goes at about $10,000. If the portapak is the Volkswagen, this is the Porsche of individual artists' video. For editing control the system of escalation in color runs parallel to black and white. The model of ultimate refinement and control is the television industry's two-inch system, and since that's what you see in action in any motel over the TV set, interesting or not, everyone takes it for the state of the art.

These conditions may not seem promising, but artists are as good at surviving as cockroaches, and they've developed three basic strategies for action. They can take the lack of technical refinements as a given and explore the theater of poverty. They can beg, borrow, or steal access to technical wealth and explore the ambiguous role of the poor relation, the unwelcome guest, the court jester, the sycophant, or the spy. This isn't a common solution; the studios don't make their facilities available so readily. But it includes works done by Allan Kaprow, Peter Campus, Les Levine, Nam June Paik, and numerous others. Artists can also raid the technology as a set of found objects or instruments with phenomenological implications in installation pieces. There are numerous examples from the work of Peter Campus, Dan Graham, Nam June Paik, Frank Gillette, etc. To a great extent the significance of all types of video art derives from its stance with respect to some aspect of television, which is itself profoundly related to the present state of our culture. In this way video art embarks on a curiously mediated but serious critique of the culture. And this reference to television, and through it to the culture, is not dependent on whether or not the artist sees the work in relation to television. The relation between television and video is created by the shared technologies and conditions of viewing, in the same way the relation of movies to underground film is created by the shared conditions of cinema. Nevertheless, an artist may exploit the relation very knowingly and may choose any aspect of the relation for attack.

If Nancy Holt's *Underscan* is an innocent masterpiece that narrates in its toneless voice a terrifying, impoverished story over a sequence of simple photographic images ruined twice over by the television raster, the correlated Benglis *Collage* and Morris *Exchange* are cunning parodies that use the cheesy video image to depreciate a filmic genre that would sensuously exploit the personal glamour of stars like Elizabeth Taylor and Richard Burton, replaced here by the mock glamour of two pseudocelebrities in a visual soup. Holt calls into question anything that the medium has ever represented as documentary with her sheer simplicity of means, while Morris and Benglis produce a total burlesque of the public figure through the manifest absurdity of their claims.

Acconci's *Undertone* is an even more precise example of this type of burlesque. In a visual style of address exactly equivalent to the Presidential address, the face-to-face camera regards The Insignificant Man making the Outrageous Confession that is as likely as not to be an Incredible Lie. Who can escape the television image of Nixon?

In Baldessari's wonderful *Inventory*, the artist presents to the camera for thirty minutes an accumulation of indiscriminate and not easily legible objects arranged in order of increasing size and accompanied by a deadpan description—only to have the sense of their relative size destroyed by the continual readjustment of the camera's focal length that is required to keep them within the frame. Who can forget Adlai Stevenson's solemn television demonstration of the "conclusive photographic evidence" of the Cuban missile sites, discernible over the TV screen as only gray blurs?

What the artists constantly re-evoke and engage with is television's fundamental equivocation and mannerism, which may really be the distinctive feature of the medium. But they may do this from two diametrically opposed angles, either by parodying the television system and providing some amazing bubble or by offering to demonstrate how, with virtually no resources, they can do all the worthwhile things that television should do or could do in principle and has never yet done and never will do.

Terry Fox's *Children's Tapes* exhibit nothing more nor less than the simple laws of the physical world in terms of small common objects—a spoon, a cup, an ice cube, a piece of cloth. They make use of a single camera, adjusted only enough to get the objects and events into the frame, and no edits. The hands crumple a spoon handle, place an ice cube in it over a small piece of cloth, balance it at the neck over the rim of a cup. You watch. It takes how long for you to figure out that the ice cube will melt? That the cloth will absorb the water. That the balance will be upset. But which way? Will the water absorbed into the cloth be drawn further from the fulcrum and increase the downward movement on the ice cube side? Or will the water dripping from the spoon reduce the downward movement and send the spoon toppling into the cup? You watch as though waiting for an explosion. It takes minutes to come and you feel relieved. It has the form of drama. You'll never see anything like it on educational television or any other television. It takes too much time, intelligence, and intensity of attention to watch—except on video. There are, I believe, twenty-two of them. They have the brilliance of still life and the intelligence of a powerful didactic art. But it is also a critique of means. Other works similar in this respect of means are Richard Serra's *Prisoners' Dilemma* and Eleanor Antin's *The Ballerina and the Bum.*

The Serra piece shamelessly adapts a casual stage skit and a contest show format to illustrate hilariously and with absolute simplicity a moral-logical dilemma with grave implications for human action. The problem is apparently simple. There are two prisoners, A and B. Each is offered a chance to betray the other and go free—but here is the first catch—provided the other refuses to betray him. In the event that this happens the prisoner who refuses to betray will receive the maximum sentence—this is the second catch. The other alternatives are that both prisoners will refuse to betray each other—this will get both prisoners the second lightest penalty; or that both prisoners will attempt to betray each other, which will get each prisoner the second gravest penalty. On the face of it we have a straightforward 2x4 matrix with four outcomes for each player, but all the outcomes are linked pairs: You go free only if he gets life imprisonment and he goes free only if you get life imprisonment; you both get away with two years' imprisonment if you both hold out against betrayal; you both get ten years' imprisonment if you both try betrayal. If each player plays the game as a zero-sum game for his own advantage, he will inspect the reward columns and come to the single conclusion that the worst possible outcome is life imprisonment, which can only happen if he refuses to betray. This prevents the other player from screwing him and leaves the original player the chance of screwing his opponent. Since both players—regarded as unrelated individuals who will consider their own individual advantage—will both play to minimize their loss, they will each play to cut their losses and inevitably come out with the next-to-worse payoff, ten years in prison. There is no way to win and no way to play for mutual nonbetrayal, because failure to betray always risks total loss. But the video piece is more brilliant than that. It sets up two precise illustrations—comic, yes; casual, yes—but elegant in the way it demonstrates that any two unrelated prisoners—say a pair of suspected criminals picked up in the street—will inevitably betray each other and take the consequences. But any two prisoners who have a real community bond between them have no choice but to play for nonbetrayal, because they must consider the value of the outcome in terms of its value for both players. Obviously, the differences in negative weights assigned to the penalties will work differently in deciding the outcome. Still, nothing in the world of this low-budget game could make Leo Castelli betray Bruce Boice in public. This low-budget marker calls up beautiful improvisational acting from all of the players and loose styles from all of the collaborators in this group piece. The logical structuring of the piece owes a great deal to Robert Bell, who occupies a role somewhere between scriptwriter and director, and to all of the actors, whose improvisatory performances contribute markedly to the final outcome of the piece, which must be considered a community venture, with Richard Serra assuming the producer's role. This piece is also of a sort that will never appear on television and has the force of a parable.

Antin's *Ballerina and the Bum,* another low-budget job, with single portapak camera and two improvising actors, declares itself, from its five-minute opening shot, against television, time, and money. The camera changes position only if it has to, to keep something in view, pans once along three cars of a freight train to count them, moves inside the car. The mike has no windscreen. The sounds of the world of 1974—cars, airplanes, children, and chickens—intermittently penetrate the film-style illusion of the image of a Sylphides-costumed, New York-accented ballerina "from the sticks" and a twenty-five-year-old grizzled bum on the way to the big city. Nothing happens but what they say and do. She practices ballet, sets up light housekeeping in the boxcar, they daydream of success, he cooks some beans, she eats them, the train goes nowhere. Everything else is moving—cars, planes, and other trains. A whole Chaplin movie for the price of a good dub.

Other successful examples of this low-budget strategy are Andy Mann's *One-Eyed Bum* and Ira Schneider and Beryl Korot's *4th of July in Saugerties,* which bring to bear the video of limited means upon documentary as a kind of artist's reminder of the ambiguities of "honesty" and "simplicity." It is no accident that the best of these works have, at least in part, a didactic and moral element behind them and are "exemplary." And even the tapes that are not specifically presented in an exemplary mode become exemplary in their fundamental disdain for television time.

But the theater of poverty isn't the only way. Peter Campus somehow infiltrated WGBH-TV, Boston, to produce a single deadly piece precisely aimed through their expensive equipment. A man holds a photograph, seemingly of himself. You see him set fire to it and watch it burn from all four sides. Gradually you notice that the photograph is breathing, its eyes are blinking. This is the image of television.

From *Video Art*. Edited by Ira Schneider and Beryl Korot. New York: Harcourt Brace Jovanovich, 1976, pp. 174-83. Reprinted with permission of the Institute of Contemporary Art, University of Pennsylvania from the catalogue to the exhibition "Video Art," 1975.

NOTES
1. Frank Gillette, *Frank Gillette Video: Process and Metaprocess*. Jodson Rosenbush, ed. (Syracuse, N.Y.: Everson Museum of Art, 1973), p. 21.
2. Hollis Frampton, "The Withering Away of the State of Art," *Artforum* (Dec. 1974): p. 50.
3. Jud Yalkut, "TV As a Creative Medium at the Howard Wise Gallery," *Arts Magazine* (Sept. 1969): p. 18.
4. Edward Stasheff and Rudy Bretz, *The Television Program: Its Writing, Direction, and Production* (New York: A.A. Wyn, 1951), p. 3.
5. Ibid., p. 6.
6. Ibid., p. 8.
7. Ibid.
8. Bruce Boice, "Lynda Benglis at Paula Cooper Gallery,„ *Artforum* (May 1973): p.83.
9. Les Levine, "Exerpts from a Tape: 'Artistic'," *Art-Rite* (Autumn 1974): p. 27.

Truth or Consequences:
American Television and Video Art

David Ross

We have an inconsequential literature, which not only takes pains to have no consequences itself, but goes to a great deal of trouble to neutralize its readers by picturing all objects and situations without their consequences.
Bertolt Brecht, 1927[1]

T HERE WAS ALWAYS something particularly disturbing about "Truth or Consequences," a prototypical 1950s American game show hosted by a smarmy announcer named Bob Barker in which members of the studio audience were made to look foolish as a consequence of answering a trivial question incorrectly. Perhaps it was the fact that one developed the idea that consequences were always undesirable and that if one could always tell the "truth" one might avoid them. Consequences were for suckers, the kind of people who actually went to sit in the audience of TV game shows to entertain those of us smart enough to keep our distance. Perhaps what was really feared was exposing the shallow mystery that was TV in its early period. This mystery was a great comfort to children of all ages, as the saying goes, for it effectively neutralized us all in precisely the manner in which Brecht had predicted it might.

The ways in which our neutralized status was reinforced by television over the years are in themselves quite fascinating. First there was the unstoppable character of television itself, which rated right up there with the earth's rotation in terms of natural phenomena. Television's velocity was constant—it kept its pace whether you were watching or not, whether you were eating, sleeping, studying, playing, or paying attention. It was oblivious of you, and you (in return) were offered the opportunity to become oblivious of it and (by extension) anything else you chose to ignore. Equally as important was the TV-bred illusion of endless choice. Change channels whenever you like. Never be bored. Live free or die. Bill Viola's "seven-channel childhood" has expanded to 105, and it's still growing! This illusion of choice was so well developed that it actually promoted the notion that there was significant difference between the essentially identical offerings "competing" with each other for the lucrative privilege of capturing an audience. Of course, once captured, you (the audience of free individuals) were delivered to the same prisons—one in which your consumer desires would be rehabilitated en masse and your sense of self either perverted or retarded. Finally there was the seamless representation of a world populated by essentially good, middle-class, white people in which powerless women and other victims were intimidated, threatened, and often harmed by essentially evil, non-white or ethnic types. In other words, the problem of pernicious content. As America and its television "greened" in the '70s, these representations were modified and reformed, providing perhaps *the* critical illusion of the medium: that TV is reformable on the basis of its content alone.

As a result, well-meaning activist organizations like the highly visible and powerful Action for Children's Television (ACT) carefully monitored television violence aimed at youth markets and observed with equal concern the content and methods of TV advertising directed towards children. They have lobbied for and brought about significant content reform. Numerous women's groups monitored and lobbied against the sexist representation of women on television, and nearly every ethnic minority and religious community continually monitors its basic media portrayal. The result has been a rapid TV industry sophistication in regard to program development, script editing, and most of all pre-testing of viewer response. Little, if anything, is left to chance. In fact, the programming of commercial broadcasting reflects the same market-tested methods that government itself does. At this point in time, the linkage between TV program development and political power development is direct: the attendant processes are identical. Selling based on illusion reigns supreme in America.

In the context of such finely crafted illusion—one developed and maintained by America's most sophisticated media minds and technologies—video art has been slowly developing for the past twenty years. Its development has been steady, marked by the work of some important artists whose aesthetic orientation has ranged widely (from

Vito Acconci and Bruce Nauman to Nam June Paik and Stephen Beck, from Eleanor Antin and Howard Fried to Mary Lucier and Bill Viola), and by many artists whose work in video resulted from a specific need generated by previous work in painting, sculpture, photography, ceramics, dance, performance, and of course film. It would be untrue to state that television, or to be precise, broadcast television—what David Antin termed video's "frightful parent"—was the sole or even the primary referent in the body of work that has emerged from the past two decades. But it would be completely misleading and actually untrue to attempt to describe the activity of American video art outside of the clear and—in some instances—critical relationship that video art has had with broadcast commercial television. But this relationship has less to do with a critique of television content, and its inconsequentiality, than with the manner in which television creates and reinforces the neutralizing effect of a consequence-free universe.

Recently, broadcast television, in its increasing sophistication, has managed to re-use its own rich (or at least dense) history of characters, plot formulae, and trivia to create what seems a parody of its own past. In fact, using the collective memory of a generation thoroughly schooled in television, TV has created a veneer constituting a metacritical strategy rather than the indication of a willingness or a fundamental ability to change. In this same climate, opportunistic Luddites like ex-advertising executive Jerry Mander publish tracts calling for the "elimination" of television, ridiculing the idea of a meaningful critique of television. Ironically, it has been the avant-garde artists working in video whose work has constituted the only meaningful critique of television's form and practice. Rather than simple parody, artists like Nam June Paik and Dara Birnbaum have used what the literary critic Fredric Jameson terms pastiche to explore and develop a grammar appropriate to a television of consequence.

To make this assertion, one must begin by assuming that the content-based critique of commercial television is, by the very nature of its intention, a modernist enterprise, linked to the rejection of "that whole landscape of advertising, motels, Hollywood B movies," and other aspects of culture that Jameson describes as "*Reader's Digest* culture." According to Jameson, pastiche, as opposed to parody, is blank, humorless, and based wholly on the primary post-modernist assumption that "stylistic innovation is no longer possible, all that is left is to ... speak through the masks and with the voices of the styles in the imaginary museum."[2] The results of this kind of thinking, whether they be the *film noir* appropriations of Betty Gordon or Vivian Dick, the stylistic appropriations of David Salle or Robert Longo's painting, the wholesale appropriation of photographic images by Sherrie Levine, or the video works of Birnbaum and Paik and others, is work which functions both directly as art and indirectly as a critique of the style, manner, and nature of the forms on which it is based.

When in 1965 Nam June Paik took a magnet to the face of a television image and physically twisted the flow of electrons that had previously formed recognizable imagery on the screen so that the resulting image had the tortured look of comic-book surrealist imagery, we finally recognized a gesture that seemed to do justice to the face of a Richard Nixon or Marshall McLuhan. The simple gesture, though demonstrably after the fact in relation to the production of those images (and by extension their power sources), robbed these images of more than their propriety. The distortion of these images constituted a primary and, in a way, profoundly liberating appropriation of the notion of media-image power.

Paik's subsequent attack on the notion of "real-time" in his earliest videotape manipulation pieces can also be seen as an extension of this emerging post-Pop sensibility. In *Variations on George Ball on Meet the Press* (1967), an off-screen recording of Johnson-era, Under-Secretary of State George Ball (who had recently resigned his post in ostensibly moral opposition to the Vietnam War), the image of Ball speaking moves first at the pace of real-time, and then in intervals determined by Paik's manual manipulations of the recording reels. The resulting tape work serves as a clear example of the kind of pastiche that Jameson later defined—in this case not in relation to speech itself, but to the representation of speech that constitutes such an integral part of the television grammar—TV time itself.

The overt satirical device of taking the powerful and making them look foolish is not in itself novel, nor in this case the really significant operating level of this work and others like it from the same period. Rather it is the double assertion of the value of the insertion of the hand of the artist into the process of media—which at this point in time was indeed novel and significant—and the relative nature of truth as communicated through this medium.

An earlier piece, *Variations on Johnny Carson vs. Charlotte Moorman* (1966), provides a link between the magnetic distortions, and the Ball piece. In this work, a simple offscreen tape of Paik's collaborator, Charlotte Moorman, conversing with and later performing a John Cage piece for Johnny Carson, is the subject of the work. This is to say, the tape itself is the subject, rather than the content of the re-recorded discussion and performance. Paik placed a live wire across the tape erasing a thin line of material directly below the wire itself. The resulting tape features the Carson-Moorman interaction periodically interrupted by a momentary erasure. The regular period of the interruption becomes shorter as the reel plays towards its core, ending in pure uninterrupted static. Again, the comic effect is there, but it's not as funny as it is disturbing. The sense of some intervening random event interfering with our vision of this representation gives way to a recognition of the pattern of the interruption which in turn shifts the work's significance to the implied critique of the reality represented rather than the content itself. Ironically—for pastiche of this sort need not be empty on this level—the tape features Carson doing his patented eyes-rolled-up double takes as Moorman first explains avant-garde music, and later as she performs the Cage piece. The use of the Cage work as a matrix, and the Carson "critique" implied by his gestures and patronizing attitude towards Moorman, only fortifies the power of Paik's meta-critique.

Like other artists of this era (late sixties, early seventies), Paik sought to build a strategy through which aspects of culture as well as understanding of culture itself might be transformed by the act of appropriation and by the will to reconstruct commonly accepted phenomena as works of art. As an early goal of Pop Art, this objective seemed unattainable before the liberating effect of the politicization of the art world during this time. Though Paik's works were seemingly dealing directly with television, they dealt more directly with the ideology of television, the structure of its controlling components, and in true Fluxus spirit, with intellectualized violence and applied chaos. As Paik's work has developed, his concentration on the broader cultural and ideological critique has become more focused as well.

For a brief though influential period, Paik focused on the invention of hardware, an essentially sculptural activity linking the lessons of electronic music composition and his guerrilla robotics in a focused attempt to re-invent the grammar of television from within the TV apparatus. If the early manipulated tapes demonstrated a resigned awareness of the artists' post-facto position in relation to television as both a technology and a universal model of society, the invention of video image-manipulating devices constituted a metaphorical and practical attempt to position the artist within. From the crudely manipulated or "prepared" television sets in his ground-breaking 1963 Wuppertal exhibition, Paik developed the idea of moving his point of entry further "upstream," into the source of the electronic flow itself. His well-known (but widely misunderstood) sculptural collaboration with the engineer Shuya Abe, known as the Paik-Abe Video Synthesizer, was a device that allowed the artist to re-scan, distort, colorize, and in other ways (that seems positively tame by 1984 technical standards) process the video image produced by a live or tape source. The visually distinctive imagery that the synthesizer produced provided the artist with a signature style, and allowed him to occupy a novel position relative to straight television imagery. Paik's images were, in the McLuhanesque terms of the time, cool, less resolved, less representational of the normal television language of recognizable signs. In short, they indicated an attempt to generate pastiche rather than parody, to reinvest emptied, well-understood forms, and refill them for distinctly different purposes.

Underlying the invention of the synthesizer was something besides the simple desire to create a video equivalent of the psychedelic "posterized" photography of the late sixties. Though his 1967 four-hour broadcast of Beatles' music and randomly generated synthesizer imagery produced by anyone who happened by the WGBH Boston studios that evening did constitute a landmark of stoned television, it was not the point of the exercise. A more subtle critique of the development of television as *the* invention of late 20th-century capitalism was also implied. The direction and progress of television's invention was brought into relief by Paik's comic intervention in that process.

The playwright Bertolt Brecht noted that "these people who have a high opinion of radio have it because they see in it something for which 'something' can be invented. They would see themselves justified," he continued, "at the moment when 'something' was discovered for the sake of which radio would have to be invented if it did not already exist."[3] Leaping over the predictions of cultural enrichment for the masses predicted by television's early defenders, Paik offers his television-art produced as a response to the clear fact that the television product and indeed the television grammar itself developed with no significant artist's participation. This is stated by Paik's invention as well as the work of the Vasulkas and others in clear counterdistinction to the development of film's grammar which *was* forged by artistic genius.

But perhaps more important than Paik's response to Brecht's analysis of the rationale supporting radio's suspect invention is Paik's overriding concern for the other thrust of Brecht's essay. Brecht asserts that "by continuous, unceasing proposals for better employment of the apparatus in the interest of the community we must destroy the social basis of that apparatus and question their use in the interest of the few."[4] Brecht questions the implicit order of one-way broadcast as model of societal control. In whose interest, one implies from Brecht's statement, does the one-way nature of broadcast (television) exist, and for what reasons did the invention take that form? Paik questions this nature of television the invention, as surely as he explores the nature of television the cultural form.

Like Brecht, Paik's work aspires towards consequence embodied metaphorically as participation. "Participation TV" was the subtitle of the exhibition of Paik's 1965 synthesizer exhibition in the Bonino Gallery. Not only positioning the artist inside the production process (or

more correctly the distortion of deconstruction process), the synthesizer opened the production process to public manipulation. Compared to most kinetic sculpture Paik's went further than any of the essentially inconsequential playthings offered up by the makers of
mechanical art purporting to hail or eulogize the end of the mechanical
age. Paik's art, to paraphrase the artist, was not "cybernetic art, but art
for cybernetic times;" it was kitsch in the true meaning of the word
Another of Paik's early participation pieces featured a device that
transformed the viewer's voice into a burst of video color on the screen.
In this work, talking back to your television set was transformed from
an act of alienation or slight craziness to a real metaphorical act. Giving
the functionally mute, passive viewer/receiver a voice was not merely
playful, it was the creation of an act of consequence, in which the
ephemeral nature of the act reinforced the real condition of the viewer
and framed his or her awareness of that condition as a work of art.

Paik's broadcast works, and live broadcast performance pieces, represent the extent of his development in this direction. Starting with *The
Selling of New York* and *Waiting for Commercial* (both 1972), Paik
began to create broadcast tapes, fully aware of the context for the
works. That is to say, Paik was fully aware of the general broadcast condition and the viewer's relation to television viewing as a physical
phenomenon and sociological situation. Though these tapes were produced to be aired on noncommercial, public television (ostensibly
differing in style and intention from their commercial cousins), it was
immediately clear that Paik projected no differentiation between the
broadcast types in his approach to the form. In *Selling*, Paik created
spots to be inserted into the late-night programming schedule of New
York's WNET-TV. The core of the work, operating below the rather
flat parody of New York's ongoing effort to sell itself as the major
media market in the U.S., is the view of "normal" people, going about
their everyday lives oblivious to the constant droning of the television
sets in their midst. Inserted as punctuation into these black-out skits,
with origins in broadcast's own penchant for defusing self-parody, are
off-the-air commercials for American products (i.e. Pepsi) produced
and aired on Japanese TV for the major industrial market in Asia. Like
Brecht's Marxist monologues, delivered in the middle of the dramatic
entertainment, these commercials are used not so much to sell a product or ideological shift as to warn the viewer and wake the sleeper.
What Paik refuses to do is idealize the conceptual process of viewing or
assign a passive role to the spectator. In these early broadcast works
Paik asserts, through the use of ironic juxtaposition, the necessity of an
active, non-neutral position for the viewer and the artist.

In 1975, in a remote "live-on-tape" broadcast emanating from Paik's studio, the artist had the rare opportunity to produce a work in the context of a highly rated, late-night network "talk" program, the now defunct Tom Snyder "Tomorrow" show. In many ways, this program allowed Paik to create his most successful two-way piece. Speaking with the host in a mock video-phone set-up, Paik led Snyder on a short tour of his studio, a tour which constituted a small retrospective of his career. Selling all the while, Paik ended the tour at his interactive video sculpture known as the *TV Chair*. On the monitor located below the transparent seat of the chair was a silent tape of Snyder, recorded off the air on the previous evening. Maintaining his polite banter all the while, Paik then sat himself atop of Snyder's silent/talking face. Like the simple gesture of erasing the Carson tape, this action confirmed the emergence of a new role for artists relative to mass media, a role characterized by the willingness and capability to appropriate and transform media power. Needless to say, Snyder was not amused.

In his New Year's Day 1984 broadcast work *Good Morning, Mr. Orwell*, Paik produced and aired a work that earlier tapes like the 1973 *Global Groove* served as studies for. This "entertainment" also took as its form the broadcast variety-talk show. This program, a live simulcast between WNET in New York and the Pompidou Center in Paris, featured real-time intercontinental interactive performance works, not-so-successful parodies of video telephony, some new music, and some talk. Though flawed by technical problems, the work demonstrated a strong sense of consequence and a profound understanding of the nature of its two-way TV context.

Dara Birnbaum's work has developed in a wholly different, though completely sympathetic, manner. Unlike Paik who emerged from an essentially musical context into the visual arts, Birnbaum came to video from a background in architecture and painting. Her video work represents the generation of artists whose exposure to Paik and the other early seventies videomakers and theorists (in her case, Dan Graham was an important influence) allowed for the creation of quite powerful and original video works based on assumptions about television that did not exist in 1963.

This is not to intimate that Birnbaum's work is academic or secondhand. Indeed, Birnbaum has wrestled with the complexities of contemporary psychoanalytic film and television theory, with Lacan and Freud on the one hand and Mulvey and Heath on the other, and has emerged from the struggle with a work that is both theoretically sound while joyous and accessible at the same time. Like Paik's, Birnbaum's video is both about consequence, truth, and the spiritual values that link them. Also like Paik, Birnbaum makes use of clearly understood cultural artifacts and popular forms to communicate with an audience she positions and charges in a manner that denies them a passive or neutral point of view.

Prior to the Faust series, which I will not discuss here as it is still in progress, Birnbaum's work divides essentially into single-channel tapes and multi-channel installation works. This division, which mirrors the exhibition opportunities developed by video artists during the seventies, allows for several things to take place. First, within the conventions of the single-channel tapes, the literal appropriation of the television program is given prominence. Within this context, Birnbaum chose to combine an exploration of the codes and grammar of commercial television with the production of a new cultural form, the music video. Also addressed, as a subtext in effect, are issues relating to concerns regarding the representation of women. But, at the risk of unintentionally denigrating Birnbaum's feminist politics, these concerns seem subsumed by primary concerns for the operation of the medium within a broader cultural situation.

Secondarily, Birnbaum has expanded her investigation by re-editing her material to conform with sculpturally-based site-specific installation environments. In these works she has been able to create spatial extensions of the concepts that were introduced in the single-channel tapes.

The first works were, in her own words, "an attempt to deal with some of the basic dichotomies intrinsic to the medium."[5] In the work *Technology/Transformation* (1978), Birnbaum focuses on the dual nature of Wonder Woman's transformation from regular (powerless) woman to Wonder (superpower) Woman in a pyrotechnic display straight out of the vocabulary of the vaudeville magician. This action, repeated dozens of times, is depleted of its magical impact and made as banal and commonplace as the concept of magically empowering the "regular-woman." Beyond the repeated pyrotechnic transformation itself, Wonder Woman confronts her image in a hall of mirrors, and again in repeated action, finds it only possible to break through her image by cutting her mirror image's throat, symbolically sacrificing her intelligence and voice in the process. This text, created entirely through the use of video quotations, is then inserted into an alien sound track; one composed of off-air synch sound and a syntho-pop disco song, which derives its energy from a rhythmic repetition of the wondrous secret desires that the idea of a "wonder" woman might generate in a "regular" man. This seemingly perverse notion of the moral wonders of which our specially empowered heroine is visibly capable should establish a sort of running self-parody but in fact it does not. The lyrics "This is your Wonder Woman talkin' to you/Said I want to take you down/Show you all the powers I possess/and o-o-u-u-u-u/(Shake thy wonder maker)/Make sweet music to you" are sung/spoken in a breathless stage seduction manner as a kind of footnote to the previous disco video transformation sequences. The implied footnote reads: there is no transformation, there is only one possible "power" you might possess, and it has nothing to do with change of your passive condition.

To reduce this to a simplified formula, Birnbaum presents an action (transformation from powerless to empowered, helpless to savior) and suggests its consequence (intensified object of desire, no change in status, voice, or sensibility.) Compared to the standard TV formula based on the illusion of empowerment in which the action (transformation) transpires without consequence, Birnbam's Wonder Woman, though comic as a result of the repetition of her video-edited actions and disco ridicule, seems far more plausible—almost realistic. The effect is reminiscent of the repetition of the Kennedy assassination in the Ant Farm/T.R. Uthco co-production *The Eternal Frame* (1975) in which a series of re-stagings of the Zapruder film at first seemed to parody the grim document, but finally reveal the nature of media-mythology as a function of enforced redundancy. Numbing, desensitizing, trivializing the use of repetition in video edition, as in Klaus vom Bruch's *propellertape* (1979) or earlier (and perhaps in its best utilization) in Paik's *Guadalcanal Requiem* (1977), underscores the way in which far more subtle repetition works to neutralize the viewer and render him passive, even as he perceives his "liberation." Birnbaum's next tape, *Kiss the Girls: Make Them Cry* (1979), is a far more sophisticated examination of television grammar. The work focuses almost exclusively on the body gestures of a Hollywood celebrity whose feminine giggle and throw of the head is set against a fast zoom, and the hint of seductive private communication to the home viewer is cut into a syntho-pop disco number. In this work, the repeated body gesture and unspoken language, which work into the rhythmic nature of the song, giving it (the music) the leading role, also allow us to focus on the exquisite qualities of the gesture, emptying it of its original intent (a standard silly hello on a daily game show) and allowing it to be filled with the intent gleaned from the song's lyrics. This is not, as some have suggested, an extension of the notion of found art, in which the artist's will, invested in a common artifact, object, or situation, critically alters the meaning of the original. In this case, appropriated material is consciously stripped of its references to its original setting, so that it can be reinvested with meaning which draws specific attention to the nature of the original surrounding context. That reinvestment results in more than a representation of the original in a new context; it results in new understanding of the original from within a novel critical framework.

In an important and relatively early essay on the relationship between video art and broadcast television ("Video: The Distinctive Features of the Medium",1975),[6] the poet and critic David Antin discussed what he termed television's "money metric," or the way in which the TV hour was methodically and unwaveringly divided up into segments based on the primary need to accommodate commercials, but as importantly, to provide a structure to the velocity of television time which must function irrespective of the dramatic value of the material being aired in order to maintain a captive audience for the selling process. Birnbaum explores just those linguistic subtleties created by the "money metric," re-applying the close-up, the fast-cut, and other devices that both propel television while supplying virtually hypnotic illusions of novelty and significance to pacify a marginally attentive mass audience. In the installation work *P.M. Magazine* (1982), arguably her most finely tuned completed work to date, the referent is the most prominent broadcast format of the seventies, the feature magazine show. These shows are essentially "life-style" digests, and like their print magazine counterparts, they deliver continual reports on the condition of upper-middle-class leisure life and hints at how to get there or appear to be there. In Jameson's world view, this is the stuff that pastiche thrives on, the meat and potatoes of postmodernism, America at its high-tech kitsch zenith.

Using an electronically altered sound track centered on the Doors' classic *L.A. Woman*, Birnbaum constructs a fast paced, image-text-music montage which runs slightly out of sync within a three-part billboard framework. The images, taken from the *P.M. Magazine* introduction montage (which ironically is itself an unconscious homage to the kind of editing Paik pioneered in the early seventies) as well as from an out-of-date (but essentially timeless) commercial for Wang office automation hardware, combine with the driving sound track, a German translation of the Doors' lyrics (the piece was originally commissioned for Documenta 7), to produce a far more disquieting work than any of Birnbaum's single-channel works seem capable of. Its effectiveness quite clearly results from the radical reconstruction of a novel environment built with utterly familiar elements. In contrast to *Kojak/Wang* (1980), one of Birnbaum's Pop-Pop videotapes in which the same office miracle (the emanation of a rainbow from the keyboard of an office machine following the gentle touch of an ethereal office worker) is intercut with a cycle of violence and recrimination from a seventies detective show (*Kojak*) and a set of color bars with a tuning tone, *P.M. Magazine* places the Wang woman in a context in which there are no visual contradictions. All is upbeat, modern, pleasant, and leisure-bound. At least, it appears that way. The Doors track consists of an edit of *L.A. Woman* which emphasizes the loneliness and alienation of the postmodern condition. "Never saw a woman so all alone/So all alone/ Alone alone alone" emanates from three sets of speakers, which, as stated above, play slightly out of sync to underscore the singularity (aloneness) of each of the three channels playing in apparent concert. All of the elements of this work support the confrontation of appearance and effect. The video and sound are displayed on monitors set into billboard-size blowups of stills from the tapes mounted on metal strut frames reminiscent of trade show displays. This display condition emphasizes the uncomfortable nature of the exhibition environment (the art gallery), adding yet another level of dissonance to the work. It is finally this active dissonance which activates the viewer of the work, and charges the viewer in a manner that rules out passive response— without resorting to overt melodramatic manipulation of the audience.

In effect, what Birnbaum creates, based in part on her own sensibilities and in part on understandings of the American television culture that she shares with many artists of her generation, is the model for a new game show, one in which truth and consequence are not mutually exclusive concepts.

From *The Luminous Image (Het Lumineuze Beeld)*. (Exhibition catalogue). Amsterdam: Stedelijk Museum, 1984, pp.72-84

1. Bertolt Brecht, "Radio as a Means of Communication," *Screen*, Vol. 20, no. 3/4 (Winter 1979/80). London: Society for Education in Film and Television, p. 25.
2. Fredric Jameson, "Postmodernism and Consumer Society," *The Anti-Aesthetic: Essays on Postmodern Culture*, ed. Hal Foster (Port Townsend, WA: Bay Press, 1983), p. 115.
3. Brecht, "Radio as a Means of Communication," p. 27.
4. Ibid.
5. Dara Birnbaum, *'60-'80 Attitudes/Concepts/Images* (Amsterdam: Stedelijk Museum (catalogue supplement), 1982), p. 35.
6. Reprinted in this volume, pp. 147-66.

Video:
The Aesthetics of Narcissism

Rosalind Krauss

IT WAS A commonplace of criticism in the 1960s that a strict application of symmetry allowed a painter "to point to the center of the canvas" and, in so doing, to invoke the internal structure of the picture-object. Thus "pointing to the center" was made to serve as one of the many blocks in that intricately constructed arch by which the criticism of the last decade sought to connect art to ethics through the "aesthetics of acknowledgment." But what does it mean to point to the center of a TV screen?

In a way that is surely conditioned by the attitudes of pop art, artists' video is largely involved in parodying the critical terms of abstraction. Thus when Vito Acconci makes a videotape called *Centers* (1971), what he does is literalize the critical notion of "pointing" by filming himself pointing to the center of a television monitor, a gesture he sustains for the twenty-minute running time of the work. The parodistic quality of Acconci's gesture, with its obvious debt to Duchampian irony, is clearly intended to disrupt and dispense with an entire critical tradition. It is meant to render nonsensical a critical engagement with the formal properties of a work or, indeed, a genre of works—such as "video." The kind of criticism *Centers* attacks is obviously one that takes seriously the formal qualities of a work or tries to assay the particular logic of a given medium. And yet, by its very mise-en-scène, *Centers* typifies the structural characteristics of the video medium. For *Centers* was made by Acconci's using the video monitor as a mirror. As we look at the artist sighting along his outstretched arm and forefinger toward the center of the screen we are watching, what we see is a sustained tautology: a line of sight that begins at Acconci's plane of vision and ends at the eyes of his projected double. In that image of self-regard is configured a narcissism so endemic to works of video that I find myself wanting to generalize it as *the* condition of the entire genre. Yet, what would it mean to say, "The medium of video is narcissism?"

For one thing, that remark tends to open up a rift between the nature of video and that of the other visual arts. Because that statement describes a psychological rather than a physical condition, and while we are accustomed to thinking of psychological states as the possible subject of works of art, we do not think of psychology as constituting their medium. Rather, the medium of painting, sculpture, or film has much more to do with the objective, material factors specific to a particular form: pigment-bearing surfaces, matter extended through space, light projected through a moving strip of celluloid. That is, the notion of a medium contains the concept of an object-state, separate from the artist's own being, through which his intentions must pass.

Video depends—in order for anything to be experienced at all—on a set of physical mechanisms. So perhaps it would be easiest to say that this apparatus—both at its present and at its future levels of technology—comprises the television medium, and leave it at that. Yet with the subject of video, the ease of defining it in terms of its machinery does not seem to coincide with accuracy; and my own experience of video keeps urging me toward the psychological model.

Everyday speech contains an example of the word *medium* used in a psychological sense; the uncommon terrain for that common-enough usage is the world of parapsychology: telepathy, extrasensory perception, and communication with an afterlife, for which people with certain kinds of psychic powers are understood to be mediums. Whether or not we give credence to the fact of mediumistic experience, we understand the referents for the language that describes it. We know, for instance, that configured within the parapsychological sense of the word *medium* is the image of a human receiver (and sender) of communications arising from an invisible source. Further, this term contains the notion that the human conduit exists in a particular relation to the message, which is one of temporal concurrence. Thus, when Freud lectures on the phenomenon of telepathic dreams, he tells his audience that the fact insisted upon by reports of such matters is that the dreams occur at the *same time* as the actual (but invariably distant) event.

Now, these are the two features of the everyday use of *medium* that are suggestive for a discussion of video: the simultaneous reception and projection of an image; and the human psyche used as a conduit, because most of the work produced over the very short span of video art's existence has used the human body as its central instrument. In the case of work on tape this has most often been the body of the artist-practitioner. In the case of video installations it has usually been the body of the responding viewer. And no matter whose body has been selected for the occasion, there is a further condition that is always present. Unlike the other visual arts, video is capable of recording and transmitting at the same time—producing instant feedback. The body is therefore as it were centered between two machines that are the opening and closing of a parenthesis. The first of these is the camera; the second is the monitor, which reprojects the performer's image with the immediacy of a mirror.

The effects of this centering are multiple. And nowhere are they more clearly named than in a tape made by Richard Serra, with the help of Nancy Holt, who made herself its willing and eloquent subject. The tape is called *Boomerang* (1974), and its situation is a recording studio in which Holt sits in a tightly framed close-up wearing a technician's headset. As Holt begins to talk, her words are fed back to her through the earphones she wears. Because the apparatus is attached to a recording instrument, there is a slight delay (of less than a second) between her actual locution and the audio feedback to which she is forced to listen. For the ten minutes of the tape, Holt describes her situation. She speaks of the way the feedback interferes with her normal thought process and of the confusion caused by the lack of synchronism between her speech and what she hears of it. "Sometimes," she says, "I find I can't quite say a word because I hear a first part come back and I forget the second part, or my head is stimulated in a new direction by the first half of the word."

As we hear Holt speak and listen to that delayed voice echoing in her ears, we are witness to an extraordinary image of distraction. Because the audio delay keeps hypostatizing her words, she has great difficulty coinciding with herself as a subject. It is a situation, she says, that "puts a distance between the words and their apprehension—their comprehension," a situation that is "like a mirror reflection ... so that I am surrounded by me and my mind surrounds me ... there is no escape."

The prison Holt both describes and enacts, from which there is no escape, could be called the prison of a collapsed present, that is, a present time that is completely severed from a sense of its own past. We get some feeling for what it is like to be stuck in that present when Holt at one point says, "I'm throwing things out in the world and they are boomeranging back ... boomeranging ... eranginging ... anginging." Through that distracted reverberation of a single word—and even word fragment—there forms an image of what it is like to be totally cut off from history, even, in this case, the immediate history of the sentence one has just spoken. Another word for that history from which Holt feels herself to be disconnected is *text*.

Most conventional performers are of course enacting or interpreting a text, whether that is a fixed choreography, a written script, a musical score, or a sketchy set of notes around which to improvise. By the very fact of that relationship, the performance ties itself to the fact of something that existed before the given moment. Most immediately, this sense of something having come before refers to the specific text for the performance at hand. But in a larger way it evokes the more general historical relationship between a specific text and the history constructed by all the texts of a given genre. Independent of the gesture made within the present, this larger history is the source of meaning for that gesture. What Holt is describing in *Boomerang* is a situation in which the action of the mirror reflection (which is auditory in this case) severs her from a sense of text; from the prior words she has spoken, from the way language connects her both to her own past and to a world of objects. What she comes to is a space where, as she says, "I am surrounded by me."

Self-encapsulation—the body or psyche as its own surround—is everywhere to be found in the corpus of video art. Acconci's *Centers* is one instance, another is his *Air Time* (1973). In *Air Time* Acconci sits between the video camera and a large mirror, which he faces. For thirty-five minutes he addresses his own reflection with a monologue in which the terms *I* and *you*—although they are presumed to be referring to himself and an absent lover—are markers of the autonomous intercourse between Acconci and his own image. Both *Centers* and *Air Time* construct a situation of spatial closure, promoting a condition of self-reflection. The response of the performer is to a continually renewed image of himself. This image, supplanting the consciousness of anything prior to it, becomes the unchanging text of the performer. Skewered on his own reflection, he is committed to the text of perpetuating that image. So the temporal concomitant of this situation is, like the echo effect of *Boomerang*, the sense of a collapsed present.

Bruce Nauman's tapes are another example of the double effect of the performance for the monitor. In *Revolving Upside Down* (1968) Nauman films himself through a camera that has been rotated so that the floor on which he stands is at the top of the screen. For sixty very long minutes, Nauman slowly moves, turning on one foot, from the depths of his studio forward toward the monitor and then back again, repeating this activity until the tape runs out.

In Lynda Benglis's *Now* (1973), there is a similar leveling out of the effects of temporality. The tape is of Benglis's head in profile, performing against the backdrop of a large monitor on which an earlier tape of herself doing the same actions, but reversed left and right, is being replayed. The two profiles, one "live," the other taped, move in mirrored synchrony with one another. As they do, Benglis's two profiles perform an autoerotic coupling, which, because it is being recorded, becomes the background for another generation of the same activity. Through this spiral of infinite regress, as the face merges with the double and triple reprojections of itself merging with itself, Benglis's voice is heard either issuing the command "Now!" or asking, "Is it now?" Clearly, Benglis is using the word *now* to underline the ambiguity of temporal reference: We realize that we do not know whether the sound of the voice is coming from the live or the taped source, and if from the latter, which level of taping. Just as we also realize that because of the activity of replaying the past generations, all layers of the "now" are equally present.

But what is far more arresting in *Now* than the technological banality of the question "Which 'now' is intended?" is the way the tape enacts a collapsed present time. In that insistence it connects itself to the tapes by Nauman and Acconci already described, and ultimately to *Boomerang*. In all these examples the nature of video performance is specified as an activity of bracketing out the text and substituting for it the mirror reflection. The result of this substitution is the presentation of a self understood to have no past and, as well, no connection with any objects that are external to it. For the double that appears on the monitor cannot be called a true external object. Rather it is a displacement of the self that has the effect—as Holt's voice has in *Boomerang*—of transforming the performer's subjectivity into another, mirror, object.

It is at this point that one might want to go back to the proposition with which this argument began and raise a particular objection. Even if it is agreed, one might ask, that the medium of video art is the psychological condition of the self split and doubled by the mirror reflection of synchronous feedback, how does that entail a "rift" between video and the other arts? Isn't it rather a case of video's using a new technique to achieve continuity with the modernist intentions of the rest of the visual media? Specifically, isn't the mirror reflection a variation on the reflexive mode in which contemporary painting, sculpture, and film have successfully entrenched themselves? Implicit in this question is the idea that autoreflection and reflexiveness refer to the same thing—that both are cases of consciousness doubling back upon itself in order to perform and portray a separation between forms of art and their contents, between the procedures of thought and their objects.[1] In its simplest form this question would be the following: Aside from their divergent technologies, what is the difference, *really*, between Vito Acconci's *Centers* and Jasper Johns's *American Flag*?

Answer: The difference is total. Reflection, when it is a case of mirroring, is a move toward an external symmetry; whereas reflexiveness is a strategy to achieve a radical asymmetry, from within. In his *American*

Flag, Johns uses the synonomy between an image (the flag) and its ground (the limits of the picture surface) to unbalance the relationship between the terms *picture* and *painting*. By forcing us to see the actual wall on which the canvas hangs as the background for the pictorial object-as-a-whole, Johns drives a wedge between two types of figure/ ground relationships: the one that is internal to the image and the one that works from without to define this object as Painting. The figure/ ground of a flat, bounded surface hung against a wall is isolated as a pri- mary, categorical condition, within which the terms of the process of painting are given. The category Painting is established as an object (or a text) whose subject becomes this particular painting—*American Flag*. The flag is thus both the object of the picture *and* the subject of a more general object (Painting) to which *American Flag* can reflexively point. Reflexiveness is precisely this fracture into two categorically dif- ferent entities that can elucidate one another insofar as their separate- ness is maintained.

Mirror reflection, on the other hand, implies the vanquishing of separateness. Its inherent movement is toward fusion. The self and its reflected image are of course literally separate. But the agency of reflec- tion is a mode of appropriation, of illusionistically erasing the differ- ence between subject and object. Facing mirrors on opposite walls squeeze out the real space between them. When we look at *Centers*, we see Acconci sighting along his arm to the center of the screen we are watching. But latent in this setup is the monitor that he is, himself, look- ing at. There is no way for us to see *Centers* without reading that sus- tained connection between the artist and his double. So for us as for Ac- conci, video is a process that allows these two terms to fuse.

One could say that if the reflexiveness of modernist art is a *dédouble- ment*, or doubling back, in order to locate the object (and thus the ob- jective conditions of one's experience), the mirror reflection of absolute feedback is a process of bracketing out the object. This is why it seems inappropriate to speak of a physical medium in relation to video. For the object (the electronic equipment and its capabilities) has become merely an appurtenance. And instead, video's real medium is a psycho- logical situation, the very terms of which are to withdraw attention from an external object—an Other—and invest it in the Self. There- fore, it is not just any psychological condition one is speaking of. Rather, it is the condition of someone who has, in Freud's words, "abandoned the investment of objects with libido and transformed object-libido into ego-libido." And that is the specific condition of narcissism.

By making this connection, then, one can recast the opposition be- tween the reflective and reflexive into the terms of the psychoanalytic project. Because it is there, too, in the drama of the couched subject, that the narcissistic reprojection of a frozen self is pitted against the analytic (or reflexive) mode.[2] One finds a particularly useful description of that struggle in the writing of Jacques Lacan.

In *The Language of the Self* Lacan begins by characterizing the space of the therapeutic transaction as an extraordinary void created by the silence of the analyst. Into this void the patient projects the monologue of his own recitation, which Lacan calls "the monumental construct of his narcissism." Using this monologue to explain himself and his situation to his silent listener, the patient begins to experience a very deep frustration. And this frustration, Lacan charges, although it is initially thought to be provoked by the maddening silence of the analyst, is eventually discovered to have another source:

> Is it not rather a matter of frustration inherent in the very discourse of the subject? Does the subject not become engaged in an ever-growing dispossession of that being of his, concerning which—by dint of sincere portraits which leave its idea no less incoherent, of rectifications which do not succeed in freeing its essence, of stays and defenses which do not prevent his statue from tottering, of narcissistic embraces which become like a puff of air in animating it—he ends up by recognizing that this being has never been anything more than his construct in the Imaginary and that this construct disappoints all his certitudes? For in this labor which he undertakes to reconstruct this construct *for another*, he finds again the fundamental alienation which made him construct it *like another one*, and which has always destined it to be stripped from him *by another*.[3]

What the patient comes to see is that this "self" of his is a projected object and that his frustration is due to his own capture by this object with which he can never really coincide. Further, this "state" that he has made and in which he believes is the basis for his "static state," for the constantly "renewed status of his alienation." Narcissism is characterized, then, as the unchanging condition of a perpetual frustration.[4]

The process of analysis is one of breaking the hold of this fascination with the mirror; and in order to do so, the patient comes to see the distinction between his lived subjectivity and the fantasy projections of himself as object. "In order for us to come back to a more dialectical view of the analytic experience," Lacan writes, "I would say that the analysis consists precisely in distinguishing the person lying on the analyst's couch from the person who is speaking. With the person listening [the analyst], that makes three persons present in the analytical situation, among whom it is the rule that the question ... be put: Where is the *moi* of the subject?"[5] The analytic project is then one in which the patient disengages from the "statue" of his reflected self and, through a method of reflexiveness, rediscovers the real time of his own history. He exchanges the atemporality of repetition for the temporality of change.

If psychoanalysis understands that the patient is engaged in a recovery of his being in terms of its real history, modernism has understood that the artist locates his own expressiveness through a discovery of the objective conditions of his medium and their history. That is, the very possibilities of finding his subjectivity necessitate that the artist recognize the material and historical independence of an external object (or medium).

In contradistinction to this, the feedback coil of video seems to be the instrument of a double repression: For through it consciousness of temporality and of separation between subject and object are simultaneously submerged. The result of this submergence is, for the maker and the viewer of most video art, a kind of weightless fall through the suspended space of narcissism.

There are, of course, a complex set of answers to the question of why video has attracted a growing set of practitioners and collectors. These answers would involve an analysis of everything from the problem of narcissism within the wider context of our culture to the specific inner workings of the present art market. Although I should like to postpone that analysis for a future essay, I do wish to make one connection here. And that is between the institution of a self formed by video feedback and the real situation that exists in the art world from which the makers of video come. In the last fifteen years that world has been deeply and disastrously affected by its relation to mass media. That an artist's work be published, reproduced, and disseminated through the media has become, for the generation that has matured in the course of the last decade, virtually the *only* means of verifying its existence as art. The demand for instant replay in the media—in fact the creation of work that literally does not exist outside of that replay, as is true of conceptual art and its nether side, body art—finds its obvious correlative in an aesthetic mode by which the self is created through the electronic device of feedback.

There exist, however, three phenomena within the corpus of video art that run counter to what I have been saying so far, or at least are somewhat tangential to it. They are: (1) tapes that exploit the medium in order to criticize it from within; (2) tapes that represent a physical assault on the video mechanism in order to break out of its psychological hold; and (3) installation forms of video, which use the medium as a subspecies of painting or sculpture. The first is represented by Richard Serra's *Boomerang*. The second can be exemplified by Joan Jonas's *Vertical Roll* (1972). And the third is limited to certain of the installation works of Bruce Nauman and Peter Campus, particularly Campus's two companion pieces *mem* (1974) and *dor*.

I have already described how narcissism is enacted in *Boomerang*. But what separates it from, say, Benglis's *Now*, is the critical distance it maintains on its own subject. This is primarily due to the fact that Serra employs audio rather than visual feedback. Because of this, the angle of vision we take on the subject does not coincide with the closed circuit of Holt's situation, but looks onto it from outside. Further, the narcissistic condition is given through the cerebrated form of language, which opens simultaneously onto the plane of expression and the plane of critical reflexiveness.

Significantly, Serra's separation from the subject of *Boomerang*, his position outside it, promotes an attitude toward time that is different from many other works of video. The tape's brevity—it is ten minutes long—is itself related to discourse: to how long it takes to shape and develop an argument and how long it takes for its receiver to get the "point." Latent within the opening situation of *Boomerang* is its own conclusion; when that is reached, it stops.

Vertical Roll is another case where time has been forced to enter the video situation, and where that time is understood as a propulsion toward an end. In this work access to a sense of time has come from fouling the stability of the projected image by desynchronizing the frequencies of the signals on camera and monitor. The rhythmic roll of the image, as the bottom of its frame scans upward to hit the top of the screen, causes a sense of decomposition that seems to work against the grain of those 525 lines of which the video picture is made. Because one recognizes it as intended, the vertical roll appears as the agency of a will that runs counter to an electronically stabilized condition. Through the effect of its constant wiping away of the image, one has a sense of a reflexive relation to the video grid and the ground or support for what happens to the image.

Out of this is born the subject of *Vertical Roll*, which visualizes time as the course of a continuous dissolve through space. In it a sequence of images and actions are seen from different positions—both in terms of the camera's distance and its orientation to a horizontal ground. With the ordinary grammar of both film and video these shifts would have to be registered either by camera movement (in which the zoom is included as one possibility) or by cutting. And while it is true that Jonas has had to use these techniques in making *Vertical Roll*, the constant sweep of the image renders these movements invisible. That is, the grammar of the camera is eroded by the dislocating grip of the roll. As I have said, the illusion this creates is one of a continuous dissolve through time and space. The monitor, as an instrument, seems to be winding into itself a ribbon of experience, like a fishing line being taken up upon a reel, or like magnetic tape being wound upon a spool. The motion of continuous dissolve becomes, then, a metaphor for the physical reality not only of the scan lines of the video raster, but of the physical reality of the tape deck, whose reels objectify a finite amount of time.

Earlier, I described the paradigm situation of video as a body centered between the parenthesis of camera and monitor. Due to *Vertical Roll*'s visual reference through the monitor's action to the physical reality of the tape, one side of this parenthesis is made more active than the other. The monitor side of the double bracket becomes a reel through which one feels prefigured the imminence of a goal or terminus for the motion. That end is reached when Jonas, who has been performing the actions recorded on the tape, from within the coils of the camera/monitor circuit, breaks through the parenthetical closure of the feedback situation to face the camera directly—without the agency of the monitor's rolling image.

If it is the paired movement of the video scan and the tape reel that is isolated as a physical object in *Vertical Roll*, it is the stasis of the wall plane that is objectified in Campus's *mem* and *dor*. In both of the Campus works there is a triangular relationship created between: (1) a video camera, (2) an instrument that will project the live camera image onto the surface of a wall (at life- and over-life-size), and (3) the wall itself. The viewer's experience of the works is the sum of the cumulative positions his body assumes within the vectors formed by these three elements. When he stands outside the triangular field of the works, the viewer sees nothing but the large, luminous plane of one of the walls in a darkened room. Only when he moves into the range of the camera is he able to realize an image (his own) projected onto the wall's pictorial field. However, the conditions of seeing that image are rather special in both *mem* and *dor*.

In the latter the camera is placed in the hallway, leading to the room that contains the projector. Inside the room, the viewer is out of the range of the camera and therefore nothing appears on the wall surface. It is only as he leaves the room, or rather is poised at the threshold of the doorway that he is both illumined enough and far enough into the focal range of the camera to register as an image. Since that image projects onto the very wall through which the doorway leads, the viewer's relation to his own image must be totally peripheral; he is himself in a plane that is not only parallel to the plane of the illusion but continuous with it. His body is therefore both the substance of the image and, as well, the slightly displaced substance of the plane onto which the image is projected.

In *mem* both camera and projector are to one side of the wall plane, stationed in such a way that the range of the camera encompasses a very thin corridorlike slice of space that is parallel to, and almost fused with, the illumined wall. Due to this, the viewer must be practically up against the wall in order to register. As he moves far enough away from the wall in order to be able to see himself, the image blurs and distorts, but if he moves near enough to place himself in focus, he has formed such closure with the support for the image that he cannot really see it. Therefore in *mem*, as in *dor*, the body of the viewer becomes physically identified with the wall plane as the "place" of the image.

There is a sense in which we could say that these two works by Campus simply take the live feedback of camera and monitor, which existed for the video artist while taping in his studio, and re-create it for the ordinary visitor to a gallery. However, *mem* and *dor* are not that simple, because built into their situation are two kinds of invisibility: the viewer's presence to the wall in which he is himself an absence and his relative absence from a view of the wall that becomes the condition for his projected presence upon its surface.

Campus's pieces acknowledge the very powerful narcissism that propels the viewer of these works forward and backward in front of the muralized field. And through the movement of his own body, his neck craning and head turning, the viewer is forced to recognize this motive as well. But the condition of these works is to acknowledge as separate the two surfaces on which the image is held—the one the viewer's body, the other the wall—and to make them register as absolutely distinct. It is in this distinction that the wall surface—the pictorial surface—is understood as an absolute Other, as part of the world of objects external to the self. Further, it is to specify that the mode of projecting oneself onto that surface entails recognizing all the ways that one does not coincide with it.

There is, of course, a history of the art of the last fifteen years into which works like *mem* and *dor* insert themselves, although it is one about which little has been written. That history involves the activities of certain artists who have made work that conflates psychologistic and formal means to achieve very particular ends. The art of Robert Rauschenberg is a case in point. His work, in bringing together groupings of real objects and found images and suspending them within the static matrix of a pictorial field, attempts to convert that field into something we could call the plane of memory. In so doing, the static pictorial field is both psychologized and temporally distended. I have argued elsewhere[6] that the impulse behind this move arose from questions that have to do with commodity fetishism. Rauschenberg, among many other artists, has been working against a situation in which painting and sculpture have been absorbed within a luxury market—absorbed so totally that their content has been deeply conditioned by their status as fetish prizes to be collected, and thereby consumed. In response, Rauschenberg's art asserts another, alternative relationship between the work of art and its viewer. And to do this, Rauschenberg has had recourse to the value of time: to the time it takes to read a text or a painting, to rehearse the activity of cognitive differentiation that that entails, to get its point. That is, he wishes to pit the temporal values of consciousness against the stasis of the commodity fetish.

Although responsive to the same considerations, the temporal values that were built into the minimalist sculpture of the 1960s were primarily engaged with questions of perception. The viewer was therefore involved in a temporal decoding of issues of scale, placement, or shape—issues that are inherently more abstract than, say, the contents of memory. Pure, as opposed to applied psychology, we might say. But in the work of certain younger sculptors, Joel Shapiro for example, the issues of minimalism are being inserted into a space that, like Rauschenberg's pictorial field, defines itself as mnemonic. So that physical distance from a sculptural object is understood as being indistinguishable from temporal remove.

It is to this body of work that I would want to add Campus's art. The narcissistic enclosure inherent in the video medium becomes for him part of a psychologistic strategy by which he is able to examine the general conditions of pictorialism in relation to its viewers. It can, that is, critically account for narcissism as a form of bracketing out the world and its conditions at the same time as it can reassert the facticity of the object against the grain of the narcissistic drive toward projection.

From *New Artists Video*, edited by Gregory Battcock. New York: E.P. Dutton, 1978, pp. 43-64.

NOTES
1. For example, this completely erroneous equation allows Max Kozloff to write that narcissism is "the emotional correlate of the intellectual basis behind self-reflexive modern art." See "Pygmalion Reversed," *Artforum* 14 (Nov. 1975): 37.
2. Freud's pessimism about the prospects of treating the narcissistic character is based on his experience of the narcissist's inherent inability to enter into the analytic situation: "Experience shows that persons suffering from the narcissistic neuroses have no capacity for transference, or only insufficient remnants of it. They turn from the physician, not in hostility, but in indifference. Therefore they are not to be influenced by him; what he says leaves them cold, makes no impression on them, and therefore the process of cure which can be carried through with others, the revivification of the pathogenic conflict and the overcoming of the resistance due to the repressions, can-

not be effected with them. They remain as they are." Sigmund Freud, *A General Introduction to Psychoanalysis*, trans. Joan Rivere (New York: Permabooks, 1953), p. 455.

3. Jacques Lacan, *The Language of the Self*, trans. Anthony Wilden (New York: Delta, 1968), p. 11.

4. Explaining this frustration, Lacan points to the fact that even when "the subject makes himself an object by striking a pose before the mirror, he could not possibly be satisfied with it, since even if he achieved his most perfect likeness in that image, it would still be the pleasure of the other that he would cause to be recognized in it." *Ibid.*, p. 12.

5. *Ibid.*, p. 100. Although *moi* translates as "ego," Wilden has presumably retained the French here in order to suggest the relationship between the different orders of the self by the implicit contrast between *moi* and *je*.

6. "Rauschenberg and the Materialized Image," *Artforum* 13 (Dec. 1974).

The Fact of Television

Stanley Cavell

OF COURSE THERE ARE interesting facts *about* television, facts about its technology, about the history of its programs, about the economic structure of the networks that produce it. Most of these facts I do not know, but I think I know what it would be like to learn them, and to start to learn what they add up to. By speaking of the fact of television, I mean to call attention to something else, something I do not, in the same way, think I know how to learn more about, something like the sheer fact that television exists, and that this existence is at once among the most obvious and the most mysterious facts of contemporary life. Its obviousness is that television has conquered, like the electric light, or the automobile, or the telephone. Its mystery is twofold: first, *how* it has conquered; and second, how we (we, for example, who write for and read *Daedalus*) have apparently remained largely uninterested in accounting for its conquering. (What it has conquered, I wish to leave, or to make, a question, part of the mystery. Has it conquered as a form of popular, or mass, entertainment? Popular as opposed to what? And what happened to the forms over which television triumphed?)

The twofold mystery comes to a twofold assumption, with which I begin, that there is something yet to be understood concerning both the interest in television and the refusal of interest in it. The latter half of the assumption is that the absence of critical or intellectual attention to television—both in kind and extent—is not satisfactorily understandable as a straightforward lack of interest, as if the medium were inherently boring. Individual intellectuals will, of course, straightforwardly find no interest there, as they may not in film. But the absence of interest in the medium seems to me more complete, or studied, than can be

accounted for by the accidents of taste. That the absence is not acciden-
tal or straightforward is epitomized, I think, in the familiar disapproval
evinced toward television in certain educated circles. Members of these
circles would apparently prefer not to permit a TV set in the house; but
if unable to hold to this pure line, they sternly limit the amount of time
the children may watch, regardless of the content. If this line has in turn
been breached, and the choice is between letting the kids watch at
home or at a neighbor's house, they are apt to speak guiltily—or at any
rate awkwardly—about their and their children's knowledge of its programs. As if in reaction, other intellectuals brazen out a preference for
commercial over public television.

   Such behavior suggests to my mind a fear of television for which I
have heard no credible explanation. Sometimes people say, loosely I
suppose, that television is addictive. And of course it would be a plausible explanation of both television's attraction and its repulsion if it
were credible to attribute addictive powers to it, to believe quite literally that the tube is not only in the service of boobs, but that it turns
otherwise useful citizens into boobs. (I will cite such a view toward the
end of these remarks.) But I have no acquaintance with anyone who
treats television in all seriousness as if it were the equivalent of, say, her-
oin. Even if marijuana presented a more analogous level of fear, no
adult worried about its effects would make it available to their children,
even on a strictly limited basis, unless perhaps they were already dealing with addiction. Nor does the disapproval of television seem to me
very close to the disapproval of comic books by an earlier generation of
parents, described so well by Robert Warshow in "Paul, the Horror
Comics, and Dr. Wertham."[1] Like any concerned parent who wants to
provide his or her children with the pleasures of cultivation, and who
does not underestimate how exacting those pleasures are to command,
Warshow was worried—having investigated and dismissed as ground-
less the then fashionable claim that comics incited their readers to violence—about the sheer time comics seems to steal from better things.
But he decided that his son's absorption would pass and that less harm
would be done by waiting it out than by prohibiting it. The difference I
sense from the disapproval of television may be that Warshow was not
himself tempted by a craving to absorb himself in comic books, so that
he had firsthand evidence that the absorption would die naturally,
whereas adults today may have no analogous evidence from their own
experience of television, fearing their own addictiveness. Or is there
some surmise about the *nature* of the pleasure television provides that
sets off disapproval of it, perhaps like surmises that once caused the disapproval of novel-reading or, later, of movie-viewing? If this were the
case, one might expect the disapproval to vanish when television comes

of age, when its programs achieve an artistic maturity to match that of the great novels and movies. Is this a reasonable faith?

Certainly I have been among those who have felt that television cannot have come of age, that the medium *must* have more in it than what has so far been shown. True, I have felt, at the same time, that so much money and talent have been lavished on it, that *if* there is anything more in the medium, it could hardly have escaped discovery. From this thought, one of two conclusions may be drawn: that there is indeed nothing more to be discovered and that the medium is accordingly one of poverty and boredom (I once found myself in a discussion of these matters impatiently observing that television is no more a medium of art than the telephone, the telegraph, or the telescope); or, since this is not quite credible, that the poverty lies not in the medium's discoveries, but rather in our understanding of these discoveries, in our failure as yet to grasp what the medium is for, what constitutes its powers and its treasures.

Since I am inclined to the latter of the conclusions, to speculate on what might constitute a better route of understanding is what I conceive my task here to be (together with some speculation about what kind of issue "the understanding of a medium" is). This means that I accept the condition of both conclusions, namely that television *has* come of age, that *this*, these programs, more or less as they stand, in what can appear to be their poverty, is what there *is* to understand. For suppose we agree that television's first major accomplishments can be dated no later than 1953, the time of the coverage of the first Eisenhower Inauguration. In that case, it has had thirty years in which to show itself. If Griffith's major films around 1915 are taken to date the birth of film as a medium of art, then it took only ten more years to reach the masterpieces of Chaplin and Keaton; and over the next fifteen years, America, to go no further, established a momentum in producing definitive movies—movies that are now among the permanent pleasures of art theaters, of museum programs, of film studies programs, and of late night television—that was essentially slowed (or so the story goes) only with the help of the rising television industry. One of our questions should be: Did television give back as good as it took away?

The acceptance of television as a mature medium of art further specifies what I mean in calling my subject here the fact of television. A further consequence of this characterization, or limitation of my subject, is that I am not undertaking to discuss the progress and results of experimental video artists. This is not meant to imply that I am uninterested in what might be called "the medium of video." On the contrary, it would be a way of describing my motive here as an interest in what television, as it stands, reveals about this medium. I do not mean to assume that this description captures a topic of assured significance or fruitfulness. I do hope, rather, that it is one way of picking up the subject of this issue of *Daedalus*, concerning the supposed general influence of video on our culture at large, on a par with the influence of print. In developing my contribution, I will take my bearings from some thoughts I worked with in speculating about the medium of film in *The World Viewed*.[2] That book also addresses what I am calling the nature of the medium, by asking what the traditional masterpieces, or successes, among movies reveal it to be, not especially what experimental work finds it to be. It is a guiding thesis of that book that major films are those in which the medium is most richly or deeply revealed. (This remains controversial. A reviewer of my recently published *Pursuits of Happiness: The Hollywood Comedy of Remarriage*[3] found that book pretentious and sometimes preposterous, in part because he cannot believe that even the best of Hollywood films are self-reflective, or intelligent, about their source in the medium of film—if, in a sense, less explicit—as is the work of "modernist self-referential artists" like Godard and Antonioni. Hollywood is a mythical locale, part of whose function is to cause people to imagine that they know it without having taken its works seriously, like America.)

An immediate difference presents itself between television and film. To say that masterpieces among movies reveal the medium of film is to say that this revelation is the business of individual works, and that these works have a status analogous to traditional works of art: they last beyond their immediate occasions; their rewards bear up under repeated viewings; they lend themselves to the same pitch of critical scrutiny as do any of the works we care about most seriously. This seems not to be true of individual works of television. What is memorable, treasurable, criticizable, is not primarily the individual work, but the program, the format, not this or that day of "I Love Lucy," but the program as such. I say this "seems" to me to be so, and what I will have to say here depends on its being so. But my experience of television is much more limited than my experience of movies and of pretelevision radio, so my views about the treasuring of television's works may be especially unreliable. Still, I think that people who have been puzzled by the phenomenon of television as I have been—evidenced by being more grateful, if grudgingly so, to some of it, than familiar aesthetic concepts will explain—must commonly have had the thought, or intuition, that its value is a function of its rule of format. My speculations here are intended as something like experiments to test how far one would have to go to follow this intuition, with reasonable intellectual satisfaction, through the aesthetic range of the phenomenon we know as television.

I have begun by citing grounds on which to deny that the evanescence of the instance, of the individual work, in itself shows that television has not yet come of age aesthetically. (Even were it to prove true that certain television works yet to be made become treasured instances, as *instances*, such as the annual running of *The Wizard of Oz*—which serves to prove my case, since this is not an object made by and for television—my topic here remains television as it stands in our lives now.) But movies also, at least some movies, maybe most, used to exist in something that resembles the condition of evanescence, viewable only in certain places at certain times, discussable solely as occasions for sociable exchange, almost never seen more than once, and then more or less forgotten. For many, perhaps still for most people, this is still the fate of film. (It is accordingly also true that some people, perhaps still most, would take it as true of movies that individual works do not bear up under repetition and criticism. That this is a possible way to take film, I was just asserting, and I was implying that it is also partial. I will give a name to this way of taking it presently.) But from the beginning of the art of film, there have been those who have known that there was more to movies, more to think about, to experience, in their ordinary instances, than met the habitual eye. In recent years, this thought is becoming increasingly common (though not at all as common, I believe, as certain people living on the East and West coasts and in certain other enclaves imagine); whereas, as I have indicated, my impression is that comparatively few people maintain an aesthetic interest in the products of network television. A writer like Leslie Fiedler asserts a brazen interest in network television, or perhaps it is a sterling interest. But he insists that the source of his interest lies precisely in television's not producing art, in its providing, so to speak, a relief from art. And then again, it seems to me that he has said the same thing about movies, all movies, anyway all American movies. And if someone did appear to take the different interest, my question would persist: What is it he or she is taking this interest in?

A further caution—as it were, a technological caution—also conditions the remarks to follow. If the increasing distribution of videocassettes and disks goes so far as to make the history of film as much a part of the present experience of film as the history of the other arts is part of their present—hence, in this dimension, brings film into the condition of art—it will make less respectable the assumption of the evanescence of the individual movie, its exhaustion under one viewing, or always casual viewings; or rather, it will make this assumption itself evanescent, evidently the product of historical conditions, not inevitable. At the same time, if the distribution of videocassette recorders and cable television increases, as appears to be happening, to the size of the distribution of television itself, or to a size capable of challenging it, this will make problematic whether television will continue to exist primarily as a medium of broadcasting. I am not so much interested in predicting that such developments will actually come to establish themselves as I am in making conceptual room for understanding the aesthetic possibilities of such developments.

To say that the primary object of aesthetic interest in television is not the individual piece, but the format, is to say that the format is its primary individual of aesthetic interest. This ontological recharacterization is meant to bring out that the relation between format and instance should be of essential aesthetic concern. There are two classical concepts in talking about movies that fit the requirements of the thing I am calling a format, as it were, an artistic *kind*: the concepts of the serial and of the genre. The units of a serial are familiarly called its episodes; I will call the units of a genre its members. A thesis it seems to me worth exploring is that television, for some reason, works aesthetically according to a serial-episode principle rather than according to a genre-member principle. What are these principles?

In traditional terms, they would not be apt to invoke what I mean by different principles of composition. What is traditionally called a genre film is a movie whose membership in a group of films is no more problematic than the exemplification of a serial in one of its episodes. You can, for example, roughly *see* that a movie is a Western, or gangster film, or horror film, or prison film, or "woman's film," or a screwball comedy. Call this way of thinking about genre, genre-as-cycle. In contrast, in *Pursuits of Happiness*, the way I found I wanted to speak of genre in defining what I call the Hollywood comedy of remarriage, I will call genre-as-medium.

Because I feel rather backed into the necessity of considering the notion of a genre, I feel especially in need of the reader's forbearance over the next half dozen or so paragraphs. It seems that the notion of a genre has lately been receiving renewed attention from literary theorists, but the recent pieces of writing I have started to look at on the subject (so far, I realize, too unsystematically) all begin with a sense of dissatisfaction with other writing on the subject, either with the way the notion has so far been defined, or with the confusion of uses to which it has been put, or both. I am not interested here in joining an argument but rather in sketching the paths of two (related) ideas of a genre; it is an interest in coming to terms with what seem to me to be certain natural confusions in approaching the notion of a genre. In *Pursuits of Happiness* I was letting the discussion of certain individual works, which, so far as I know, had never been put together as a group, lead me, or push me, into sketching a theory of genre, and I went no further with it than the concrete motivations in reading individual works seemed to me to demand. With that in mind, in the present essay I am beginning, on the contrary, with certain intuitions concerning what the general aesthetic powers of video turn upon, and I am hoping to get far enough in abstracting these powers from the similar, hence different, powers of film, to get in a position to test these intuitions in concrete cases. (I may, however, just mention that two of the books I have been most helped by are Northop Frye's *A Natural Perspective*[4] and Tzvetan Todorov's *The Fantastic.*[5])

Before going on to give my understanding of the contrasting notions of a genre, I should perhaps anticipate two objections to my terminology. First, if there is an established, conventional use of the word "genre," and if this fits what I am calling genre-as-cycle—why not keep the simple word and use some other simple word to name the further kind of kind I am thinking of, the kind I am calling genre-as-medium— why not just call the further kind a set or a group or a pride? Second, since film itself is thought of as a medium (for example, of art), why insist on using the same word to characterize a gathering of works *within* that medium? As to this second objection, this double range of the concept of a medium is deployed familiarly in the visual arts, in which painting is said to be a medium (of art, in contrast, say, to sculpture or to music—hardly, one would think, the same contrast), and in which gouache is also a medium (of painting, in contrast to water color or oil or tempera). I wish to preserve, and make more explicit—or curious— this double range in order to keep open to investigation the relation between work and medium that I call the revelation, or acknowledgment, of the one in the other. In my experience, to keep this open means, above all, resisting (by understanding) the temptation to think of a medium simply as a familiar material (for instance, sound, color, words), as if this were an unprejudicial observation rather than one of a number of ways of taking the material of a medium, and recognizing instead that only the art can define its media, only painting and composing and movie-making can reveal what is required, or possible (what means, what exploits of material), for something to be a painting, a piece of music, a movie. As to the first objection—my use of "genre" in naming both of what I claim are different principles or procedures of composition—my purpose is to release something true in both uses of the word (in both, there is a process of generating in question), and to leave open to investigation what the relation between these processes may be. The difference may be consequential. I think, for example, that it is easier to understand movies as some familiar kind of commodity or as entertainments if you take them as participating not in a genre-as-medium but in genres-as-cycles, or if you focus on those movies that *do* participate, without remainder, in genres so conceived. Movies thought of as members of genres-as-cycles is the name of the way of taking them that I earlier characterized as evanescent. The simplest examples of such cycles used to be signaled by titles such as *The Son of X, The Curse of X, X Meets Dracula*, and so on. Our sophistication today requires that we call such sequels *X II, X III*, and so on, like Super Bowls. It is part of Hollywood's deviousness that certain sequels may be better than their originals, as perhaps *The Bride of Frankenstein* is, or Fritz Lang's *The Return of Frank James*.

Still another word about terminology, before going on to consider the thesis that television works according to a serial-episode rather than a genre-member principle. In picking up the old movie term "serial" to mark the contrast in question, I am assuming that what used to be called serials on film bears some internal relation to what are called serials on television. But what I am interested in considering here is the idea of serialization generally, wishing again to leave open what the relations are between serials and series (as I wish to leave open, hence to recall, the occurrence of serialization in classical novels, in photographs, in music, in comic strips). One might find that the closest equivalent on television to the movie serial is the soap opera, since this shares the feature of more or less endless narration across episodes, linked by crises. But in going on now to consider a little my thesis about serialization in television, I am exploring my intuition that the repetitions and recurrences of soap operas bear a significant relation with those of series, in which the narrative comes to a classical ending each time, and indeed that these repetitions and recurrences are modes of a requirement that the medium of television exacts in all its formats. A program such as "Hill Street Blues" seems to be questioning the feature of a series that demands a classical ending for each instance, hence questioning the distinction betwen soap opera and series. Similarly, or oppositely, the projected sequence of movies instanced by *Star Wars* and *The Empire Strikes Back* seems to be questioning the distinction between a serial and a cycle by questioning the demand of a serial (a narrative that continues over an indefinite number of episodes) *not* to come to a classical ending before the final episode. This would bring the sequence closer in structure to literary forms such as (depending on individual taste) the King Arthur legends, the Shakespeare Henry plays (perhaps a Lamb-like retelling), or Tolkien's *Lord of the Rings* trilogy.

A genre, as I use the notion in *Pursuits of Happiness*, and which I am here calling genre-as-medium, behaves according to two basic "laws" (or "principles"), one internal, the other external. Internally, a genre is constituted by members, about which it can be said that they share what you might picture as every feature in common. In practice, this means that, where a given member diverges, as it must, from the rest, it must "compensate" for this divergence. The genre undergoes continuous definition or redefinition as new members introduce new points of compensation. Externally, a genre is distinguished from other genres, in particular from what I call "adjacent" genres, when one feature shared by its members "negates" a feature shared by the members of another. Here, a feature of a genre will develop new lines of refinement. If genres form a system (which is part of the faith that for me keeps alive an interest in the concept), then in principle it would seem possible to be able to move by negation from one genre through adjacent genres, until all the genres of film are derived. Hitchcock's corpus provides convenient examples: his *North by Northwest* shares an indefinitely long list of features with remarriage comedies, which implies, according to my work on the subject, that it is about the legitimizing of marriage. In this film, as in other adventures, by Hitchcock and by others, legitimacy is conferred by a pair's survival together of a nation-saving adventure.[6] But that film can further be understood as negating the feature of the remarriage genre according to which the woman has to undergo something like death and revival. When this happens in Hitchcock, as in *Vertigo*, the Hitchcock film immediately preceding *North by Northwest*, it causes catastrophe. In *North by Northwest* it is the man who undergoes death and revival (and for a reason, I claim, having to do with the structure of the remarriage form). A dozen years earlier, in *Notorious*, Hitchcock compensates for the feature of the woman's death and revival (hence, maintaining the happiness of a remarriage ending) by emphasizing that her death and revival are not the condition of the man's loving her, but the effect of his failure to acknowledge her (as happens, seminally, according to my discussion of the genre, in *The Winter's Tale*).

The operations of compensation and negation are meant to specify the idea of a genre in *Pursuits of Happiness*, in contrast to what I take to be the structuralist idea of a genre as a form characterized by features, as an object is characterized by its properties, an idea that seems to me to underlay, for example, Todorov's work on the fantastic tale.

> An alternative idea ... is that the members of a genre share the inheritance of certain conditions, procedures and subjects and goals of composition, and that in primary art each member of such a genre represents a study of these conditions, something I think of as bearing the responsibility of the inheritance. There is, on this picture, nothing one is tempted to call *the* features of a genre which all its members have in common (p. 28).

Such operations as compensation and negation are not invoked either in genre-as-cycle or in serial-episode procedure. So I am saying that they are made by serialization as opposed to the generation in genre-as-medium. But in neither sense of genre are the members of a genre episodes of a continuing story of situation or setting. It is not the same narrative matter for Frankenstein to get a bride as for Rhoda (in a popular television series of a few years ago bearing her name) to get a husband. The former is a drama on its own; the latter serves a history, a before and after.

In speaking of a procedure of serialization, I wish to capture what seems to me right in the intuition of what are called narrative "formulas." When theorists of structural or formal matters speak of "formulas" of composition, they are thinking, I believe, of genre-as-cycle or of serial-episode construction, in which each instance is a perfect exemplification of the format, as each solution of an equation, or each step in a mathematical series, is a perfect instance of the formula that "generates" it. The instances do not compete with one another for depth of participation, nor comment upon one another for mutual revelation; and whether an instance "belongs" to the formula is as settled by the formula as is the identity of the instance. (Such remarks are really recipes—most untested—for what a formula would look like; hence, for what would count as "generation" in this context. I am taking it that no item of plot need be common to all the episodes of, say, "Rhoda" so that the formula that does the generating is sufficiently specified by designating the continuing characters and their relations with one another [characters and relations whose recurrent traits are themselves specifiable in definite ways.] This is the situation in the situation comedy. A certain description of the situation would constitute the formula of the comedy. Then the substitution of the unknown new element to initiate the generation, the element of difference, can be any event that alters the situation comically—Rhoda develops a rash; her sister is being followed by the office lothario; her mother's first boyfriend has just showed up; and so on. A minimum amount of talent is all it takes to write out the results of the generation competently—which of course does not mean salably; a much higher order is required to invent the characters and relations, and cast them, in such a way as to allow new generations readily and consistently to be funny.) Whereas in genre-as-medium none of this is so. In what I call the genre of remarriage comedy, the presence or absence of even the title feature of the genre does not insure that an instance does or does not belong to the genre. Belonging has to be won, earned, as by an argument of the members with one another; as adjacency of genre must be proved, something irrelevant to the existence of multiple series, which, further, raise no issue of the definition and refinement a genre undergoes. ("Belonging has to be won, as by an argument. . . ." Here is an allegory of the relation of the principal pair in such comedies. In their adventures of conversation, the pair are forever taking each other by surprise, forever interesting each other anew. To dream up these surprises and interests demands an exercise of talent that differs not only, or primarily, in its degree of energy from the energies I imagine in connection with developing a series, but differs in its order of deployment: here, the initiating idea is next to nothing compared with the details of the working out, which is what one would expect where the rule of format is, so to speak, over-thrown. Here, what you might call the formula, or what in *Pursuits of Happiness* I call the myth, is itself under investigation, or generation, by the instances.)

What difference does any of this make? I expect no simple or direct answer to the question of the difference between generation and serial-ization. Perhaps they name incompatible ways of looking at human ac-tivities generally, or texts. It might be thought, for example, that a series and its formulas specify the construction of the popular arts, whereas genre-as-medium and its arguments specify the construction of the higher arts. John G. Cawelti's *Adventure, Mystery, and Romance: Formula Stories as Art and Popular Culture*[7] perhaps suggests this. Charles Rosen's *The Classical Style*[8] states a related distinction within high art, between the great and the mediocre, or between the original and the academic. Vladimir Propp's classical analysis of the fairy tale virtually declares that you would not expect a sophisticated work of art to obey formulas in that way.[9] But this merely transfers the question: What is "that way"?

One wants to answer by saying something like, "Mechanically or au-tomatically (or formulaically?)." But maybe this is specific to fairy tales, not to all forms you might call popular. Are black-figure and red-figure vase paintings less formulaic? And are they less than high art? Ameri-can quilts of the nineteenth century are surely not less formulaic, yet the effect of certain of them is breathtaking, not unlike the directness of certain nonobjective paintings. Like those paintings (I think of certain works of Rothko, Louis, Noland, Olitski, Stella), these examples exist essentially as items of a series. It would follow that the concept of exis-tence in a series, of being composed according to a serial-episode prin-ciple, does not distinguish popular from high arts, only if, for instance, one accepts such painting as high art, something not everyone does. And it would follow only if the concept of a series in painting (or quilts) captures the same thought as the concept of a serial in film and a series in television. So far as the thought is one of establishing a formulaic relation between instances, the relation between paintings in a series certainly seems at least as strong (as, so to speak, mechanical) as the relation of episodes to one another. In fact, the relation between the paintings seems *too* strong to yield works of art: here, the instances seem purely generated, or determined, by a format with finite features, each of which can be specified and varied to yield new items. (I think here of Stella's Z-forms, or Noland's Chevrons or Ribbons, or Louis's Unfurleds.) The relation between members is exhaustively constituted, one may say, by their mutual differences, as if to illustrate a linguist's vision, or that of the more advanced of today's textualists, according to which language, and meaning, and hence whatever replaces or precedes art, is constituted not by signs (inherently) possessing or containing meaning, but by the weave of the relation of difference among them (say their synthesis of distinctive features). But at the same time, the idea of the series can be taken to dispute the linguistic or textualist appeal to difference, since this appeal generally accompanies, even grounds, a claim that the sensuous properties of the signs themselves are arbitrary. What painting in series argues is rather the absolute *non*-arbitrariness of format, because the artistic discovery is precisely that *this* synthesis of features generates instances, each of which maintains itself as a proposal of beauty. The achievement may be felt as something like an empirical discovery of the a priori—not unlike a certain aspiration of philosophy. (The implications of the fact of series for modern painting's disputing of received ideas of craft and style and medium, and its proposal of surprising consequences for thinking about the relation of painting and photography, is the subject of a pivotal chapter, "Excursus: Some Modern Painting," in *The World Viewed*.)

Another home of the idea of the formulaic is jazz, whose improvisations over most of its history are explicitly made possible by shared formulas, say of riff and progression. But the role of the formulaic in improvisation is familiar in other arenas of performance—in other regions of music (say, in improvising cadenzas), in other recitations (say, the singing of epics), and in other theater (say, Commedia dell'Arte). When people say they miss television as it was when it was produced live, what they may be missing is the sense of the improvisatory. And it may be that the diminished role of improvisation on television is an instance of a familiar process in certain phases of the history of performance, during which the scope of improvisation is progressively diminished in favor, let us say, of the literary; in which, for example, it is no longer open to the performer to fill in the continuo part or to work out his or her own cadenza, for these are instead written out, fixed. Yet room remains for the improvisatory in television's formats, which I will specify after saying something about what those formats are, or are of. I note here that the idea of improvisation has internal, and opposite, associations with the idea of serialization. In movie serials and in soap operas, the sense of suspense turns on the necessity for improvisation, of manner as well as of plot—humanity as expressed by the power and the readiness to improvise, as much as by the power and the readiness to endure. The issue is how the hero and heroine can survive *this*, this unprecedented precipice; how the authors can get themselves out. The issue has its comic equivalents, emotional and intellectual. It may be this connection of serialization with improvisation that links serialization with the idea or the fact of the popular. Contrariwise, serialization in music and in painting are as if made to reduce improvisation to a minimum, as if to prove that necessities can be found that are as beautiful in their consequences as contingencies can prove to be.

The point of going into the distinction of two modes of composition was to get at television's way of revealing its medium; it represents an effort to get at something one can see as the aesthetic interest of television. That there is such an interest invited by it, related to, but different from, an interest in what we call its economy, its sociology, and its psychology, and that this interest is still insufficiently understood—which contributes to an insufficiently developed critical tradition concerning television—is the way I am taking the issue of this issue of *Daedalus*. It is the point from which any contribution I may make to it is apt to proceed. If it proves sensible to locate television's aesthetic interest in a serial-episode mode of composition, as contrasted with a genre-member mode, then an investigation of the fact of television ought to contribute to understanding why there should be two principles of aesthetic composition.

What I have said they are principles of is the revelation (I habitually call this the acknowledgment) of an artistic medium. I specify this revelation in *The World Viewed*, by way of articulating what I call there "the material basis" of film. While I propose to continue here to be guided by such an idea, I do not mean just to assume that this idea makes good sense. I claim at most merely that what I am saying here makes sense *if* the procedures of *The World Viewed* make sense. This is far from certain, but there is more evidence of their working out there than anything I can provide here.

About halfway through *The World Viewed*, I give a provisional summary characterization of the material basis of movies, apart from which there would be nothing to call a movie, just as without color on a delimited two-dimensional support there would be nothing to call a painting; I call the basis *a succession of automatic world projections*.[10] To capture my intuition of the comparable material basis of the (aesthetic) medium of television, I begin by recurring to the one remark about television that crops up in *The World Viewed*. The moment is one at which I am at pains to distinguish the fact of movies in relation to the fact of theater, on the blatant ground that in a theater the actors appear in person and in a film they do not. I quote a response André Bazin gives to this blatant ground,[11] one in which he downplays the difference in question, denying that "the screen is incapable of putting us 'in the presence of' the actor": Bazin wishes to say that it relays the actor's presence to us as by mirrors. My response is to note that Bazin's idea here really fits the fact of live television, in which what we are presented with is happening simultaneously with its presentation. This remains reasonably blatant, anyway unsurprising. What surprised me was to find myself going on to object: "But in live television what is present to us while it is happening is not the world, but an event standing out from the world. Its point is not to reveal, but to cover (as with a gun), to keep something on view" (p. 26).

Taking this tip, I will characterize the material basis of television as *a current of simultaneous event reception*. This is how I am conceiving of the aesthetic fact of television that I propose to begin portraying. Why the ideas of *a current* and of *simultaneity* fit here in place of the ideas of *succession* and of *the automatic*, and why that of *event* than of *world*, and why *reception* than *projection*, are not matters decidable in advance of the investigation of each of these concepts. The mode of perception that I claim is called upon by film's material basis is what I call viewing. The mode of perception I wish to think about in connection with television's material basis is that of *monitoring*. The cause for this choice, initially, seems to be that, in characterizing television's material basis, I have not included transmission as essential to it; this would be because I am not regarding broadcasting as essential to the work of television. In that case, the mysterious sets, or visual fields, in our houses, for our private lives, are to be seen not as receivers, but as monitors. My claim about the aesthetic medium of television can now be put this way: its succeesful formats are to be understood as revelations (acknowledgments) of the conditions of monitoring, and by means of a serial-episode procedure of composition, which is to say, by means of an aesthetic procedure in which the basis of a medium is acknowledged primarily by the format rather than primarily by its instantiations.

What are the formats, or serializations, of television? I mean to be referring to things perfectly, grossly obvious: sitcoms, game shows, sports, cultural coverage (concerts, opera, ballet, etc.), talk shows, speeches and lectures, news, weather reports, movies, specials, and so on.

A notable feature of this list is the amount of talk that runs across the forms. This is an important reason, no doubt, for the frequent description of television as providing "company." But what does this talk signify, how does it in particular signify that one is not alone, or anyway, that being alone is not unbearable? Partly, of course, this is a function of the simultaneity of the medium—or of the fact that at any time it might be live and that there is no sensuous distinction between the live and the repeat, or the replay: the others are *there*, if not shut in this room, still caught at this time. One is receiving or monitoring them, like callers; and receiving or monitoring, unlike screening and projection, does not come between their presence to the camera and their present-ness to us.

I recognize that even in the present sketch of a way to approach mat-ters, this appeal to the idea of "no sensuous distinction" between the live and the repeat, or the replay or the delayed, and the connection of this distinction with a difference in modes of presence and presentness, is going too fast over consequential issues. It doesn't even include the fact that television can work in film as well as in tape. William Rothman has suggested to me that since television can equally adopt a movie mode or a video mode, we might recognize one dimension of televi-sion's "company" in the understanding of the act of switching from one mode to another as the thing that is always live, that is, effected simul-taneously with our watching. This points to the feature of the current (suggesting the contemporary as well as indicating the continuous) in my articulation of this aesthetic medium's physical basis. It is internal to television formats to be made so as to participate in this continuity, which means that they are formed to admit discontinuities both within themselves and between one and another, and between these and com-mercials, station breaks, news breaks, emergency signal tests, color charts, program announcements, and so on, which means formed to allow these breaks, hence these recurrences, to be legible. So that switching (and I mean here not primarily switching within a narrative but switching from, say, a narrative to one or another breaks, for a sta-tion or for a sponsor, and back again) is as indicative of live as—in ways to be specified—monitoring is.

(I think in this context of the as yet undefined aesthetic position of commercials. Foreigners to commercial television often find them merely amusing or annoying interruptions [or of course, in addition, marks of a corrupt civilization]; native explainers will sometimes affect to find them more interesting than the so-called programs they inter-rupt. Surely, ordinary people, anyway people without either of these axes to grind, can feel either way on occasion. Nor do I doubt, in all soberness, that *some* commercials just are more interesting than *some* programs. What the effort, or claim, to favor commercials over pro-grams suggests to me is that the aesthetic position of commercials, what you might call their possibility—what makes them aesthetically possible rather than merely intolerable—is not their inherent aesthetic interest [one would not sit still, with mild interest, for periodic minute-length transmissions of, say, a passage of Garbo's face or of a Chaplin routine: these glimpses of the masterful would be *pointless*], but the fact that they are readable, not as interruptions, but as *interludes*. Of course they can be handled all but intolerably, like late-night used car ads, or offers of recordings "not sold in any store." But even in these cases, the point of tolerability is the requirement of live switching—life, moreover, that is acknowledged by the habitual invitation at these peculiar late hours to "come on down" or to order by writing or by "calling now." Where there's life, there's hope.)

The fact of television's company is expressed not simply by the amount of talk, but by the massive repetitiveness of its formats for talk. Here I am thinking not merely of the shows explicitly *of* talk, with their repetitious sets and hosts and guests. Broadcasts of sports events are embedded in talk (as sports events are), and I can see the point even of game shows as providing occasions or covers for talk. Of course these shows are reasonably exciting, visually and aurally, with their obligatory jumping and screaming; and even, some of them, mildly educational. But is this excitement and education sufficient to account for the willingness to tune them in endlessly, for the pleasure taken endlessly in them? Nor am I satisfied to cite the reputed attractions, or fantasies, of striking it rich—anymore than, in thinking about the attractions of Hollywood thirties comedies, was I satisfied to account for their popularity by the widespread idea that they were fairy tales for the depression. I am struck by the plain fact that on each of the game shows I have watched, new sets of contestants are introduced to us. What strikes me is not that we are interested in identifying with these ordinary people, but simply that we are introduced to them. The hardest part of conversation, or the scariest part, that of improvising the conventional phrases of meeting someone and *starting* to talk, is all there is time for on these formats; and it is repeated endlessly, and without the scary anticipation of consequences in presenting the self that meetings in reality exact. The one who can get us perennially acquainted, who faces the initiation time and again, who has the power to create the familiar out of strangeness—the host of the show—is heavily rewarded for his abilities; not, indeed, by becoming a star, but by becoming a personality, even a celebrity, famous for nothing but being visible and surviving new encounters.

The appearance just now, or reappearance, of the idea of improvisation indicates the principal room I said was left for the improvisatory in television's persistent formats, its dimension of talk. I would not wish exactly to say that improvisation is localized there, since the dimension of talk is itself all but universally present; but each format for talk will have its own requirements or opportunities for improvisation. The most elaborate of these are, naturally, presented by talk shows themselves, with their monologues, and hence the interruptions and accidents that expert monologues invite, and with their more or less extended interviews. Here, the fact that nothing of consequence is said matters little compared with the fact that something is spoken, that the momentarily famous and the permanently successful are seen to have to find words for their lives, even as you and I. The gift of the host is to know how, and how far, to put the guests recurrently at ease and on the spot, and to make dramas of overcoming the one with the other, and both his or her capacity at any time to top what has been said. This is not the same as turning every event into a comic routine, as Jonathan Winters and Robin Williams have the talent and imagination to do. They are too anarchic to entertain guests, or too relentlessly absorbed by their inventions, as if inhabited by them, to invite and prepare for conversation. Johnny Carson is so good at taking conversation near, but not over, the abyss of embarrassment, he has made so good an alliance, not to say conspiracy, with the camera, that he can instruct his audiences' responses with a glance in our direction (i.e., in the direction of the camera)—a power the comedian shares with the lion tamer. Again, it is rather beside the point that the so-called color commentaries for sports events are not particularly colorful, since the point of the role is rather the unpreparedness of response itself. So hungry are we for the unrehearsed, the unscripted, that the persons at news desks feel obliged to please us by exchanging pleasantries with each other (sometimes abbreviated to one of them pleasantly speaking the other's name) as transitions between stories. This provides a primitive version of the complex emotion in having an actor step outside his or her character as part of her or his performance—as, for example, in Bergman's *The Story of Anna*, or Godard's *Two or Three Things I Know About Her.* Since the practice of exchanging pleasantries reveals that the delivery of news is a form of acting (it may, I suppose, have been meant to conceal the fact)—hence, that for all television can bring out, the news itself is as likely as not to be fictional, if only because theatricalized—there must be something else television brings out that is as important to us as the distinction between fact and fiction, some matter of life and death. This would be its demonstration that, whether fact or fiction, our news is still something that can humanly be responded to, in particular, responded to by the human power of improvisation. But what news may be so terrible that we will accept such mediocre evidence of this power as reassuring? I will at the end give an answer to this question.

A more immediate question is this: If I am right in taking improvisation to be as apt a sign of human life as we have to go on, and a sign that survives the change from live to taped production, why is it that people who miss the live on television do not recognize where the quality of the live is preserved? It may be that they miss the life primarily of television's old dramatic productions. But it is not television's obligation to provide its audience with the experience of live theater—beyond going out into the world to bring us worthwhile actual performances (live or on tape). Why is the live not seen where it can still be found, and first of all in the improvisations of talk, of exchange? Is this region too tawdry for those who have pictures of something higher? I do not deny a certain paradoxicality in finding life in what is reputedly the dullest, deadest feature of television, namely the omnipresent "talking head." Then the question for us should be: Where did this feature get its deadly reputation?

The remaining category of the material basis of television, after *current* and *simultaneity* and *reception*, the category of the event, is equally to the point here, but to bring out its significance, it will help to look first at the formats that are not made primarily for talk—for example, sports and cultural coverage. These make up the bulk of the television fare ingested by many of my acquaintances (and, except for movies, by me). The characteristic feature of these programs is that they are presented as events, that is to say, as something unique, as occasions, something out of the ordinary. But if the event is something the television screen likes to monitor, so, it appears, is the opposite, the *uneventful*, the repeated, the repetitive, the utterly familiar. The familiar repetitions of the shows of talk—centrally including here situation comedies—are accordingly company because of their embodiment of the uneventful, the ordinary.

To find comfort or company in the endlessly uneventful has its purest realization, and emblem, in the literal use of television sets as monitors against the suspicious, for example, against unwanted entry. The bank of monitors at which a door guard glances from time to time— one fixed, say, on each of the empty corridors leading from the otherwise unattended points of entry to the building—emblematizes the mode of perception I am taking as the aesthetic access to television.

The multiplicity of monitors, each linked to a more or less fixed camera, encodes the denial of succession as integral to the basis of the medium. In covering a sports event, a network's cameras are, similarly, placed ahead of time. That their views are transmitted to us one at a time for home consumption is merely an accident of economy; in principle, we could all watch a replica of the bank of monitors the producer sees. In that case, we might speak of television's material basis by putting simultaneity into the plural. When there is a switch of the camera whose image is fed into our sole receiver, we might think of this not as a switch of comment from one camera or angle to another camera or angle, but as a switch of attention from one monitor to another monitor. Succession is replaced by switching, which means that the move from one image to another is motivated not, as on film, by requirements of meaning, but by requirements of opportunity and anticipation—as if the meaning is dictated by the event itself. As in monitoring the heart, or the rapid eye movements during periods of dreaming—say, monitoring signs of life—most of what appears is a graph of the normal, or the establishment of some reference or base line, a line, so to speak, of the uneventful, from which events stand out with perfectly anticipatable significance. If classical narrative càn be pictured as the progress from the establishing of one stable situation, through an event of difference, to the reestablishing of a stable situation related to the original one, serial procedure can be thought of as the establishing of a stable condition punctuated by repeated crises or events that are not developments of the situation requiring a single resolution, but intrusions or emergencies—of humor, or adventure, or talent, or misery—each of which runs a natural course and thereupon rejoins the realm of the uneventful; which is perhaps to say, serial procedure is undialectical.

As I do not wish to claim that generation and serialization exhaust the field of narration, so I do not wish to claim that they are exclusive. So in saying that television organizes its formats in ways that explore the experience and the concept of the event, and hence of the experience and the concept of the uneventful, I am not saying that film lacks an analogous exploration, only that each medium will work out its stabilities in its own way. The ways will be as close as monitoring is to viewing, and to define such a closeness, and distance, is the sort of task my remarks here are meant to interest us in doing. For example, film and video may occupy themselves with nature, but if the distinction I have pointed to between viewing and monitoring is a valid one, then our experience of nature, its role in this stretch of our lives, should split itself over the different presentations. In *The World Viewed* I suggest a sense in which

> the film frame generally ... has the opposite significance of the frame in painting. Following Bazin's suggestion that the screen works as much by what it excludes as by what it includes, that it functions less to frame than to mask (which led me to speak of a photograph as of a segment of the world as a whole), I interpreted the frame of a film as forming its content not the way borders or outlines form, but rather the way looms and molds form (p. 200).

In such a light, I was led to say, "we are told that people seeing the first moving pictures were amazed to see the motion, as if by the novelty. But what movies did at first they can do at last: spare our attention wholly for *that* thing *now*, in the frame of nature, the world moving in the branch.... It is not novelty that has worn off, but our interest in our experience" (ibid.). Now, sparing our attention and expending it wholly is not a characterization of monitoring, which is rather preparing our attention to be called upon by certain eventualities. The world is not in the monitored branch, whose movement is now either an event (if, say, you are watching for a sign of wind) or a mark of the uneventful (a sign that the change has not yet come). The intimacy of such a difference prompts me to emphasize that by monitoring and viewing, I mean to be calling attention to aspects of human perception generally, so that film and video will not be expected to capture one of these aspects to the exclusion of the other, but rather to stress one at the expense of the other—as each may be stressing different aspects of art; video of its relation to communication, film of its relation to seduction.

My use of the concept of the uneventful is produced by my understanding of the *Annales* historians' interest in getting beyond the events and the dramas of history to the permanencies, or anyway to the longer spans, of common life.[12] This is worth making explicit as a way of emphasizing that the concepts in which I have been speaking of the phenomena of television and movies are as much in need of investigation as are the phenomena themselves. Everything seems to me so doubtful, or intangible, in this area. I would like to have useful words in which to consider why the opera and the ballet I have seen on television in recent years have seemed to me so good, whereas films I recall of opera and of ballet have seemed to me boring. Is it that television can respect the theatricality or the foreign conventionality of those media without trying, as film greedily would, to reinterpret them? And is this well thought of as television's ability to respect the independence of the theatrical event? I did like Bergman's *Magic Flute*, but I also felt that the piece looked like a television production. The question is this easy to beg. And does the idea of respecting the event go into the reason puppets and muppets are at home on television in a way they are not in the movies?

Here an answer suggests itself to a question my assumption of the primacy of format might at any time raise: Isn't the television "special" an exception to the rule of this primacy, since, by definition, a special occurs uniquely? The answer is not merely that uniqueness proposes a television format (like farewells, awards, roasts) that any number of stars and celebrities can occupy, and occupy again and again, so long as not regularly, that is, serially. The answer has also to specify what the format is that can occur outside a series. Take the fact that the entertainment special, designed to showcase a star or celebrity, familiarly takes the form of a variety show. The fittingness of the variety show format for television I can now attribute to the fact that a variety show just is a *sequence of events*, where events are interpreted as autonomous acts or routines constituted by incidents of excitement that are understandable as essentially repeatable, in another show and in another town. The concept of event here captures the sense of the variety and the discreteness—that is, the integrity—of the items of such shows, as it does in naming the items of track and field meets, and of bouts on a fight card.

The broadcasts of cultural events may also seem another set of exceptions to the rule of format, other instances of unique occurrences. But what is unique here, and what is above all memorable, is the performance itself, say of Balanchine's ballet on Stravinsky's *Agon*, the performance at which the pair of dancers of the difficult canon passage got off to a false start and had to begin again. Beyond the performance, the television presentation itself may be of interest, perhaps because of its novel camera installations, which make for a greater fidelity to the details of the performance, or because it was the first to use subtitles in a particular way. But these features of the presentation form an essentially repeatable format, usable and refinable in future broadcasts of ballet performances. If, however, the television presentation becomes so integral to the performance, the performance itself having been designed to incorporate the possibilities of presentation into its own integrity, that the ideas of "repeating" the format or of refining such things as camera "installations" no longer make clear sense, then the television format would have been led to the condition genre-as-medium. I have seen too little in the way of such works to have any useful response to them. They must in any case be part of the realm of experimental video art, which, as said, I am here leaving out of account.

I note that the variety format also fit the requirements of radio in its network days. It is, I think, commonly said that in its beginning, television "took over" many programs, or ideas for programs, from radio. Empirically or legally, no one could deny this, but ontologically, so to speak, or aesthetically, it should be wondered why radio was so ready a source for television. The better thought may be that television took its formats from many of the same places radio had taken them, for example, from vaudeville, and that the reason they could share these sources is that both are forms of broadcasting and monitoring, that is, currents of simultaneous event reception. Since one of these currents is made for the ear and the other also for the eye, it may be wondered what ratio of these senses is called upon by various events. Why, for example, is the weather given its own little dramatic slot on news programs, whereas the performance of the stock market is simply announced? Does this have to do with the weather's providing more visual interest than the market, or with its natural involvement in drama, or with its perennial role as a topic of conversation between strangers, or with its being an allegory of our gathering frame of mind, or simply with the fact of interest in predicting it (as if retaining some control over the future)? If the interest in predicting it were exhausted by its practical bearing on our plans for the days ahead, announcing it would serve as well as dramatizing it or making a little lecture about it. Prediction is of interest with respect to the stock market only, on the whole, to those who have a specialized connection with it, those, for example, who play it, for whom not just a day's outcome, but a day's events of fluctuation or stability, matter.

Of more fateful interest concerning the format of news is its invitation of the television item I have perhaps most notably omitted in my more or less informal itemizing of formats, namely, that of the event shaped expressly for the possibilities of television coverage itself, something that came upon most viewers' consciousness most memorably with the civil rights and antiwar demonstrations of the sixties, and subsequently with the staging of terrorist actions. In citing the theatricality of scripted news recitation, and in emphasizing television's tropism toward the event, I am indicating what the possibilities of the medium are that shaped events seek to attract; but the fact of television no more explains the occurrence of such events than it explains the effects of weather on our consciousness. For what would have to be explained, as my reference to the *Annales* historians is intended to register, is exactly our continued attraction by events, our will to understand our lives, or to take interest in them, from their dramas rather than from their stabilities, from the incident and the accident rather than from the resident, from their themes rather than from their structures—to theatricalize ourselves. But this is something that Thoreau, for one, held against the interest in reading newspapers a century and a half ago, an interest he described as amounting virtually to an addiction.

The *Annales* historians' idea of the long time span oddly applies to the altogether extraordinary spans of narrative time commanded by serialization. The ultimate span is that commanded by successful soap operas, in which the following of its yarns can go on off and on for years. I said a while ago that serial procedure is undialectical. Here I might add that the span of soap operas can allow them to escape history, or rather to require modification of the concept of history, of history as drama, history as related to the yarns of traditional novels. The lapse of fictional time in a soap world can be immeasurably shorter (or slower) than that of the span of time over which one may watch them. (Forty or so years ago my mother frequently tuned the radio to a fifteen-minute serial called "Helen Trent," as she and I were getting ready to go off, respectively, to work and to school. The idea of the serial was announced each morning by asking whether a woman can find romance after thirty-five, or maybe it was forty. I can imagine that this serial still persists. But if so, Helen Trent must still be something like thirty-five or forty years old.) However dire their events, they are of the interminable everyday, passages and abysses of the routine, which may help explain the ease with which members of their audience take their characters (so it seems) as "real." Without attempting to account for the specialized features of the stories and audiences that make soap operas possible, I call attention to the fact that most prestigious, even sensational efforts originating on television in recent years have been serials—either the snobby sort the BBC has patented ("Upstairs/Downstairs," "The Forsythe Saga," "Tinker Tailor," "Brideshead Revisited"), or the anti-snobby American sort ("Roots," "Dallas"). Here I am merely assuming, without argument, that eleven weekly hour-length episodes of, say, "Brideshead Revisited" command an order of time incommensurate with film time. It is equivalent in its effect neither to something on film that would last eleven hours, nor to something that would last eleven weeks (whatever such things would be), nor, I think, to eleven films of an hour each. Not only does an hour signify something in television time that has no bearing on film time, but it is internal to the establishment of its formats that television obeys the rhythm, perhaps even celebrates the articulations, the recurrences, of the order of the week, as does Genesis. The way in which it celebrates this, by further dividing and repeating the day in terms of minutes and seconds, would be a function of television's establishment in industrialized societies, with their regimentation of time.

It may be thought that one of the formats I listed earlier itself proves that one should make much less of the differences between film and video than I am inclined to make, or rather proves the emptiness of the differences: I mean the perfectly common format of running movies on television. Of course, no one would claim that the experience of a movie is just the same run on television as projected on a screen, and everyone will have some informal theory or other about what the difference consists in—that the television image is smaller, that the room is not otherwise dark, that there is no proper audience, hence that the image is inherently less gripping, and so on. But how much difference do such differences make? It seems to me that subtleties here can be bypassed or postponed, because a difference, sufficient to give us to think, between the medium of film and that of video is that, in running a film on television, the television set is (interpretable as) a moviola; though unlike a moviola, a monitor may be thought of as a device for checking a film without projecting it. A way to begin characterizing the difference, accordingly, is that the experience of a film on television is as of something over whose running you have in principle, a *control*; you are not *subjected* to it, as you are by film itself or television itself.

But to go further with this line of difference would require a theory of the moviola, or editing viewer; I mean a theory of the relation between the experience of this way of screening a film and that of its full or public screening. The moviola may be thought of as providing a reproduction of the original, or as a reduction of it. In the latter case, we need to think, for example, that a piano reduction of a symphonic score is not merely a reduction of physical scale; perhaps it should be thought of as an extreme case of reorchestration. Equally, a piece for piano can be transcribed for orchestra, and so on. Are there analogous intermediate and reciprocal operations lending comprehensibility, or perspicuousness, to the relation between small and large screens? (Naturally, it may seem that the relation between small and large screens, being merely mechanical, should be clearer than the relation between transcriptions and their originals. My point is that as a matter of fact, of the fact of experience, this is not so.) In the former case, that of reproduction, we need a theory of the reproduction, which can cover everything from a black-and-white half-page photograph in an art book of a fresco a hundred times its size, to a duplicate cast of a statue.

It is a contrary of the long time span that applies to individual episodes, whose events are, however dramatic, transient. So the aesthetics of serial-episode construction comes to a suggestion that what is under construction is an argument between time as repetition and time as transience. Without considering that this is a way of characterizing the thinking of Nietzsche's *Zarathustra*, and following that, of Heidegger's *What Is Called Thinking?* I surmise that something had better be said, in conclusion, about what these speculations seem to add up to.

I go back to the fear or repulsion or anxiety that I have found television to inspire in what I called educated circles, and I ask whether the considerations we have been assembling provide a realistic level of explanation for this fact of television. To indicate the depth of the level required, I mention a book recommended to me by several sources as I was casting about for touchstones in starting notes for my present remarks. *Four Arguments for the Elimination of Television*, by Jerry Mander.[13] The book wishes to convince its readers that television, like "tobacco, saccharin, some food dyes, certain uses of polychlorinated biphenyls, aerosols, fluoroscopes and X rays to name a few" may cause cancer and for that reason alone ought to be banned. And there

are plenty of other reasons it is addictive, and "qualifies more as an instrument of brainwashing, sleep induction and/or hypnosis than anything that stimulates conscious learning processes"; it is a form of sense
deprivation, causing disorientation and confusion; it suppresses and
replaces creative human imagery; it is an instrument of transmutation,
turning people into their TV images; it contributes to hyperactivity; "it
accelerates our alienation from nature and therefore accelerates the
destruction of nature." Is this a disturbance merely of style? Perhaps
the most astonishing stretch of what I have been able to read of this
book is its section in praise of Victor Tausk's description of the "Influencing Machine." Mander is convinced that television *is* the realization of the ultimate influencing machine. But the point of Tausk's extraordinary paper is that to think there are in reality such machines is
symptomatic of schizophrenia.[14] I cannot tell whether Mander knows
this, and whether, if he does, he is declaring that he is schizophrenic,
and if he is, whether he is claiming that television has driven him so,
even as it is so driving the rest of us, and perhaps claiming that it is a
state in which the truth of our condition has become particularly lu-
cid to him. Without telling these things, I am still prepared to regard
this book, the very fact that numbers of reasonable people apparently
take it seriously, as symptomatic of the depth of anxiety television can
inspire.

The depth of it seems to me also expressed in the various more or less
casual hypotheses one hears about, for example, the role of television in
determining reactions to the Vietnam War. Some say it helped end this
war, others (understandably) that it made the war seem unreal. One of
the most haunting images I know from television is the footage of the
Vietnamese priest immolating himself in protest against the war.
Bergman considers this image in *Persona*, as if considering at once the
refuge there is in madness and its silence, and the refuge there is in television. The maddened, speechless heroine stares at the burning priest
both as if she has been given an image of her pain, even a kind of explanation of it, and as if she is the cause of such pain in the world, as of its
infection by her.

But the role of television in explanations of catastrophe was in preparation before the war in Vietnam. Consider that the conquering of television began just after World War II, which means, for the purposes of
the hypothesis I wish to offer here, after the discovery of concentration
camps and of the atomic bomb; of, I take it, the discovery of the literal
possibility that human life will destroy itself; that is to say, that it is *willing* to destroy itself. (This, too, had been in sufficient preparation; it
was realistically described by Nietzsche. In my taking this as a lesson of
the Second World War, the lesson there seems no way for us to learn

realistically, I detect the lingering effect, for all its excess, of a once well-known essay of Norman Mailer's, "The White Negro.") And the conquering continued with the decline of our cities and the increasing fear of walking out at night, producing the present world of shut-ins. Not to postpone saying it any longer, my hypothesis is that the fear of television—the fear large or pervasive enough to account for the fear of television—is the fear that what it monitors is the growing uninhabitability of the world, the irreversible pollution of the earth, a fear displaced from the world onto its monitor (as we convert the fear of what we see, and wish to see, into a fear of being seen). The loss of this inhabitability would mean, on Heidegger's view, the loss of our humanity, whether or not we remain alive. Of course children may not have contracted the fear; and the child in us is capable of repressing the fear, ambivalently. My hypothesis is meant to respond to the mind's demand of itself to take up the slack of mismatch between the fact of television and the fact of our indifference to its significance—as though this slack were itself an expression of the fact that a commodity has conquered, an appliance that is a monitor, and yet that what it monitors, apart from events whose existence preceded its own (cultural coverage, sports, movies), are so often settings of the shut-in, a reference line of normality or banality so insistent as to suggest that *what* is shut out, that suspicion whose entry we would at all costs guard against, must be as monstrous as, let me say, the death of the normal, of the familiar as such.

I am not unaware that the charge of psychosis may well now be shifted in my direction. If so, it should have been leveled at me at least a decade ago, when *The World Viewed* appeared, since the concluding paragraph of that book prepares such a hypothesis:

> A world complete without me which is present to me is the world of my immortality. This is an importance of film—and a danger. It takes my life as my haunting of the world, either because I left it unloved or because I left unfinished business. So there is reason for me to want the camera to deny the coherence of the world, its coherence as past: to deny that the world is complete without me. But there is equal reason to want it affirmed that the world is coherent without me. That is essential to what I want of immortality: nature's survival of me. It will mean that the present judgment upon me is not yet the last.

The development I have introduced here lies in the thought that the medium of television makes intuitive the failure of nature's survival of me.

I suppose it is a tall order for the repetitions and transiences of television, the company of its talk and its events, to overcome the anxiety of the intuition the medium embodies. But if I am right, this is the order it more or less already fulfills, proving again the power of familiarity, for good and ill, in human affairs; call it our adaptability. And who knows but that if the monitor picked up on better talk, monitored habitually the talk of people who actually had something to say, and if it probed for intelligible connections and for beauty among its events—who knows but that it would alleviate our paralysis, our pride in adaptation, our addiction to a solemn destiny, sufficiently to help us allow ourselves to do something intelligent about its cause.

From *Daedalus* "Print Culture and Video Culture," vol. III, no. 4 (Fall 1982), pp. 75-96.

NOTES

A set of comments William Rothman prepared on the basis of a reading of the first version of these remarks caused changes on every other page as I prepared a second version. This was then read by Norton Batkin, Gus Blaisdell, Jay Cantor, and Arnold Davidson, whose comments I used as I prepared the present version. I am, as before, grateful to these friends.

1. In *The Immediate Experience* (New York: Anchor Paperback, 1964).
2. Enlarged edition, Cambridge, Harvard University Press, 1979.
3. Cambridge, Harvard University, 1981.
4. New York, Columbia University Press, 1965.
5. Translated by Richard Howard (Ithaca: Cornell University Press, 1975).
6. I spell this out in "North by Northwest," *Critical Inquiry*, (Summer 1981).
7. Chicago, University of Chicago Press, 1976.
8. New York, Viking, 1971.
9. *Morphologie du conte*, translated by Marguerite Derrida (Paris: Editions du Seuil, 1970).
10. P. 72; this is taken further and modified to characterize cartoons in "More of The World Viewed," pp. 167ff.
11. *What Is Cinema?* translated by Hugh Gray (Berkeley: University of California Press, 1967), p. 97.
12. See, for example, the essays collected in Fernand Braudel, *On History*, translated by Sarah Matthews (Chicago: University of Chicago Press, 1980).
13. New York, Morrow Quill Paperbacks, 1978, pp. 348, 394.
14. An English translation of Tausk's paper, "On the Origin of the 'Influencing Machine' in Schizophrenia," originally published in 1919, is included in *The Psychoanalytic Reader*, edited by Robert Fliess (New York: International Universities Press, 1948), pp. 31-64.

La Vie, Satellites, One Meeting—One Life

Nam June Paik

I T IS SAID that all the sciences can trace their roots to Aristotle; but the science of cosmic aesthetics started with SARUTOBI Sasuke, a famous *ninja* (a samurai who mastered many fantastic arts, including that of making himself invisible, chiefly to spy upon an enemy). The first step for a *ninja* is learning how to shorten distances by shrinking the earth, that is, how to transcend the law of gravity. For the satellite, this is a piece of cake. So, just as Mozart mastered the newly-invented clarinet, the satellite artist must compose his art from the beginning suitable to physical conditions and grammar. The satellite art in the superior sense does not merely transmit existing symphonies and operas to other lands. It must consider how to achieve a two-way connection between opposite sides of the earth; how to give a conversational structure to the art; how to master the differences in time; how to play with improvisation, in determinism, echoes, feedbacks, and empty spaces in the Cagean sense; and how to instantaneously manage the differences in culture, preconceptions, and common sense that exist between various nations. Satellite art must make the most of these elements (for they can become strengths or weaknesses) creating a multi-temporal, multispatial symphony.

These factors complicated matters immensely for the broadcast of "Good Morning, Mr. Orwell," which was transmitted simultaneously on two channels from New York, San Francisco, and Paris, and received simultaneously in the U.S.A., France, West Germany, parts of Canada, and Korea.

First of all, there was the difference in time. There is a six-hour time difference between New York and Paris. It was impossible for it to be prime time in both countries, so I chose a cold winter Sunday. Noon in

New York (Sunday, January 1, 1984) would be freezing cold, so most people would still be at home (with a hangover). Twelve noon in New York is 6:00 p.m. in Paris. I figured that even the worst philanderer would take his dinner at home on New Year's Day. In Korea, this unfortunately turned out to be 2:00 a.m. on January 2.

A second difficulty was the difference in general knowledge and language. Orwell's *1984* has become so well known in English-speaking countries as to be almost stale. Obviously, it needs no explanation. In French-speaking countries, however, it has been out of print since the '50s, and, what is more, there is only one critical work dealing with it. Therefore, French TV required a long, long, fifteen-minute commentary both prior to and in the middle of the broadcast. These differences made this difficult avant-garde art even more difficult.

There is no rewind button on the BETAMAX of life. An important event takes place only once. The free deaths (of Socrates, Christ, Bo Yi and Shu Qi) that became the foundations for the morality of three civilizations occurred only once. The meeting of person and person, of person and specific era are often said to take place "one meeting-one life," but the bundle of segments of this existence (if segments can come in bundles) has grown much thicker because of the satellite. The thinking process is the jumping of electrical sparks across the synapses between brain cells arranged in multilayered matrices. Inspiration is a spark shooting off in an unexpected direction and landing on a point in some corner of the matrix. The satellite will accidentally and inevitably produce unexpected meetings of person and person and will enrich the synapses between the brain cells of mankind. Thoreau, the author of *Walden, Life in the Woods*, and a nineteenth-century forerunner of the hippies, wrote, "The telephone company is trying to connect Maine and Tennessee by telephone. Even if it were to succeed, though, what would the people say to each other? What could they possibly find to talk about?" Of course, history eventually answered Thoreau's questions (silly ones, at that). There developed a feedback (or, to use an older term, dialectic) of new contacts breeding new contents and new contents breeding new contacts.

"Good Morning, Mr. Orwell" of New Year's Day 1984 produced all kinds of feedback. Cage and Beuys are friends, but they have never performed together. Beuys and Ginsberg are two artists who have many things in common (active political involvement, heated performance, complete anti-nuclear naturalism, similar age, romanticism), but have never met. The heavenly stars (Mars, Saturn, Altair, Vega, etc.) meet periodically, but the earthly ones do so very rarely. When I ponder what mysteries the encounter with other people holds for our insubstantial lives, I feel it is a terrible shame that great geniuses may pass their prime without ever meeting. And even when such encounters have actually taken place (for example, Cage and McLuhan; Cage and Buckminster Fuller), no camera has recorded the event. What a loss for the history of human civilization! In 1963, French television recorded a meeting between Edgar Varèse and Marcel Duchamp. Now that both of these giants have passed away, I find it a stirring moment no matter how many times I watch it. The satellite will no doubt amplify these mysteries of encounters by geometric progression. If I may relate a personal experience, I was surprised to find a photograph of myself and my respected friend Beuys at our first encounter (at the "Zero" exhibition held at the Galerie Schmela, Düsseldorf, 1961) in the catalogue *Zero International Antwerpen*. Indeed, I had not even known that such a picture existed.

Thanks to the satellite, the mysteries of encounters with others (chance meetings) will accumulate in geometric progression and should become the main nonmaterial product of post-industrial society. God created love to propagate the human race, but, unawares, man began to love simply to love. By the same logic, although man talks to accomplish something, unawares, he soon begins to talk simply to talk.

It is a small step from *love* to *freedom*. To predefine freedom is a paradox in itself. Therefore, we must retrace the development of freedom historically in order to understand it. The progressive American journalist Theodore White once wrote how impossible it was to explain the difference between *liberty* and *greed* to the leaders of the Chinese Communist Party at Yánān during the Second World War. There are 2,500,000,000 two-character permutations and combinations of the 50,000 Chinese characters. *Zìyóu*, the two-character word for *freedom*, however, did not come into being until the nineteenth century. Just as it is harder to translate *rén* (benevolence, humanity) and *lǐ* (ceremony, etiquette) into English than *dào* (the way [of life, etc.]), it is extremely difficult to translate *liberty* and *freedom* into Chinese. It seems that *gòngchǎn*, the word *communist* as in the Chinese Communist Party, is a loanword from Japan; perhaps *zìyóu* originated in a similar fashion. Even in bright and free ancient Greece, there was the term *free man*, referring to a social class, but there was no philosophical concept of freedom. The passionate idea of freedom is said to have been born under the most unfree, dark domination, of medieval Christianity. Moreover, it was amidst the rise of fascism and the decadence of the Russian Revolution and after the loss of bourgeois freedom before and after the Second World War that man was most strongly and keenly aware of this passionate idea. The existentialism of Camus, Sartre, and Berdyaev was once again forgotten by West European society from the 1960s on, when it experienced a return of freedom and prosperity. In any case, freedom is not a concept inherent in man (it is found neither in the *Koran* nor in the *Analects* of Confucius) but is an artificial creation like chocolate or chewing gum.

The "increase in freedom" brought about by the satellite (from a purely existential point of view, an "increase in freedom" is paradoxical; freedom is a qualitative idea, not a quantitative one) may, contrary to expectation, lead to the "winning of the strong." (Although the imported concepts of freedom and equality may appear to be close brothers, they are in fact antagonistic strangers.)

Recently, an Eskimo village in the Arctic region of Canada started establishing contact with civilization. So far they only have four stores. The first is a general store. The second is a candy shop. (They had not even tasted sugar until quite recently.) The third is, of all things, a video cassette rental shop!!!

Video has immeasurable magical powers. This means that the Eskimos' ancient traditional culture is in danger of being rapidly crushed by the bulldozers of Hollywood. The satellite's amplification of the freedom of the strong must be accompanied by the protection of the culture of the weak or by the creation of a diverse software skillfully bringing to life the qualitative differences in various cultures. As the poets of the beat generation learned from Zen, Phillip Glass obtained hints from the music of India, and Steve Reich looked to the music of Ghana in their creation of original forms of late twentieth-century high art, it is not an impossible task.

As long as the absorption of a different culture makes up the greater part of the pleasure of tourism, the satellite may be able to make every day a sight-seeing trip. So, SARUTOBI Sasuke not only embodies the origins of cosmic aesthetics but also the ethnic romanticism that must always be the companion of satellite art.

P.S. I dedicate this exhibition to my esteemed, one meeting-one life friend Shuya Abe.

From *Nam June Paik—Mostly Video* (exhibition catalogue). Translated by Yumiko Yamazaki. Tokyo: The Tokyo Metropolitan Art Museum, 1984, pp. 12-14.

FILM AND VIDEO: DIFFERENCES AND FUTURES

Art, Entertainment, Entropy

Gene Youngblood

It is easier to copy than to think, hence fashion. Besides, a community of
originals is not a community.

Wallace Stevens

THE CURRENT GENERATION is engaged in an unprecedented
questioning of all that has been held essential. We question traditional concepts of authority, ownership, justice, love, sex, freedom,
politics, even tradition itself. But it's significant that we don't question
our entertainment. The disenfranchised young man who dropped out
of college, burned his draft card, braids his hair, smokes pot, and digs
Dylan is standing in line with his girl, who takes the pill, waiting to see
The Graduate or *Bonnie and Clyde* or *Easy Rider*—and they're reacting
to the same formulas of conditioned response that lulled their parents
to sleep in the 1930s.

We've seen the urgent need for an expanded cinematic language. I
hope to illustrate that profit-motivated commercial entertainment, by
its very nature, cannot supply this new vision. Commercial entertainment works against art, exploits the alienation and boredom of the
public, by perpetuating a system of conditioned response to formulas.
Commercial entertainment not only isn't creative, it actually destroys
the audience's ability to appreciate and participate in the creative process. The implications become apparent when we realize that, as leisure
time increases, each human will be forced to become a creative, self-
sufficient, empirical energy laboratory.

D.H. Lawrence has written: "The business of art is to reveal the relation between man and his circumambient universe at this living mo-

ment. As mankind is always struggling in the toil of old relationships, art is always ahead of its 'times,' which themselves are always far in the rear of the living present." Jean-Jacques Lebel stated the same idea in different terms when he described art as "the creation of a new world, never seen before, imperceptibly gaining on reality." [1]

We've seen that man [sic] is conditioned by, and reacts to, certain stimuli in the man-made environment. The commercial entertainer is a manipulator of these stimuli. If he employs a certain trigger mechanism, we're guaranteed to react accordingly, like puppets, providing he manipulates the trigger properly. I'm not saying the artist doesn't resort to audience manipulation; we know he often does. The point, however, is the motivation in doing so. If the artist must resort to trigger mechanisms to make himself clear, he will; but it's only a means to his end. In the case of the commercial entertainer, however, it's the end in itself.

Plot, story, and what commonly is known as "drama" are the devices that enable the commercial entertainer to manipulate his audience. The very act of this manipulation, gratifying conditioned needs, is what the films actually are about. The viewer purchases it with his ticket and is understandably annoyed if the film asks him to manipulate himself, to engage in the creative process along with the artist. Our word poetry derives from the Greek root *poiein* meaning "to make" or "to work." The viewer of commercial entertainment cinema does not want to work; he wants to be an object, to be acted upon, to be manipulated. The true subject of commercial entertainment is this little game it plays with its audience.

By perpetuating a destructive habit of unthinking response to formulas, by forcing us to rely ever more frequently on memory, the commercial entertainer encourages an unthinking response to daily life, inhibiting self-awareness. Driven by the profit motive, the commercial entertainer dares not risk alienating us by attempting new language even if he were capable of it. He seeks only to gratify preconditioned needs for formula stimulus. He offers nothing we haven't already conceived, nothing we don't already expect. Art explains; entertainment exploits. Art is freedom from the conditions of memory; entertainment is conditional on a present that is conditioned by the past. Entertainment gives us what we want; art gives us what we don't know we want. To confront a work of art is to confront oneself—but aspects of oneself previously unrecognized.

The extent to which blatant audience manipulation not only is tolerated but extolled is alarming. Alfred Hitchcock, for example, in his interview with François Truffaut, finds merit in his ability to manipulate preconditioned needs for formula stimulus. Speaking of *Psycho*,

Hitchcock frankly admits: "It wasn't a message that stirred them, nor was it a great performance, or their enjoyment of the novel ... they were aroused by the construction of the story, and the way in which it was told caused audiences all over the world to react and become emotional."[2]

It is essential to understand that Hitchcock openly admits that he didn't even try to expand awareness or to communicate some significant message, but only exploited a universal tradition of dramatic manipulation in order to supply his audience with the gratification it paid for. The audience sees itself and its dreams reflected in the film and reacts according to memory, which Krishnamurti has characterized as being always conditioned. "Memory," says Krishnamurti, "is always in the past and is given life in the present by a challenge. Memory has no life in itself; it comes to life in the challenge [preconditioned formula stimulus]. And all memory, whether dormant or active, is conditioned."[3] It is this process that the entertainment industry calls audience identification.

To a healthy mind, anything that is primarily art is also immensely entertaining. It seems obvious that the most important things should be the most entertaining. Where there's a difference between what we "like" and what we know to be vital, we have a condition of schizophrenia, an unnatural and destructive situation. I speak deliberately of a "healthy" mind as one capable of creative thinking. Filmmaker Ken Kelman: "The old cinema removes experience, making us see things along with (or through) a protagonist with whom we identify, and a plot in which we are caught. Such an approach tends toward not only a lack of viewpoint, of definition of *whose* experience it is, but also filters the power of sight into mere habit, dissolves insight into vicariousness. The spectator is reduced to a voyeur—which is, increasingly, the individual's role in society at large."[4]

Minimalist painter David Lee: "When people do not trust their senses they lack confidence in themselves. For the last few centuries people have lacked confidence. They have not trusted their experience to provide a standard for knowing how to act."[5] It is quite obvious that most of us not only don't know much about art, we don't even know what we like. Krishnamurti: "One of the fundamental causes of the disintegration of society is copying, which is the worship of authority."[6]

Imitation is the result of inadequate information. Information results in change. Change requires energy. Energy is the result of adequate information. Energy is directly proportional to the amount of information about the structure of a system. Norbert Wiener: "Information is a name for the content of what is exchanged with the outer world as we adjust to it and make our adjustment felt upon it ... to live effectively is to live with adequate information."[7] From the cinema we receive conceptual information (ideas) and design information (experiences). In concert they become one phenomenon, which I've described as the experiential information of aesthetic conceptual design. This information is either useful (additive) or redundant. Useful information accelerates change. Redundant information restricts change. If sustained long enough, redundant information finally becomes misinformation, which results in negative change.

In communication theory and the laws of thermodynamics the quantity called entropy is the amount of energy reversibly exchanged from one system in the universe to another. Entropy also is the measure of disorder within those systems. It measures the lack of information about the structure of the system. For our purposes "structure of the system" should be taken to mean "the human condition," the universal subject of aesthetic activity. Entropy should be understood as the degree of our ignorance about that condition. Ignorance always increases when a system's messages are redundant. Ignorance is not a state of limbo in which no information exists, but rather a state of increasing chaos due to *mis*information about the structure of the system.

The First Law of Thermodynamics states that energy is constant: it cannot be created or destroyed; its form can change, but not its quantity. The Second Law states that the amount of energy within a local system is naturally entropic—it tends toward disorder, dissipation, incoherence. And since energy is defined as "a capacity to rearrange elemental order," entropy, which runs counter to that capacity, means less potential for change. We've learned from physics that the only anti-entropic force in the universe, or what is called negentropy (negative entropy), results from the process of feedback. Feedback exists between systems that are not closed but rather open and contingent upon other systems. In the strictest sense there are no truly "closed" systems anywhere in the universe; all processes impinge upon and are affected by other processes in some way. However, for most practical purposes, it is enough to say that a system is "closed" when entropy dominates the feedback process, that is, when the measure of energy lost is greater than the measure of energy gained.

The phenomenon of man, or of biological life on earth taken as a process, is negentropic because its subsystems feed energy back into one another and thus are self-enriching, regenerative. Thus energy is wealth, and wealth, according to Buckminster Fuller, is "the number of forward days a given system is sustainable." Biologist John Bleibtreu arrived at a similar conclusion when he noted that the concept of time can best be viewed as a function of the Second Law of Thermodynamics—that the measure of entropy in a system is a measure of its age, or the passage of time since the system originated.[8] In other words, the degree of a system's entropy is equal to redundancy or stasis whereas its negentropy is equal to kinesis or change. So information becomes energy when it contributes to the self-enriching omni-regenerative wealth of the system. When it's not contributing (i.e., redundant) it is allowing the natural entropy to increase.

"It is possible to treat sets of messages as having an entropy like sets of states of the external world ... in fact, it is possible to interpret the information carried by a message as essentially the negative of its entropy ... that is, the more probable the message the less information it gives. Clichés, for example, are less illuminating than great poems."[9] Thus the more information concerning the human condition that the artist is able to give us, the more energy we have with which to modify ourselves and grow in accord with the accelerating accelerations of the living present.

Commercial entertainment may be considered a closed system since entropy dominates the feedback process. To satisfy the profit motive the commercial entertainer must give the audience what it expects, which is conditional on what it has been getting, which is conditional on what it previously received, ad infinitum. Inherent in the term "genre," which applies to all entertainment, is that it must be probable. The content of westerns, gangster movies, romances, etc., is probable in that it can be identified and comprehended simply by classification. The phenomenon of drama itself usually is not considered a genre, but is in fact the most universal and archetypical of all genres. Drama, by definition, means conflict, which in turn means suspense. Suspense is requisite on the expectation of known alternatives. One cannot expect the unknown. Therefore expectation, suspense, and drama are all redundant probable qualities and thus are noninformative.

Drama requires a plot that forces the viewer to move from point A to point B to point C along predetermined lines. Plot does not mean "story" (beginning-middle-end). It simply indicates a relatively closed structure in which free association and conscious participation are restricted. Since the viewer remains passive and is acted upon by the experience rather than participating in it with volition, there's no feedback, that vital source of negentropy. Norbert Wiener: "Feedback is a method of controlling a system by reinserting into it the results of its past performance ... if the information which proceeds backward from the performance is able to change the general method and pattern of performance, we have a process which may well be called learning."[10] Fuller: "Every time man makes a new experiment he always learns more. He cannot learn less."[11]

In the cinema, feedback is possible almost exclusively in what I call the synaesthetic mode, which we'll discuss presently. Because it is entirely personal it rests on no identifiable plot and is not probable. The viewer is forced to create along with the film, to interpret for himself what he is experiencing. If the information (either concept or design) reveals some previously unrecognized aspect of the viewer's relation to the circumambient universe—or provides language with which to conceptualize old realities more effectively—the viewer re-creates that discovery along with the artist, thus feeding back into the environment the existence of more creative potential, which may in turn be used by the artist for messages of still greater eloquence and perception. If the information is redundant, as it must be in commercial entertainment, nothing is learned and change becomes unlikely. The noted authority on communication theory, J.R. Pierce, has demonstrated that an increase in entropy means a decrease in the ability to change.[12] And we have seen that the ability to change is the most urgent need facing twentieth-century man.

The notion of experimental art, therefore, is meaningless. All art is experimental or it isn't art. Art is research, whereas entertainment is a game or conflict. We have learned from cybernetics that in research one's work is governed by one's strongest points, whereas in conflicts or games one's work is governed by its weakest moments. We have defined the difference between art and entertainment in scientific terms and have found entertainment to be inherently entropic, opposed to change, and art to be inherently negentropic, a catalyst to change. The artist is always an anarchist, a revolutionary, a creator of new worlds imperceptibly gaining on reality. He can do this because we live in a cosmos in which there's always something more to be seen. When finally we erase the difference between art and entertainment—as we must to survive—we shall find that our community is no longer a community, and we shall begin to understand radical evolution.

From *Expanded Cinema*. New York: E.P. Dutton and Co., Inc., 1970, pp. 59-65.

NOTES
 1. Jean-Jacques Lebel, "On the Necessity of Violation," *The Drama Review* (Fall 1968).
 2. François Truffaut, *Hitchcock* (New York: Simon & Schuster, 1968), p. 211.
 3. J. Krishnamurti, *The First and Last Freedom* (Wheaton, Ill.: Quest Books, 1968), p. 54.
 4. Ken Kelman, "Anticipation of the Light," *The New American Cinema*, ed. Gregory Battcock (New York: Dutton Paperbacks, 1967), pp. 24, 25.
 5. David Lee, "A Systematic Revery from Abstraction to Now," *Minimal Art*, ed.

Gregory Battcock (New York: E.P. Dutton, 1968), p. 195.

6. Krishamurti, *The First and Last Freedom*, p. 41.
7. Norbert Wiener, *The Human Use of Human Beings* (New York: Avon Books, 1967), pp. 26, 27.
8. John N. Bleibtreu, *The Parable of the Beast* (New York: Collier Books, 1969), p. 15.
9. Wiener, *The Human Use of Human Beings*, p. 31.
10. *Ibid.*, p. 84.
11. R. Buckminster Fuller, *Operating Manual for Spaceship Earth* (Carbondale, Ill.: Southern Illinois University Press, 1969), p. 92.
12. J.R. Pierce, *Symbols, Signals and Noise* (New York: Harper & Brothers, 1961).

Art and Technology: The Panacea That Failed

Jack Burnham

T ODAY'S SCIENCE has spawned a wealth of technical gadgetry, while on the other hand, modern visual artists have been notoriously unsuccessful in utilizing much of it in the making of socially acceptable art. Why should it be so? Some forms of technology seem to lend themselves to art which has gained museum status, yet even with the aid of millions of dollars in grants and private donations (plus the assistance of some of the biggest names in contemporary American art, e.g., Rauschenberg, Oldenburg, Warhol, Kaprow, Lichtenstein, Morris, and Smith), the results have fared from mediocre to disastrous when artists have tried to use what has euphemistically been referred to as the electronic technology of "postindustrial culture."

Precisely what succeeds in the context of art and what fails? Simple mechanical devices based on balanced catenary links such as Alexander Calder's mobiles or George Rickey's weighted blades seem to be the only kinetic sculpture fully accepted by the art world. In terms of luminous sculpture (which saw a dazzling revival in the 1960s), only Dan Flavin's unexotic fluorescent fixtures have gained permanent status in museum collections. Certain hand-manipulated objects such as the water boxes of Hans Haacke, the optical reliefs of Jesus Soto, and the Signals of the Greek Takis have some artistic validity. Curiously enough, the only machine-driven or electrically powered art that has maintained its status through the 1970s are the fantastic robots and constructions of the Swiss Jean Tinguely, which are programmed in many instances to break down or malfunction. It must be remembered that during the 1920s Francis Picabia, Max Ernst, Man Ray, Marcel Duchamp, and Tristan Tzara joined in the systematic subversion of the machine as an artistic force. Moreover, one wonders if the Constructivist-Dadaist Congress in Weimar in 1922 was really an accident of accommodation as some of the participants later insisted, or if there was subconscious and interior motivation to the juxtaposition of dada's brand of chaotic destruction with the mechanistic ideology of constructivism. Why should the only successful art in the realm of twentieth-century technology deal with the absurdity and fallibility of the machine? And why should electrical and electronic visual art prove to be such a dismal failure?

At its ideological core, advanced technology has always maintained some of the chimerical effect that the perpetual motion machine had before the twentieth century; we are led to believe in its eternal stability, omnipotence, and its ability to perpetuate human enlightenment. We have been seduced into not doubting technology's efficacy because of its palpable short-term advantages. Yet why have the majority of artists spurned advanced technology, and why have others so bungled its use in producing new art forms? Is it possible that the schism between art and sophisticated technology is far deeper than we suspect, that, in fact, these differences may lie embedded in the neural programs of artists' and scientists' minds? Or are there teleological reasons for this schism, perhaps based on the theological foundations of the Judaic-Christian tradition? If so, let us review some of the recent evidence before surmising the reasons for it.

In Paris the dealer Denise Renée opened an exhibition entitled "Le Mouvement" in 1953 with the help of K.G. Pontus Hultén and her partner Victor Vasarely. Included in "Le Mouvement" were Duchamp, Soto, Tinguely, Calder, Bury, and Agam. In March of 1961 the first "International Exhibition of Art and Motion" opened at the Stedelijk Museum in Amsterdam where it caused a *succès de scandale* for the organizers, in part because of the public response and the bitter tensions which prevailed between the Neo-dadaists and the kinetic constructivists. In April of that same year the Australian sculptor Len Lye mesmerized an audience at the Museum of Modern Art in New York City with an evening of "Revolving Harmonic" polished rods which created virtual forms at various speeds. Thus began a propensity for art in motion and light during the last decade which in 1967 *Time* magazine was to caption "The Kinetic Kraze." The rationale behind much of this aesthetic was a simple one; namely, if so much of twentieth-century art was concerned with the depicted effects of light and movement, then why not produce art which literally relied on light and movement?

Until the early 1960s museums and galleries had tended to emphasize the historical aspects of light and movement. Technically this involved simple motor-driven devices, motorized light boxes, and various static light sources such as neon, incandescent and fluorescent fixtures. Following the Amsterdam retrospective and an outstanding kinetic display at the 1964 Documenta III exhibition in Kassel, West Germany, the tendency moved towards an escalation of technical means, with a concurrent emphasis on collaborations between artists and research and engineering personnel. By the mid-1960s a division had developed between the earlier "machine art" and what could be defined as "systems and information technology." The latter includes artists' use of computer and online display systems, laser and plasma technology, light and audio-sensor controlled environments, all levels of video technology, color copy duplicating systems, programmed strobe and projected light environments using sophisticated consoles, and artificially controlled ecological sites. The definitive boundary line between the old and new technologies probably came with the New York Museum of Modern Art's 1968 exhibition "The Machine as Seen at the End of the Mechanical Age."

At this point it might prove beneficial to touch upon five major art and technology projects with which I have been tangentially or directly concerned. In some instances financial support or approximate budgets have been supplied. These are given to provide some yardstick with which to compare costs relative to standard museum exhibitions. If final evaluations for most of these projects appear overly negative, it should be remembered that these also express the general consensus of the art community and not just my opinion.

I. Experiments in Art and Technology

Dr. Billy Kluver, a Bell Telephone Laboratories' scientist specializing in laser research, had worked with top-level artists all over the world since the late 1950s when he had been an adviser for K.G. Hultén's kinetic exhibition in Amsterdam. In 1965, along with John Cage and Robert Rauschenberg, Kluver began to organize an art and technology extravaganza which became the ill-fated "Nine Evenings: Theater and Engineering," presented at the 69th Regimental Armory in New York City in October of 1966. Kluver, with the aid of some of the most prestigious names in American art, gained the support of some thirty patrons and sponsors amounting to over $100,000. The donated engineering aid was probably worth at least $150,000.

Each evening of "Nine Evenings" presented one or two uniquely designed "pieces," including large scale inflatable structures, radio-controlled dance vehicles, audio-magnified tennis games, infra-red projected "work tasks" performed in the dark, and complex musical pieces synthesized from a number of live external sources. On October

15 the theater critic Clive Barnes reported on the first performance of "Nine Evenings"; his view was more or less typical of the general audience response, particularly that of other artist spectators:

> If the Robert Rauschenberg work, "Open Score," had been a big and glorious fiasco—the kind of thing people write about in years to come rather than the next morning—it could have been a kind of little triumph. But in fact it was such a sad failure, such a limp disaster, more like an indiscretion than an offense. The level of the technology was such that the performance started 40 minutes late, a 15-minute intermission lasted 35 minutes and even a loud speaker announcement was so indistinct on the apparently unsound sound equipment that it became unintelligible. God bless American art, but God help American science.[1]

Barnes later pointed out that "Nine Evenings" was not so much an experiment in theater and engineering as it was an experiment in sociology, since it would take a particularly perverse audience to sit through and endure anything so feeble. Later defenders of "Nine Evenings," such as the critic Douglas Davis, alluded to the overall complexity and uniqueness of each performer's support system. "There was, to begin with," Davis has written, "the patchboard system. Each artist's performance was prewired; all of his equipment could be hooked up by inserting his particular patchboard. The system included amplifiers, relay decoders, tone-control units, transmitters and receivers; it also included a 'proportional control' network that made it possible to change the intensity and volume of both light and sound by moving a flashlight over sixteen photocells...."[2] Kluver and his associates insisted that "Nine Evenings" had been a qualified success, based on the excellent rapport that developed between some artists and engineers working out problems on an intimate basis, and indeed, this has become the major rationale for claiming success for many subsequent art and technology mergers.

In January of 1967 Kluver and a group of associates published their first *E.A.T. News* bulletin as an outgrowth of "Nine Evenings." The public function of Experiments in Art and Technology Inc. was to act as a service organization, to make materials, technology, and engineering advice available to contemporary artists. Because of its governmental and corporate ties, E.A.T. felt that it was in an ideal position to act as a liaison between artists and desired industries. Working from a Manhattan loft, E.A.T. held a number of seminars, lectures, and demonstrations for interested parties, and produced "Some More Beginnings" at the Brooklyn Museum in 1968. By 1970 Kluver and key members of

E.A.T. had so proselytized on a nation-wide basis that according to their files they had upwards of 6,000 members, reportedly half artists and half engineers. No doubt, E.A.T.'s greatest success was its ability to extract relatively large sums of money from the National Endowment for the Arts, the New York Arts Council, large corporations, and various patrons of the arts. Technology seemed to be the key to loosening all sorts of purse strings. If business had been the business of the United States in the 1920s, surely in the 1960s the business of the United States was to acquiesce to the mystique of technology, as epitomized by the use of the "automated battlefield" and systems analysis during the Vietnam War.

The reputation of E.A.T. was irreparably hurt by its rupture with the Pepsi-Cola Company when it planned to produce an art and technology pavilion for *Expo '70* at Osaka, Japan. As Calvin Tompkins elaborates in his brilliant article for *The New Yorker*, "Onward and Upward with the Arts," the E.A.T. people, after many delays and financial fiascos in Osaka, presented Pepsi in April 1970 with a maintenance contract for $405,000; the previously proposed sum had been $185,000.[3] Pepsi pulled out and E.A.T. gradually lost its image as a corporate mediator. Outside New York City, artist members of E.A.T. began to grumble that they were merely statistical fodder for E.A.T.'s grant proposals and that most of their serious requests to E.A.T. were simply ignored or bypassed with form letters. Once the word penetrated the art world that E.A.T. was an "elitist" organization, simply catering to the needs of its own staff and a few favored big-time artists in the New York area, its national demise was insured.

II. Cybernetic Serendipity

The first large-scale exhibition of "post-machine" art was held at the Institute of Contemporary Arts in London during the summer of 1968. Entitled "Cybernetic Serendipity," it was curated by Jasia Reichardt, an imaginative writer and vital force on the London art scene. Her catalogue-book contains a good layman's account of the historical development of digital computers, some relevant scientific projects, plus various experiments by artists that utilize feedback in machines. Other exhibits in "Cybernetic Serendipity" included computer printouts of musical analysis, computer-designed choreography, and computer generated texts and poems. But the I.C.A.'s exhibition was produced on a shoe-string budget: it did not use on-site computers or terminals and much of the available equipment was loaned. Moreover, when the exhibition was shipped to the Corcoran Gallery of Art in Washington,

D.C., the following year, a considerable portion of the contents was destroyed because of poor packing and handling. Several unpaid electrical engineers spent months salvaging parts of "Cybernetic Serendipity" for the opening, but Jasia Reichardt publicly disowned what was shown there.

III. Software

During the winter of 1969, Karl Katz, the director of the Jewish Museum in New York City, decided to mount a major exhibition based on computer technology and chose me to curate what was to become the first computerized art environment within a museum. "Software" did not open, however, until September of the following year. When I accepted, I hardly realized that the project would consume a year and a half of my life. Problems surfaced at every turn, ranging from dilemmas of conception and budgetary restrictions to malfunctioning of equipment and possibly even sabotage.

First, in planning the content of "Software," I was faced with an obvious quandary. At least two-thirds of extant "computer-art" consisted of computer programs designed to simulate existing art styles. Early on the use of the digital computer as a generative tool for creating art or music had been noted by Dr. John R. Pierce of Bell Labs. This was the case in the work of John Whitney, for example, who in the early 1960s began to program geometrical computer graphics using I.B.M. equipment. Similarly, Michael Noll had created a series of linear variations on known modernist masterpieces by using a line plotter. And there were many others: Kenneth Knowlton and Leon Harmon, Charles Csuri and Harold Cohen, to name only a few. But in spite of a wealth of official financial aid during the 1960s and early 1970s, most computer artists became profoundly disillusioned with the creative potential of tools. As Michael Noll admitted as early as 1970, "The computer has only been used to copy aesthetic effects easily obtained with the use of conventional media, although the computer does its work with phenomenal speed and eliminated considerable drudgery. The use of computers in the arts has yet to produce anything approaching entirely new aesthetic experience."[4] And in fact, except for the magazine, *Leonardo*, edited by the ex-aeronautics engineer Frank Malina, the art world has been consistently unanimous in its refusal to recognize or in any way support computer-based art. With all this in mind, I decided with "Software" to forget about "art" as such and to concentrate on producing an exhibition that was educational, viewer interactive, and open to showing information processing in all its forms.

Sponsored by the American Motors Corporation through the agency of Ruder & Finn Fine Arts, a public relations firm, "Software's" initial budget was $60,000, not a princely sum, we were to learn, for an exhibition which expected to house four computers. The Jewish Museum expected substantial help from some of the smaller computer firms, companies specializing in software design, and various university departments that relied heavily on computer technology. I.B.M., we were told, was willing to pick up the tab for all of the exhibition's hardware and software. But the Museum and American Motors correctly perceived that "Software" would all too readily become a prime-time commercial for I.B.M., and thus the offer was rejected. However, two months before the opening of "Software"—with eight major computerized exhibits—we decided that an extra $15,000 was an absolute necessity to sustain the show through a two-month exhibition period. American Motors generously added this money to our budget of $60,000. And without the donated support of various corporations such as Digital Equipment Corporation, 3M Company, Interdata, Mohawk Data Systems, two members of the Smithsonian Institution design staff, and sundry individuals in the computer field, it is doubtful that "Software" could have been mounted for less than $250,000. Yet even after our major computer, the PDP-8, had been reprogrammed a second time, it took several D.E.C. engineers six weeks to make both "Labyrinth" (the interactive catalogue) and related exhibits operational. The computer's failure to function was a mystery to everyone and a source of embarrassment to D.E.C.

This was not the only operational difficulty. The day before "Software" opened, the exhibit which one encountered upon entering the show's space—a darkened pentagon of five film loops which showed artists working or explaining their conception of "Software"—was destroyed by two of the filmmakers themselves. Involved in a dispute over titling and finances with the producer of the films, they cut the five films to pieces; it took three weeks to resolve these problems and make copies from the master prints. And the night before "Software" opened, a janitor sweeping the floors of the Museum short-circuited the entire program of the PDP-8 by breaking some wires in a terminal stand with a push broom—or at least that was the official story released by the Jewish Museum.

The fact that "Software" opened without its film and minus the use of its central computer gave gleeful satisfaction to some members of the New York art press. The reasons for this animosity may stem from the ever-growing and disproportionate influence that technology exerts on our cultural values. As a result of training and personality, many art critics consider themselves "humanists" with strong feelings concerning the encroachments of technology on nature and cultural traditions. A few have successfully advocated what might be termed "Pop Technology," e.g., cybernetic light towers, video banks, and electronic sensoriums, but most critics instinctively realize that it would damage their art-world credibility if they became serious advocates of hard technology as an aesthetic life-style. With the rash of "Tek-Art" adventures during the 1960s, substantial numbers of artists and critics feared that electronics might soon overwhelm the prestige of the traditional art media as found in painting and sculpture. At the time, the spectre of an engineer-controlled art world seemed a bit too imminent for comfort. Hence, the reviews for "Software" were decidedly mixed, containing both strong praise and condemnation.

But on the whole, Talmudic scholars and rabbis situated on the top floor of the Jewish Museum were heard to mutter darkly as to the inappropriateness of exhibiting "Software" in a museum mainly devoted to Judaica and Jewish studies. The director of the museum, Karl Katz, lost his job a month after "Software" was disassembled. And the New York Trade Commission gave American Motors a special award in 1971 for sponsoring the most ambitious and interesting cultural failure of the year in New York City, a mixed blessing which American Motors, nevertheless, accepted with gratitude.

IV. The Center for Advanced Visual Studies

One of the major attempts to wed art and technology in the United States during the last decade began formally in January 1968 with the opening of The Center for Advanced Visual Studies at the Massachusetts Institute of Technology. Its founder was the head of the Visual Design Department at M.I.T., Professor Gyorgy Kepes, who in the early 1940s had headed the photography department at the Chicago Bauhaus under László Moholy-Nagy. Invited to M.I.T. in 1946 to organize the design program for student architects and engineers, Kepes created several important light murals during the 1950s and taught a seminar in 1957 on kinetic art, considerably before kineticism became fashionable in the United States. Possessing formidable connections within the scientific and academic world, he began plans for the Center in 1965. The Center for Advanced Visual Studies was to be the fulfillment of everything his mentor, Moholy-Nagy, had written about in his seminal *Vision in Motion* during the Dessau Bauhaus period. In 1967 M.I.T. renovated its old bookstore on Massachusetts Avenue in Cambridge according to Kepes's plans. Essentially this consisted of five large, first floor studio areas, a large public work space in the basement, a small woodworking shop, plus a lavishly equipped photography darkroom.

In 1968 the German artist Otto Piene, the Greek sculptor Takis, Harold Tovish, Ted Kraynik, Wen-Ying Tsai, and I were invited to join the Center as its first fellows. Kepes's master plan for the Center was to produce a sophisticated environment where artists with a technological bent could do their own art and collaborate on large-scale group projects. In *Art and the Future*, Douglas Davis draws a fairly sympathetic portrait of Kepes's hopes and the early progress of the Center. Davis comments that the "Center's early years were lean ones financially, and that Kepes was kept from fulfilling his hopes in detail."[5] After a year at the Center my perception was at considerable variance with what Douglas Davis saw or believed.

Given the state of the American art world, Kepes initially had generous financial support, with M.I.T. and a half a dozen foundations backing him. But during the past few years support for the Center has dwindled as it has failed to produce writings, art works, or urban projects of any significance. Much of this is not the fault of the present director, Otto Piene, who has struggled to keep the Center alive. I would lay the blame in two directions: the rapid decline of technological art as one of the pet ideals of the avant garde, and the Center's lack of any concrete philosophy beyond the exploitation of available technologies. All too often artists expect their rather feeble art ideas to be rescued with the aid of exotic electronics.

Actually, except for those areas of scientific research that produced stunning photographs, such as holography, electron microscopy, and aspects of optical physics, Kepes had a strange aversion to direct involvement with sophisticated technology, particularly anything to do with the computer sciences. Due to the fact that the Center had been publicized, by virtue of its relation to M.I.T., as a technological nirvana for the artist, I found the situation mystifying. Slowly it began to dawn on me that the Center's underlying purpose was not primarily to do visual research or to make art, but to produce lavishly illustrated catalogues and anthologies that would impress foundations.

One should remember that in 1969 the Vietnam War and student-faculty protests were at their height. Speculation abounded that the Center was M.I.T.'s gesture towards the humanities, perhaps a means of focusing attention away from the presence of so many Navy and Air Force contracts. Certainly the Center never really had any concrete program outside of fulfilling the director's vague dreams of creating urban spectaculars. During my first month and a half we met twice weekly to discuss Kepes's ambitions for erecting a colossal light tower in the middle of Boston Harbor. Somehow the conversations and exchange of ideas remained maddeningly vague. I began to ask specific questions:

> Did the Center have funds for such a project or any idea of costs? *No.*

> Given that the Boston Harbor was directly in the flight patterns of Logan Airport, had the Center checked on the feasibility of the project with the local Civil Aeronautics Board, or with the Boston Harbor Authority? *No.*

> Did they understand the problems of laying underwater electrical conduit or the costs? *No.*

> What was the civic purpose of the light monument? *No one really knew.*

V. *Art and Technology*

Of all the art and technology projects instigated during the 1960s, Maurice Tuchman's five-year symbiosis at the Los Angeles County Museum (1967-71) was the most ambitious and perhaps the most revealing. In 1968 I visited the Los Angeles County Museum at the invitation of Tuchman, the Museum's Curator of Modern Art, in the capacity of consultant. From the start there was something grossly immodest about "Art & Technology" or "A & T" as the Museum called it. Tuchman managed to induce thirty-seven corporations in the Southern California area to contribute financial and technical support to resident artists. After three years of selection and various labyrinthine transactions which are documented in the "A & T" catalogue, the Museum came up with twenty-two artists who were paired to work with specific corporations. Out of these twenty-two artists, sixteen finally produced usable pieces or environments for the exhibition. Originally Tuchman proposed that the Museum contribute $70,000 towards supporting "A & T," while corporations, he felt, would contribute $140,000 in cash donations. By the Museum's own reckoning, its final budget was $140,000 for the expenses of "A & T," including three months of operating expenses. In terms of nonmonetary contributions by corporations, including materials, technical assistance, and the use of working facilities, I suspect the total outlay for "A & T" was between $500,000 and $1,000,000. If "Art & Technology" had been a critical success, or if its extravagance had not been so attacked by critics, quite likely the published budget would have been considerably higher.

By drawing up contracts for artists and supporting corporations, Tuchman made certain that there would be no abrupt pull-outs, inadequate technical assistance, or failures to furnish length of exhibition maintenance for artists' projects. In retrospect, the technical support for Los Angeles' "A & T" exhibition was probably the most thorough and proficient ever supplied for an exhibition of its kind. And yet the length and legal binding character of "A & T's" contract was a facet of the project which critics attacked with vigor. Critics saw it as a covenant between two capitalist organizations (e.g., the museum and each of its corporate benefactors), in collusion with or against all the artists involved. Even Tuchman in the catalogue intimated that most of the artists in the show would not have participated by 1971, the year "A & T" finally opened, primarily because much of the art world believed by then that there was or is a nefarious connection between advanced technology and the architects of late capitalism. In the press "Art & Technology" was decimated, and not altogether for unsound reasons.

In a review of "Art and Technology" for *Artforum*, I tried to place the exhibition in an historical perspective that would make the responses of the art world more discernible:

> No doubt "humanist" art critics are going to pan A & T as another marriage of convenience with industry that fails to measure up to Henry Geldzahler's exalted view of the last 30 years. However, like Dr. Johnson's remarks on the virtues of singing dogs, defending A & T as the "best exhibition of its kind" is also questionable. In any case, due to the particular sociopolitical malaise that has gradually engulfed the United States, this show probably will be the last technological attempt for a while. If presented five years ago, A & T would have been difficult to refute as an important event, posing some hard questions about the future of art. Given the effects of a Republican recession, the role of large industry as an intransigent beneficiary of an even more intractable federal government, and the fatal environmental effects of most of our technologies, few people are going to be seduced by three months of industry-sponsored art—no matter how laudable the initial motivation. Certainly painting and sculpture do nothing to alleviate these conditions, but at least they are less exasperating since they avoid unpleasant juxtapositions.[6]

One might look again at the large corporations supporting technological art and the artists receiving their sponsorship and conclude that both were guilty of some degree of naiveté, but hardly collusion for political purposes. While E.A.T. and other art groups held out the boon of "new discoveries" to corporations funding them, most companies were cynical and wise enough to realize that the research abilities of nearly all artists are nil. What companies could expect is a limited amount of good press for appearing "forward looking." To be sure, sociologists and several conceptual artists such as Victor Burgin and Hans Haacke have shown that pervasive philanthropy and museum-controlled "taste-making" do exert long term political control over the artistic tastes of the public. But given the costs and popular failure of technological art, it would appear an enormously inefficient means of swaying the masses, much less a means of promoting Technocracy as a successor to Capitalism.

In retrospect one could divide the artists participating into three categories: the techno-artists such as Robert Whitman, Rockne Krebs, Newton Harrison, and Boyd Mefferd who were aesthetically allied with the light and kinetic movement; New York "name" artists such as Claes Oldenburg, Roy Lichtenstein, Richard Serra, Tony Smith, Andy Warhol, and Robert Rauschenberg who were only tangentially connected with art and technology; and finally the oddballs such as James Lee Byars, Ron Kitaj, and Oyvind Falstrom who provided the show's element of serendipity. The "name" artists tended to do enlarged or elaborate variations of their standard work or to cynically build into their projects hints about the utter futility of technology as a humanistic endeavor. Yet, as I stated in my review, by its nature art depends upon social compliance and cooperation; every successful artist places his or herself in the hands of the financial establishment: "Whether out of political conviction or paranoia, elements of the Art World tend to see latent fascist aesthetics in any liaison with giant industries; it is permissible to have your fabrication done by a local sheet-metal shop, but not by Hewlett-Packard."[7]

The examples given so far—"Experiments in Art and Technology," "Cybernetic Serendipity," "Software," The Center for Advanced Visual Studies, and "Art and Technology"—are a representative cross-section of major art projects concerned with advanced "postindustrial" technology during the past ten years. Have they failed as art because of technical or aesthetic incompetency, or because they represent some fundamental dissimilarity as systems of human semiosis? Although it is clear that technical incompetency is partially to blame, I would suspect the latter is a more fundamental explanation. My experiences with semiology and iconography lead me to believe that the enormous vitality and will-to-change behind Western art is in a sense an illusion, just as technology harbors its own illusionary impulses. Only within the past ten years have we begun to accept the possibility that technological solutions are not universal panaceas. Gradually but surely, much of it in unspoken terms, we are beginning to accept evidences that scientific research and technological invention have their boundaries. Such a speculation would have been nearly unthinkable fifteen years ago when scientific grants were plentiful and the avant garde was the key to artistic success. Perhaps technology is only a matter of man-made or artificial negentropy which, because of its enormous and productive capacity and ability to aggrandize perception into convenient and coherent packages of "information," we perceive as invincible, life-stabilizing, all-meaningful, and omnipotent.

Since the scientific revolution, art has become a protected cultural sanctuary; as empiricism has gradually dominated everyday cultural values and academic standards, art has been transformed into a sort of necessary way-station for the expression of anti-social sentiments. It liberates the human spirit by its inability or reluctance to become acutely self-analytical, while at the same time art remains implicitly critical of everything around itself. One might conjecture that art remains a knife-edge or balancing fulcrum for the human psyche. By that I mean it encompasses all aspects of the psyche equally; mythic fantasy, technological skills, aesthetic idealism, manual craftsmanship, a variety of contents, but most importantly an internal semiotic consistency which prevents it from becoming absorbed by other disciplines, no matter how powerful or persuasive. If there is a teleological function to art, quite likely it is to lead us back to our psychological origins, to exhaust our material illusions by forcing us to understand the reality of mythic experience, for myths are merely the mental constructs we devise for our perception of the world, having particular properties isomorphic with the physical world. Yet increasingly we sense the fragility of art, the fact that modern rationalism tends to denude it of its most precious characteristic, its "believability."

In 1968, my book *Beyond Modern Sculpture* was published. What made the book controversial was the prediction that inert art objects would eventually exhaust themselves as a means of cultural expression (that is, lose their powers of contemplative evocation for human beings). I suggested that the art world was rapidly moving from "object" orientation towards a "systems" orientation in its perception of mundane reality. The book ended with a prophecy:

> The stabilized dynamic system will become not only a symbol of life but literally life in the artist's hands and the dominant medium of further aesthetic ventures.... As the Cybernetic Art of this generation grows more intelligent and sensitive, the Greek obsession with "living" sculpture will take on an undreamed

reality.

The physical beauty which separates the sculptor from the results of his endeavors may well disappear altogether.[8]

In a sense *Beyond Modern Sculpture* validated itself in terms of some subsequent art; where it erred gravely is in its tendency to anthropomorphize the goals of technology. As with Norbert Weiner's comparison of the ancient Jewish myth of the man-made Golem with cybernetic technology, I envisioned the resolution of art and technology in the creation of *life* itself. Yet, in a most ironic fashion, something other than that has taken place. Presently and for the near future the science of artificial intelligence has produced nothing approaching lifelike cognition, but merely pale imitations of it. The cybernetic art of the 1960s and 1970s is considered today little more than a trivial fiasco. Nevertheless, avant garde art during the past ten years has, in part, rejected inert objects for the "living" presence of artists, and by that I am referring to Conceptual Art, Performance Art, and Video Art. In the case of such artists as Chris Burden, Joseph Beuys, Christian Boltanski, James Lee Byars, and Ben Vautier, art and life activities have become deliberately fused, so that the artist's output is, in the largest sense, *lifestyle*. During his last years, Marcel Duchamp often insisted that art, after all, was only the process of "making." Thus, in a literal way, art objects are merely materials, the semiotic residue of the artist's activities. What we are seeing when we view art is a fusion of cognition and gesture; as the historical semiotic of art evolves, this becomes increasingly apparent. Gradually, the art object destabilized, imploding upon itself. What is left is a series of partitioned fragments of the entire art-making process.

In the long run, technology may, like art, be a form of cognitive bootstrapping, an illusionary form of conquest over the forces of Nature. Both are vaguely deceptive in that they hold out the possibility of human transcendence, yet they only lead us back to a point where we can understand how we are dominated by our own perceptual illusions. In technology the sense of mastery, manipulation, and "otherness" is a more implicit assumption than it is in art. The ritual-making aspects of art do not sever man so effectively from his natural origins. Ultimately, perhaps, the very weakness of art as a cultural force—its conceptual confusion and lack of utilitarian value—gives it its strength.

Any attempt to explain why art and the electronic technologies are mutually exclusive can only be conjecture. Possibly, though, the reasons for this schism are metaphysical and not technical. At its foundations art may be a cognitive discipline or exercise, one that steers us towards the most primitive regions of the human brain. Physically, the brain is a jelly-like gray mass composed of billions of neurons sending and receiving billions of weak electrical signals per second. Providing that art is primarily a form of self-understanding (*re-cognition*), it would seem likely that the principles behind the historical evolution of art contain an exclusion principle. By that I mean a principle which does not allow the aesthetic-cognitive functions of the brain to accept an electronic technology as an extension of inanimate objects. In a sense a certain rapport or similarity exists between the brain and electronic technology, although analogies between the two at this time are very gross. Traditionally the aesthetic aura or charisma of art has existed within a Pygmalion-like paradox: art "lives" although it remains consecrated in dead, inanimate materials. To challenge that paradoxical state may very well jeopardize the mythic consistency of Western art.

When one speaks of the "mythic consistency of Western Art" many alternate possibilities come to mind. What I mean by that is Western art's semiological consistency, that fabric of "believability" in contemporary thought which has possibly been best defined in Roland Barthes's illuminating essay, "Myth Today." Barthes suggests, and I feel correctly so, that virtually everything is subject to mythic interpretation, hence the limits of myth are essentially formal, not substantial.[9] Does such a broad generalization define myth out of existence? Or does it suggest that the efficacy of mythic thought is far more culturally pervasive than our intellectual conventions allow? Barthes, of course, has been a strong advocate of the second position. For him myth becomes in a sense "background," the naturalization and depoliticization of everyday speech. This suffices, as with Barthes's examples, to explain the subtleties of patriotic posters, dress codes, or bourgeois rhetoric, yet it allows us insufficient insight into the dynamic vicissitudes of equally if not more complex phenomena such as art history.

Here one might suspect that the level of historical discourse (that carried on in works of art by artists and not scholarly analysis) is essentially anagogic, having to do with the unresolved purpose of Judaic-Christian culture at the highest levels. In such a case, the linguistic conventions of signified, signifier, sign, and referent revert back to their theological forms of Father, Son, Holy Ghost, and last but not least, Man himself. The mythic consistency of the Judaic-Christian tradition is premised on a somewhat multiple assumption: namely, man cognizes by virtue of perceiving dichotomies, he acts triadically through the agency of signs, but he only comes to know himself by dissolving thought and action in the recognition of unity. The theological term "anagogic" also refers to the transformation of drives from the unconscious into constructive ideation, which is just about as succinct a definition of Western art as one could hope for.

As such, Western art leads a double existence. It operates as an unveiled and exoteric activity, taught pervasively in schools (usually badly) and subject to the most commercial exploitation. Yet it contradicts Barthes's everyday mythic invisibility because art by its very paradoxical nature (its near perfect resistance to economic, psychological, or sociological interpretation) openly signifies an apparent mystery concerning the fusion of spirit and matter. So at the highest level, secrecy and a code of concealment are imperative for its cultural survival.

Dialectically art moves in Western culture towards the disclosure of the human psyche, which I would interpret as the life force unhindered by ego and self-consciousness. Even this is accomplished paradoxically in that art appears to be constantly moving away from clarity and resolution, and towards chaos and materialism. Technology's mythic consistency is no less subtle, because it springs from the accrued conviction of the intellect's invincibility. In a sense it resembles the other side of the human personality: lacking the psychic acceptance of the artist, it places its *raison d'être* in empiricism, which tends to lead it towards its worst enemies, paradox and meaninglessness. Nevertheless, while art and technology show signs of mutual exclusiveness, at the level of anagogic significance they may actually be completely tautological.

From *The Myths of Information: Technology and Postindustrial Culture*, edited by Kathleen Woodward. Madison, Wisconsin: Coda Press, Inc. 1980, pp. 200-215.

NOTES
1. Clive Barnes, "Dance of Something at the Armory," *New York Times*, Oct. 15, 1966, p. 88.
2. Douglas Davis, *Art and the Future: A History/Prophecy of the Collaboration Between Science, Technology, and Art* (New York: Praeger, 1973), p. 69.
3. Calvin Tomkins, "Onward and Upward with the Arts," *The New Yorker*, Oct. 3, 1970: 83 ff.
4. Davis, p. 111.
5. Davis, p. 115.
6. Jack Burnham, "Corporate Art," *Artforum* (Oct. 1971): 67. This review appeared in *Artforum* along with a piece by Max Kozloff under the general heading: "The 'Art and Technology' Exhibition at the Los Angeles County Museum (Two Views)." What was interesting about this review was that both the Los Angeles County Museum and *Artforum* had asked me to write it—the former, I thought, because they trusted my objectivity, and certainly there was much of a critical nature in the 5,000 words that I wrote. But unknown to me, John Coplans, then Managing Editor of *Artforum*, sent out his most trusted critic. Max Kozloff's piece, "The Multimillion Dollar Art Boondoggle," *Artforum* (Oct. 1971): 72, was probably the most vicious, inflammatory, and irrational attack ever written on the art and technology phenomenon. It posed the Museum, Tuchman, and most of the artists connected with "A & T" as lackeys of a killer government, insane for new capitalist conquests in South East Asia. Kozloff depicted half of the artists involved as "fledgling technocrats, acting out

mad science fiction fantasies"; the more sophisticated artists he envisioned as cynical opportunists.

7. Burnham, "Corporate Art," pp. 66-67.
8. Jack Burnham, *Beyond Modern Sculpture: The Effects of Science and Technology on The Sculpture of This Century* (New York: George Braziller, Inc., 1968), p. 376.
9. Roland Barthes, *Mythologies*, trans. Annette Lavers (New York: Hill and Wang, 1972).

Cinema and Broadcast TV Together

John Ellis

THE CONVENTIONALLY ACCEPTED notion of what consti-
tutes "a film" is the product of a specific period of the history of
cinema, lasting roughly from 1915 to 1950. This period was characterized by the dominance of American interests. The intervention of
broadcast TV, which had become a mass medium in both North America and Europe by the late 1950s, radically changed cinema's methods
of working. Cinema and broadcast TV have developed, over the last
quarter century, both forms of co-existence and forms of divergence.
TV has pioneered whole genres that had a primitive or fleeting existence in cinema like news and current affairs work. It has plundered
cinema and literature for other genres, like melodrama. Within cinema,
traditional mass entertainment forms have continued to operate, some
with considerable financial success. Overall, however, cinema work has
become more fragmentary, offering possibilities that broadcast TV
cannot or will not provide. Sometimes, it is precisely because cinema
has pioneered a means of representation that broadcast TV can then
take it up. In this sense, cinema is rather more on the side of innovation
than broadcast TV can be: this is one of the implications of cinema's
production of prototypes rather than TV's industrial series production.
Hence one of the most interesting relationships has grown up between
cinema and TV. TV uses cinema to provide it with new ideas, new material, and, above all, to take its risks for it.

Since broadcast TV is a predominantly national phenomenon, the
exact relationships between cinema and TV differ from one political
situation to another. The strength of a particular state's TV operations,
its popularity, its appeal to different sectors of the population, its distinctive aesthetic strengths and weaknesses, its openness or hostility to

innovatory ideas, all of these factors affect the kind of cinema that is offered within a particular state. Platitudes abound on this topic, like the habitual assertion that British cinema (both in production and exhibition) is weak because British TV is so good. However, much of what cinema in other parts of Europe has produced is never seen either in British cinemas or on British TV. A whole dimension of work is virtually absent from the experience of most of the British population. In fact, the British situation is by no means accurately described by rather smug assertions about the supposed quality of British TV. Rather, the situation can be briefly characterized as one where cinema exhibition has been poorly managed by the conglomerates (Rank and Thorn/EMI/ABC) that effectively control it. Popular cinema exhibition in Britain has been slavishly linked to the large American distributors, and has never looked towards alternative sources of alternative kinds of material, for instance the art cinema market. Art cinema production and exhibition has never received the level of subsidy that it has in Europe. British TV for its part can be characterized as being very good at a relatively narrow range of program types: principally those of historical fiction and literary adaptation for which it has established its reputation in the international TV market. British TV has not entered into productive relationships with cinema in the way that other national TV institutions (Germany's ZDF, Italy's RAI) have done. British TV has a close relationship with British theater: its prestige work is called "drama" rather than "film"; it lionizes the writer rather than the director.

Certain generalizations can be made about cinema and TV and their relationship. Nowhere is cinema subject to more stringent censorship arrangements than broadcast TV: in some states, cinema is given a far wider freedom than broadcasting, in the USA for instance. In other states, like Britain, cinema is subject to different, less stringent, but still constricting forms of censorship. In yet other states, mostly right-wing dictatorships, cinema and TV are subject to exactly the same direct state intervention into their activities. These formal censorship mechanisms create an atmosphere where a pervasive self-censorship takes place: self-censorship being the result of the calculation that every film- or program-maker makes about what subject and what approach to that subject are feasible in a particular circumstance. Self-censorship is in most states a far more restricting form in TV than it is in cinema: the judgments that are habitually made about what "will be OK" for TV are notoriously more conservative. This is partly the result of TV's self-definition as a *mass* medium (and therefore needing to be intelligible to "everyone"), partly because of the close relationship that national TV institutions have with controlling political elites, and partly because of the industrialized production form and the consequent difficulty of working in adventurous ways. Cinema no longer works with such a rigid sense of itself as a mass medium, although the pervasiveness of such a view of cinema in the general culture is still surprising. Cinema's characteristic commodity form makes it rather more open to introducing "difference" at various levels: in the subject matter of a film, its formal construction, its method of exhibition and promotion, its production organization, etc. Hence the broad distinction can be made between the current operations of the two media, that cinema is more prone to innovative work.

Cinema work regularly appears on TV. Cinema films are consumed by TV, under a variety of financial and social arrangements that are usually rather more to TV's benefit than cinema's. Hence a major consideration in the interrelationship between the two media is what TV does with cinema, the way that it uses cinema to provide certain features to its outputs. TV tends to have contradictory relationships with the cinema films it shows. On the one hand, it looks to cinema to provide certain forms of innovation (which particular forms depends on the particular TV institution in question). On the other hand, its use of cinema films as broadcastable material elides one of the major features of cinema: the fact of cinema exhibition as a public exhibition of a high-grade image. One growing tendency in some cinema activity in recent years has been to emphasize the potential of the situation of public collective viewing. Any potential that lies in this aspect of cinema's work is denied in the way in which films are habitually broadcast; it is usually neglected in the coverage that TV gives to cinema as well.

Finally, TV has achieved a centrality in everyday life which outstrips anything that cinema could achieve. TV broadcasts have a particular kind of cultural visibility that is distinct from that still maintained by some of cinema's products. TV broadcasts are seen on one night by a huge number of people: they therefore create patterns of expectancy and publicity around that one exposure. Newspapers (themselves a daily rhythm) are the privileged arena for creating notoriety around TV broadcasts. They either publicize the expectations of "tonight's episode," or they pick up on "last night's revelation by politician X." The cultural visibility of particular TV broadcasts is thus one of a day or two's length; whereas that of a cinema film can last several months, depending on its pattern of distribution. Broadcast TV has an immediacy in the sense that its rhythm is that of everyday life. TV programs are the stuff of small-talk, of "did you see that thing last night where ... ?" However, the centrality and familiarity of broadcast TV create definite, ideological limitations to its work. TV is required to be predictable and timetabled; it is required to avoid offense and difficulty. This centrality that TV has is also responsible for creating a space of cinema, a space where everything that fits uneasily into TV's centrality can nevertheless take place.

The centrality of broadcast TV to everyday life combined with the resultant demands for timidity and predictability means that TV defines a kind of center ground from which cinema, in a variety of ways, diverges. This center ground is composed of TV's habitual attitudes and its habitual forms. TV's concentration on the domestic has already been explored as a pervasive representation resulting from the very conditions of use of TV in Western states as a private and domestic activity. This sense of the domestic is itself a representation rather than a reflection. It creates and mobilizes notions of domestic life that are at variance with the actual conditions in which a large proportion of the population lives. The representation of the domestic is one aspect of TV's center ground. Another aspect is the way in which TV (quite explicitly) seeks to speak from a central position. The current organizing notion for news and current affairs in Britain is one of "balance" between contesting official viewpoints, in which the TV institution holds a position of common sense. These two aspects of centrality are complemented by the spread of genres that TV uses. These genres define the levels of complexity and the characteristic forms of attention that are given to various areas of human life. Some forms of available social definition of the human body are used, for instance, and not others. There is the medical (*Your Life in Their Hands*), the sporting, the violent (the stuff of drama), but never the pornographic or the erotic. The domestic, the notion of balance and the habitual spread of genres constitute the core of TV's centrality in relation to cinema.

Broadcast TV displays its notions of the domestic in several ways. First, its own fictions are inclined to foreground "family life" in all its complexities. Hence soap operas are constituted around families (*The Brothers, Dallas*), the street (*Coronation Street*), or the workplace conceived of as a kind of displaced domestic life (*Crossroads*). Serious drama deals with "problems" which are usually those of a socio-sexual nature: domestic violence, the welfare state and its uneasy interaction with "real people," interpersonal conflicts at work. Where life outside the family is shown (the sphere of public life, the workplace, boardroom struggles: all fit subjects for TV fiction), these aspects of life are interpreted in psychological terms which have their central basis in the vision of domestic life that TV presents. Characters form themselves into patterns of dependency and authority that often have as their implicit (sometimes explicit) psychological model the structures of family life. Hence the privileged representation of relations between employers and employees is that of fathers to their sons; and the range of relationships between workers takes notions of "brotherhood" to sometimes ludicrous extremes. Of course, a range of TV productions go beyond these rather simple characterizations to produce more acute analyses of the relations between those in authority and those who have to (or protest against having to) submit to them. Yet even in these cases, the characters are assumed to have a family behind them, giving support, normalizing their lives.

The appearance of notions of domesticity can be charted across the whole of TV fiction, reaching a level of pandemonium in situation comedy. It is equally present in the form of address of TV: whether it is the direct address of the announcer speaking to "viewers at home" (or using them as an alibi for a certain line of questioning in an interview), and in the assumptions made about the patterns of programming. In Britain, programming presupposes certain audiences: weekday daytime TV assumes "the housewife at home" until about 4:30 when children become the target audience (commercial TV advertisements register this shift very clearly). 5:45 is the homecoming of the breadwinner, eager to hear news of the world's affairs, followed by forms of domestic familial entertainment until 9:00. At this hour, children are deemed to have retired for the night (dreaming of the toys advertised between 4:30 and 5:45), and programming changes toward more adult programs. After 10:30 only "minorities" are deemed to be awake, and it is often around this time that the "routine marginal" programs are screened. These are as varied as the up-market American soap operas of *Lou Grant* (newspapers) or *Soap* (pushing the genre conventions to their limits); or programs for racial minorities; or serious current affairs discussions like *Newsnight* (news/interviews/filmed reports) or *What the Papers Say* (sometimes astute comments on newspapers' coverage of a particular contemporary issue). A pattern of domestic life is assumed in the overall scheduling of the main channels of BBC1 and ITV. These patterns have a long and settled history. BBC2 presents a variant of this strategy, presenting its news for the late arrival (after 6:30) and its mid-evening entertainment for enthusiasts for particular activities (snooker, gardening, etc.) as well as the uncommitted family audience. The 9:00 p.m. embargo works for this channel as well. Scheduling assumes a certain domestic pattern: housewives at home; children in the late afternoon home from school; programs to eat by between 6:00 and 7:00; an evening's entertainment to settle down with for the whole family until 9:00 when the children are packed off to bed and adults enjoy themselves alone. Most of the nation is assumed to switch off at about 10:30 or 11:00, unless a particular mania or insomnia holds them a little longer. This general cozy domestic vision itself determines the balance of kinds of programs across the evening, with situation comedy, variety, made-for-TV films and police series gravitating towards the mid-evening peak hours.

The dominance of a particular image of domestic life over the whole of TV's output is only one feature defining its "centrality" in relation to cinema. The notion of "balance" that dominates the coverage of news and current affairs is another. "Balance" does not mean that two sides of any question are shown, or are presented equally. Balance is rather more a matter of official political institutions, and ensuring that those institutions have a roughly equal access to air time. Balance is scrupulously operated when it concerns political parties; it is less so when it concerns other important political institutions like trade unions, professional bodies or employers' associations. There is no operational concept of balance in relation to ordinary people. The voice of those who have no institutionalized political power is heard very rarely. When "pensioners," "the self-employed" or "housewives" are mentioned, they are used as a rhetorical point to bolster some argument about their supposed interests as presented by a politician, or by a TV interviewer or reporter. Indeed, it is difficult to see how things could be arranged otherwise, since TV's notion of current events is almost exclusively a passive one. TV claims to be reporting what is important at any one time, and the agenda of what is important is set by representative institutions or by acts of Nature. The actions of ordinary people only appear in TV's news-gaze when they are organized as "newsworthy": picket lines, random acts of violence, spectacular protests. The "newsworthy" is a particular definition that is put on all actions so that a few can be selected to compose new bulletins and the subjects of current affairs. It is the product of the hundred years' history of popular journalism, not the product of TV itself. The "newsworthy" is composed of two disparate functions. One is that of picking up on particular isolated and spectacular items, be they earthquakes or court cases; the other is that of informing the people of the intentions and actions of those in power. Sometimes, as in a strike or a war, the two come together. Most of the time, political actions are constructed according to the demands of the spectacular, so political parties "split," they do not disagree; strikes are a "confrontation" rather than a bargaining tactic. The most favored form of spectacular model for political events is that of conflict between opposing institutions: government and opposition; trade unions and employers; trade unions and governments; Britain and the world; the West and Russia, etc. This adversarial pattern has suited the dominant representation of the world; it can ignore the Third World and China, parliamentary parties like the Liberals, the whole of extra-parliamentary political activity of both left and right and new political and social forces like the feminist movement. Such political factors do not make a routine appearance as "news": their newsworthiness depends upon spectacular events: a military coup, a trade agreement with Britain, natural disasters, the disruption of a "Miss World" competition.

The adversarial definition of political events has also constructed TV's notion of "balance" in their coverage. If political events are constituted by two opposing forces, then TV's role as neutral observer, reporter and interrogator would seem to lie in the center: holding the balance between the two sides. This is, indeed, how TV's role has been interpreted in the coverage of domestic affairs. In foreign affairs, TV has every right to be as chauvinistic and racist as it likes. There may be balance within the domestic political arena, but there is none in the coverage of international affairs. So the concept of balance effectively means occupying a central position in relation to domestic political events. This central position enables the TV institution to appear both unbiased (in the sense of not favoring one or other position) and commonsensical (in the sense of representing a "possible compromise" between the two positions). This is TV's balancing act with balance. The concept of the newsworthy allied with the privileged access given to institutions of power creates the terrain upon which it can take place.

The complexities of politics are denied by this process, as are the areas of life beyond the orthodox institutions of power. Trade unions have a particularly uneasy relationship with this concept of balance. It is a concept that allows access to the trade union bureaucracy, but not to shop stewards, the base (and often "unruly" base) of the trade union movement. The result is that the politics of the trade union movement itself tends to be travestied, and the nature of labor disputes is often misapprehended by TV news.

Balance is a concept that is central to the ways in which TV constructs its vision of domestic political events. Its current use in TV implies that TV is central, holding a neutral middle ground between opposing forces, seeking a compromise position or playing "devil's advocate" by presenting the view of the right to the spokesperson of the left, and vice-versa. This has led to the elaboration of a specific TV rhetoric to describe political situations. There are "moderates" and "extremists"; "moderates" are those who are nearer to the TV central position in any particular situation. It is quite possible for those who are moderates in one situation to become extremists in another: the so-called moderate candidate in an election for an important trade union post can become an extremist in a dispute with employers or government. The categories have no meaning except as derogatory or complimentary terms from the point of view of a centralist TV position.

However, the strenuous application of this centralist position under the banner of balance has finally produced effects within the political arena. It has made possible the conception of a political party whose self-presentation is that of being "the party of the center, the party of moderation." Hence the recent emergence in British politics of the Social Democratic Party, whose rhetoric of centrality is in marked contrast to that of the other third party in British parliamentary politics, the Liberal Party. Where the Liberal Party's self-image was that of the party of mavericks, the party of ideas and originality, the Social Democratic Party has fastened on to the political rhetoric sanctioned by TV coverage of current political affairs. The SDP claims to be the party of centrality, of moderation, of compromise.

The emergence of a political party that claims the center ground as its own is a serious challenge to TV's painstaking construction of balance from a position of centrality. The whole adversarial representation of the domestic political arena, the construction of TV as a neutral, centralist institution within this adversarial system, these are both challenged by the emergence of a political party which uses the very rhetoric that TV creates from its centralist position. The institution of balance from a position of centrality has reached the summit of its achievement in the creation of a political party which makes flesh the rhetoric of TV, but it also poses a serious problem for the operation and justification of the notion of "balance."

Balance, despite its current problems and its inherent fictional nature, still constructs the institution of TV as occupying a central position in the life of the nation. TV is central in its political position of compromise and moderation; it is central in that it is a privileged means of gaining political knowledge. These centralities are further reinforced by the spread of genres that TV uses, which effectively provide a kind of lexicon of human life and emotions. The TV salesman in Sirk's *All That Heaven Allows* (1955) describes the set as giving "All the company you want: drama, comedy, life's parade at your fingertips." In the film, this is the moment of deepest hopelessness for the widow played by Jane Wyman. Appropriately enough, since TV does have an aura of presenting "the whole of life," if only because of its ever-present nature. But this presentation of everything (or everything that counts) is always under the form of various genres. These split "life's parade" into particular definitions, particular forms of attention. The spread of genres in TV defines the spread of definitions and attentions that are given to human life within the gaze of TV. Some aspects are emphasized, some disappear almost entirely; some combinations of ideas and experiences are ruled out. TV's generic system reinforces the centralist position that TV constructs for itself by the series of definitions (and consequent silences) that it involves.

The generic definition underpinning the whole of TV's broadcast output is the distinction between fact and fiction. A program has to be one or the other: at limits it can be a fictionalization based upon or using historical fact. But the corollary (a factualization of a fiction) is an impossibility. The distinction is vitally important for TV because it defines two basic forms of attention and their consequent production techniques and audience expectations. A factual program is one in which the concept of balance may well come into play (especially if it refers to a domestic political issue). It is one in which TV observes and reports the world beyond TV: the world of people or animals; of sport, model railway enthusiasts or doctors; of the conflict between man and nature, the co-existence of different species. Here the gaze of TV presents and interprets. It does not interfere, organize, construct or fictionalize events. The category of "fact" is therefore an ethical position as well as a generic definition. It implies a particular relationship between broadcast TV and the raw material for its programs. Factual programs are those in which the activity of program-making interferes to the least possible degree, aiming instead to preserve the truth and integrity of that which is presented to TV's gaze.

Fiction, on the other hand, is the area in which events are created for the gaze of TV. In fiction, the element of personal view is permitted to intrude to structure the material of the program. Hence the privileged position given to the writer and, in some areas, to the director as the structuring consciousness of fictional output. Fiction is therefore the area in which particular interpretations of events can be produced without considering the formal demands of balance. However, this means that fiction is by and large kept away from the area of contentious political events, and from public controversy that has no clear moral position implied within it. It is by no means infrequent for a British broadcasting institution to replace an advertised fiction program because its subject has become too contentious. Similarly, British TV institutions are unwilling to produce more than the isolated example of a militantly left-wing program, even though there are numerous writers and directors within an orthodox TV aesthetic who could produce such material. Fiction implies a particular vision; but the range of possible visions is distinctly limited by the fear of political controversy and possible accusations of bias that is shared by senior TV executives.

The broad distinction between fact and fiction in TV output underpins the more flexible distinctions between different program genres. These genres are defined in terms of content, for factual programs (sport, news, current affairs discussion, interview, chat show, etc.), and in terms of formal definitions, for fiction (comedy, play, film, soap opera). These broad definitions of genre are steadily refined by the use of the series form: within each genre there are different series which are distinguished both by their content and by their form of attention to it. Thus *Nationwide* treats a range of domestic/political subjects (fit for the family feeding time) with an amount of amateurish humor mixed in; but *Panorama* (later on a Monday night on the same channel) consists of a filmed report from a particular political context, with a studio debate or interview. Each item is sustained, lasting up to thirty minutes. Thus *Panorama* tends to cast its gaze upon the world's trouble-spots, and to interview prominent political personalities, interrogating them about their current positions, if any. *Nationwide* is an intensely domestic arena, presenting consumer issues, short interviews with individuals who have achieved a temporary noteriety (local councilors who have banned a film from their cinemas), and even an "eccentric" (someone carrying out research on toilet seats or slugs). Similarly, the various fiction series define different attentions to a particular topic: within police fictions there are those which concentrate on violence and the glamor of dealing with "real villains" (*The Sweeney*); those which emphasize the caring, community aspects of police work (*The Gentle Touch*); those that highlight the problems of police corruption (*The Chinese Detective*). Each centers on particular definitions of power and character within the police force; each defines its own vision of the police force which obstinately cannot be reconciled with each other.

TV's centrality is defined by its insistence on the domestic; its conception of balance in its political coverage; and use of generically defined output to "describe" the world. All of this is framed within a definition of intelligibility which is not unlike that which was developed by the American mass cinema in the classic period. Like the output of the classic mass entertainment cinema, the wide gamut of TV output is not meant to appeal to everyone indiscriminately; however, it is meant to be intelligible to everyone. Broadcast TV is the inheritor of mass cinema in this respect: it has inherited a belief in the universal intelligibility (within one nation-state) of particular sets of formal procedures. These underlie the planning of the industrial production procedure, which is designed to yield this easily intelligible set of standard forms. The rules of intelligibility encompass forms of transition and classification of material (the news transition from neutral newsreader to "subjective" on-the-spot witness reporting to "our own correspondent" producing comment, analysis and prediction). It instrumentalizes the TV image (so that one image is held until it has been used as information, then cut to another image), and uses conventions of sound/image relations (the voice-over, and synchronized dialogue both with ascribed sources). The construction of a form of intelligibility (some would call it "transparency") by TV is the final and founding component of its construction of a central position for itself: it is central to the informational and entertainment lives of its huge audiences; it is centralist in its attitudes; it is central to the culture of the moving image because it defines a norm of intelligibility against which other procedures (film or video) are implicitly judged.

However, this ideological centrality, allied with an industrial mode of program production, produces a powerful tendency towards conservatism within broadcast TV institutions. In these circumstances, TV looks toward cinema as one of the main sources for innovation. Not only does TV use cinema as a source of entertainment material, but it also looks to it as a source of new ideas, because it is very difficult to generate new ideas within the structures of TV institutions. Cinema is seen as an area in which new styles of shooting and editing can be pioneered; and equally new forms of subject matter. It was up to cinema rather than TV in the USA to develop ways of approaching the ideological problem that Vietnam represents. Hence a spate of films about Vietnam, dealing with the war itself as an incomprehensible event on to which American soldiers can project their fantasies or inadequacies (*Go Tell the Spartans*, 1978); or as an act of collective insanity (*Apocalypse Now*, 1979); or showing the problems of veterans returning to a society hostile to them as reminders of what is "best forgotten" (*Coming Home*, 1978); as well as standard forms of oblique reference to veteran as a social problem (providing motivation for dramatically interesting social misfits like muggers or bank robbers). Broadcast TV was subsequently able to ingest these approaches to the topic.

Some broadcast TV institutions acknowledge this relationship between cinema and TV. Some few of them straightforwardly subsidize radical forms of cinema production (albeit on minimal budgets), and regard the broadcasting of the resultant films as distinctly secondary to their life in the cinema. An example is the German ZDF's weekly *Das Kleine Fernsehspiel* slot, which has subsidized the work of such filmmakers as Rosa von Praunheim, Stephen Dwoskin and Helka Sander. Channel Four in Britain has institutionalized a relationship with a cinematic form of production by purchasing its production from independent producers rather than adopting an industrial production model. Whilst half of its programs come from the existing industrial giants that dominate the ITV channel, other material is produced in a way that closely resembles film production with its film-by-film pattern of production. Whether or not the adoption of this model of production will guarantee that the finished programs show any originality when compared to other British TV work is another question. It depends finally on the kind of politico-aesthetic decisions that are taken within the Channel's own hierarchy.

Hence broadcast TV's very centrality brings it into a close relationship with cinema. Cinema for its part stands or falls on its differences from this central presence of TV. Cinema no longer needs to occupy a central position, with the consequent demands for intelligibility and unexceptionability. Cinema has ceased to be dominated by a simple conception of mass cinema, although certain crucial components of this conception still remain. In particular, the conception of "a film" developed in the classic period of American cinema still survives in a series of cinema practices. However, it could be said that cinema has become more visibly fragmented than it was within the classic period. In the classic period, the pattern of an American-dominated mass cinema with a series of marginalized practices of film production and exhibition (European art cinema, non-theatrical documentary work, etc.) is the more or less stable pattern for most of the world's cinemas. Nowadays, the term "cinema" covers a series of diverse practices both of production and exhibition.

To a great extent, a complimentarity exists between cinema and broadcast TV: cinema doing (some of) the things that TV cannot, for technical, aesthetic, economic or social reasons. But the relationship between the media is not only one of complementarity; it is equally one of mutual dependence. In performing roles that TV cannot, cinema makes several direct contributions to TV. First, it can develop prototypes for new forms of fiction or new forms of textual construction that TV can then adapt and adopt. The level of automation of TV production makes any dramatic innovation very difficult; just as the Hollywood studio system once made cinematic innovation difficult. So cinema provides a point at which experimentation can be found, which often has a fairly direct influence on TV. Equally, cinema can pioneer and render more acceptable certain areas of representation, certain subject matters, so that they, too, can be taken up by TV. Second, cinema is able to provide a certain amount of material directly for TV: the practice of screening old feature films on TV is established virtually everywhere that TV is used. This provides TV with spectacular material far cheaper than it could possibly manufacture for itself, even on an international level. The practice provides more as well: it sets cinema up as a particular kind of reference point for TV. Cinema is constituted as "better" than TV (more big stars, more big spectacles, etc.), but also as more adventurous, a belief that some TV channels have used in order to introduce more adventurous material than would be possible if it were made directly for TV only, and within the institutions of TV manufacture. Both ZDF in Germany and the British Channel Four use cinema as this kind of political and aesthetic Trojan Horse.

Cinema needs TV as well: it is a relationship of mutual dependency. Cinema now has a strong financial dependency on TV for many of its diverse financial operations. The financing of large-scale feature film production takes into account the eventual sale to TV, which is often arranged as a "pre-sale," where the TV channel effectively becomes a co-producer. The financing of radical, independent work also depends on TV financing in various places where TV adopts a "Trojan Horse" strategy. Often, this dependence become excessive, as other possible sources of finance (state funding, private sources) tend to fade away, and the existence of a radical and independent sector becomes dependent upon the internal decisions of a TV channel. Cinema also depends upon TV aesthetically: a certain consciousness of the history of cinema can be gained from TV screening of old films, especially, as on French TV, where this is actively encouraged by screenings of seasons of films along with intelligent critical commentaries of various kinds, both on TV itself, and in critical magazines. Cinema also assumes a certain level of facility of reading images and sounds on the part of its audience; this, too, is a product of habitual use of TV. TV enables cinema to assume rather more from its audiences. These relationships of mutual dependency between TV and cinema are by no means easy ones: there is the perpetual accusation from cinema that TV gets films "too cheap" and is therefore directly contributing to the financial instability of cinema and the consequent closure of cinema halls. Neither are the relations between the two media the same in each country, and they are, by definition, shifting relations, taking different forms at different times.

In two distinct ways cinema has developed away from the classic model of a mass cinema with marginal forms. One direction maintains many of the features of the mass cinema: its basic conception of "a film" and its attitudes to the nature of film exhibition. The other, dealt with in the next chapter, tends to move beyond these conceptions to produce a number of "active audiences," using the public and collective nature of cinema exhibition to develop new relationships between spectators and film or video material. The first direction is that chiefly represented by the so-called commercial cinema, whose products are often re-used by broadcast TV and form a staple of the growing home video market. It produces films which can still be treated as objects for consumption, intelligible on their own to the audiences that they define for themselves. The second direction reuses material from the commercial cinema, putting it into contexts that can alter its meanings and its nature as experience. It is also the area of independent cinema production and exhibition; and of the use of film or video in a public context that often goes beyond traditional cinema halls. It has a much more hesitant and sporadic relationship with the institutions of broadcast TV.

The commercial cinema has undergone a gradual transformation since the arrival of mass broadcast TV in the early 1950s. A number of strategies were attempted, during the 1950s, to compete with broadcast TV on its own terms, particularly since the technical and aesthetic quality of early broadcast TV in the USA was not great. Cinema emphasized the physical superiority of its projected image in a series of technical "improvements" (Cinemascope, Widescreen, VistaVision, 3-D, etc.) which resulted overall in a certain loss of projected picture quality. It also boasted the superiority of its capital base in a series of spectacular productions that culminated in the débâcle of *Cleopatra* (1963). Since this initial period, another strategy has emerged, which aims to complement and supplement broadcast TV rather than to challenge it directly. There are two interlinked aspects to this strategy. The first exploits cinema's ability to produce prototypes rather than series: it produces films at a variety of budgetary levels that initiate and develop a particular narrative conception and problematic. Such films can indeed result in TV series being built from them. This conception of cinema is that which is current in the more "mainstream" or "entertainment" areas of commercial cinema: it leads to blockbusters with huge promotion budgets like *Star Wars*, and *Alien*, as well as more modestly budgeted (but equally thoroughly worked out) films like *Escape from New York* (1981) or *Twilight's Last Gleaming* (1977), to cite random but related examples. Its films are conceived of as entertainment events which require no special skills or knowledges on the part of their potential audiences, apart from the general (and culturally acquired) ability to make sense of the current fashions in narrative film-making, and the more diffuse "general knowledge" of Western culture. The particular area of this general knowledge that the film exploits will be indicated in the narrative image that surrounds and gives a context of the film from very basic presuppositions. *Twilight's Last Gleaming* assumes a public knowledge of the fact of silos containing nuclear weapons, the general belief that it is possible for such weapons to be launched by mechanical error or by individual human initiative, and a sense of the massive dislocation to the American military and its personnel caused by the Vietnam War. These knowledges lend plausibility to the film's narrative, and are developed (and hence explained, reinforced and, as it were, verified) during the course of the narration.

But *Twilight's Last Gleaming* is also a rather difficult film for British film exhibition. It was released in a cut-down version in Britain, reduced from 146 minutes to 122 minutes. Its difficulty lies chiefly in its split-screen sequences, which combine multiple images of interlinked spaces and events, shown "directly" by film, and "indirectly" by video surveillance cameras. These compress much of the action, and pose severe problems for spectatorship: the problems of knowing which way to look when; the problems of having a de-centered form of attention.

Added to this, the film aimed to make an argument about the nature of American political power and geopolitics. Faced with such a film, the British distributors opted to reduce it to its thriller aspects. So the case of *Twilight's Last Gleaming* demonstrates a trend within the commercial entertainment cinema which British interests, notoriously conservative, frequently have difficulty in dealing with. The commercial entertainment film still habitually begins from the premises that are cultural commonplaces, and with ideas that have an immediate place in the small change of everyday life. But they can then extend beyond the constructions of what they can assume everyone will know. Entertainment films can develop their narratives to the extent of launching a critique of the American governmental system that would be impossible on American TV, or indeed on British TV, if it occurred on a program made directly for TV. They can also complicate their narration by introducing elliptical or enigmatic sequences and encounters; by developing dense thematic parallels between characters and actions; by a limited use of techniques (like split-screen) that disorient the spectator. The demands of immediate and universal intelligibility no longer apply so rigidly and directly to the commercial entertainment film. They apply instead to broadcast TV.

Commercial cinema still maintains a certain level of production that appeals to an immediate intelligibility in its largest scale productions, the so-called blockbusters. Such films become general cultural events through their skillful and massive use of publicity, expenditure on which is planned to exceed expenditure on the film's production. Films like *Jaws* (1975), *Star Wars* (1977), *Raiders of the Lost Ark* (1981) or the James Bond cycle (from 1962) represent cinema's attempt to maximize its audience and to draw in spectators who rarely see films in cinemas. Hence they often conform to a simpler form of intelligibility, substituting spectacular effects for complexity of narration and event. However important such films are to the economics of the industry, and to the maintenance of the general conception of what constitutes "a film," such productions are relatively rare and isolated events in cinema film production. Signalled in advance, discussed endlessly before they are seen, they can be few in number: overproduction of blockbusters would reduce their cultural impact. Instead, the normal run of films (whose budgets are often large) normally seeks out a certain difficulty and specificity of address.

Blockbusters and more specialized films alike comprise a commercial cinema which has a central marketing function within modern society. Broadcast TV's output is largely resistant to advertising as specific cultural events; however, cinema films depend upon such marketing. So a large component of the current commercial cinema is the way in which it practices marketing of individual films and of cinema itself. Individual films are established with a particular narrative image which enhances considerably their marketability on TV as well as in cinemas. A notably successful piece of marketing was the film *Jaws* (1975), which in due time attracted a vast TV audience. This audience was much larger than that for Spielberg's earlier made-for-TV film, *Duel* (1971) could possibly have been, simply because of the cinema-based marketing to which *Jaws* was treated. But cinema's marketing does not only rebound to the benefit of individual films. Cinema, equally, is the arena in which stars can be created: actors whose contradictory images are constituted as continuing paradoxes for spectators. Cinema still remains the central place for the production of stars because it offers single self-contained films rather than series re-production of the same basic performance. Broadcast TV's patterns of repetition militate against the creation of stars from its performers because they generally become associated with one particular performance and one particular basic problematic. They also appear too intimate and domestic, lacking the dimensions of distance and difference that cinematic performance will tend to give them. Hence TV personalities are made stars through the action of cinema and its marketing devices. They can then return, enhanced, to broadcast TV activities.

The major strategy adopted by commercial cinema both in its marketing and in construction of individual films has been to produce films whose address has been quite clearly directed to a specific fraction of the population. This address does not exclude other people from the audience (i.e. still rests its appeal on generally shared cultural definitions). Rather, it is an approach that guarantees that the films will diverge from the mass conception of thematic material that dominates broadcast TV. Hence a diversity of particular "interest groups" is catered for directly in commercial cinema production. These are often groups that have a relatively large amount of disposable income, so there is a certain circularity in the process: cinema tends to address its films toward those fractions of the community that recognize themselves in various forms of activity, one of which is cinema attendance. So in addition to the obvious specific audiences that cinema addresses, those of "youth culture," gay culture, the Women's Movement, one major facet of cinema's address of its films is to the culturally sophisticated. Hence commercial films which cautiously ease themselves into areas which connote "culture": the use, for instance, of Baroque music in American films about mature problems of married life (Pachelbel in *Ordinary People* (1980); Vivaldi as the organizing structure of *The Four Seasons* (1981)). Another index of cultural sophistication is the element of self-consciousness that has invaded commercial cinema. Extensive broadcast TV screening of old entertainment films has created a new "public memory" of cinema, as well as recreating the images that compose those films by cutting about 15 per cent off their edges (the phenomenon of "video cut-off"). Despite this loss of edges, the center still holds, so contemporary cinema can be self-conscious about its narration (making some devices obvious to the viewer) because it can assume a certain knowledge of Hollywood cinema in its audience. The result is a large number of films that trade upon their knowingness, placing the audience in a position of colluding with the film in mocking a supposed naive audience. Such is the position of *Raiders of the Lost Ark*, camping in relation to the B-features and adventure serials of classic Hollywood. Equally, sophistication about the tradition and history of the cinema can lead to the work of a Robert Altman, whose career has consisted to a large degree of un-making the staple genres of classic Hollywood by frustrating and undercutting their presumptions: the war film in *M*A*S*H**, the Western in *McCabe and Mrs. Miller* (1971), the private eye movie in *The Long Goodbye* (1973).

Self-referentiality in the more or less commercial feature film has two different facets. One is that which tends to be taken up within a mainstream production that seeks to maximize its audience; the other is a feature of a more overtly specialized cinema, an "art" cinema. The first, associated still with maximization of the audience, is a level of reference to the public iconography of the movies: to those figures and genres that have some kind of circulation outside a specifically filmic set of interests. Hence it refers to certain stars whose images (in the form of posters, books of biography laced with stills, etc.) still have a general popular circulation: Humphrey Bogart, Marilyn Monroe. They refer to genres that have a fairly stable identity in the history of cinema: gangster movies, Westerns. It is reference to that small fragment of classic Hollywood that has remained in the public memory, or has been reintroduced as camp or nostalgia. This type of reference is confirming for its audience, in that spectators can "spot the reference" and tend to feel sophisticated in that recognition; it is safe for the film itself, since it can reckon on a certain level of public awareness of the myth of the history of cinema, and the few images from it that still have currency. This level of reference to films themselves cannot be taken as the structuring principle of the film, what organizes it and gives it meaning. At best it can, like *Play It Again Sam* (1972), starring Woody Allen, provide the central obsession for a character in a film. For Woody Allen, the figure of Bogart (impersonated by an actor in the shadows) provides a kind of alter ego, who would do precisely what Allen could never do. So *Play It Again Sam* is another Woody Allen film: playing over the feelings of insecurity and self-congratulating self-depreciation that Allen has made his authorial mark. The reference to Bogart (not to a more obscure star) is incidental to this process. It is a reference to a character that Bogart played only once (in *The Big Sleep*, 1946): Philip Marlowe in a trench coat, an image that has wide currency in the myth of the cinema.

The films of Robert Altman have a rather more complicated relationship to this kind of self-referentiality of modern cinema. To some extent, they remain within the simpler type of reference, which plasters a pastiche of a particular piece of film iconography on to a traditional kind of film, rather like the picture palaces of the 1920s splashed pastiches of architectural style on to brick box buildings. Sometimes, however, Altman produces a more complicated form of reference, which tends to criticize the form that is being pastiched, pointing out the personal inadequacies and idiocies of a man like Philip Marlowe, in a way that is not altogether affectionate. The films have a more uncertain career as a result: they tend to specify their audience and the demand they make on their spectators in a way that can conflict with the drive to maximize the audience.

Some of Altman's films are characterized by concerns that have more traditionally been associated with the "art cinema." This area of production and exhibition has defined its audience as "different from" the audience for mass entertainment films. To some extent, exhibition defines "art cinema" rather more than interests within film production. Films from European countries often become "art films" when exported, where they are recognized as national cinema (and rather superior as a result) in their country of origin. Such was the case with the films produced by Ealing Studios in Britain in the period 1944-56. Seen as notable entertainment films in Britain, they became "art films" abroad. They had different exhibition patterns: in Britain, they went out on the normal Rank circuit release, as first features in Odeon or Gaumont cinemas, showing for one week only, right across a particular geographic locality (North London, South London, the North-East, etc.). In the USA and France, the career of those films that were released tended to be different: they were shown typically for extended runs (more than a week) in specialized cinemas in major population centers, and were subsequently absorbed by film-clubs, college circuits, etc. Such is the pattern of art cinema exhibition, the kind of exhibition that is given to "Continental" films that are shown in Britain. However, for various reasons, Britain has scarcely developed a network of art cinema venues outside London.

This pattern of exhibition makes available films that are not considered suitable for the mass cinema circuits, and hence defines a different audience. It tends to produce an area of film production when the cinema network begins to approach financial viability. This "art cinema" in exhibition and in production has two major tendencies within it, which could be subsumed under the names of two French directors: Godard and Truffaut. The category of "director" (the creator of the art) is central to the way in which criticism deals with art cinema, so perhaps the use of these authorial titles is appropriate. Truffaut represents a rather more reactionary end of art cinema: his films are (increasingly) conservative in their form, becoming indistinguishable from the more crafted product of entertainment cinema (many of whose young personnel in USA would recognize Truffaut as "a major influence on their lives"; probably along with their mothers). Truffaut brings a characteristic "vision" to his films: they are essentially humanist, concerned with individuals trying to make sense of their world, and cautiously testing the ground in personal relations. The terms applied to his films by critics and audiences alike are those of "warmth and humanity," "understanding," "wry humor." Their concern is with individuals, whose portrayal is considerably aided by the skills in dramatic understatement developed by French cinema acting.

This humanism and conservatism of form contrasts strongly with the work of Godard, whose films throughout the 1960s created something of a scandal each time a new one appeared. Godard's films have a central concern with the problems of representation: character becomes a problem for them rather than a refuge because they seek to portray the character of individuals as constructed by circumstance (and changed by circumstance) rather than as a stable entity to be explored. Equally, the films became increasingly aware through the 1960s first of the limitations of filmic portrayal, then increasingly of the social role of filmic portrayal, and of the ideological role of images and sounds in society. Godard's films can never be said to be conservative in their form: often they are seen as puzzling or obscure, making demands on their audiences that are out of line with their expectations.

These two approaches (from directors with similar beginnings in cinema) can be taken as synoptic of two tendencies within modern art cinema, a splitting of audience into two different perspectives. One seeks a humanistic portrayal of personal problems of a kind that is not considered usual in commercial cinema. The other looks to specialized cinema to provide films that challenge them on a formal aesthetic level as well as providing a radical set of concerns on other levels as well. Both of these "tastes" still rest at the level of a traditional definition of "a film" as a self-sufficient entity, though in some areas the work inspired by Godard's films has had to move away from this conception, and much of his work in the 1970s was concerned with the possibilities of broadcast TV and video.

The work of Altman represents a new development that began in the early 1970s in which entertainment cinema, in its search for identifiable audiences, began to produce films aimed more specifically towards the audience which had traditionally identified itself with art cinema. This meant a subtle series of changes in the expectations that films made of their audiences. It became possible to produce highly elliptical narratives which substituted the longueurs and the "gaps in between" for the classic cinema's concentration on the narratively significant actions and their chains of consequences. This tendency has usually been mollified by the continued demand to maximize audiences within a more adventurous aesthetic strategy. The interests backing such commercial-art features have wanted to hedge their bets as far as possible. Nevertheless, an erosion of the action-centered nature of the classic narrative form has tended to take place during the 1970s in American production. In Europe, the tendency has been far more marked, with major American-owned distributors like United Artists financing the work of established art cinema directors like Fellini or Bertolucci. This is more the acquisition of already established commodities (star directors) than a move into new terrain as has tended to happen in the USA itself.

Commercial cinema's move towards the terrain traditionally occupied by art cinema is one aspect of a general trend within commercial film-making from the latter half of the 1960s. Commercial cinema's response to the prevalence of broadcast TV has been to move out of competition with it. The amorphous mass market has been abandoned to broadcast TV; the commercial cinema has begun to explore and exploit other definitions of audience. This is strikingly similar to the kind of strategy that gave birth to art cinema in several European countries in the 1920s. Commercial film production and exhibition has moved towards different definitions of its audience, in terms of specialized interests ("minority" groups; pornography; specialized interests like rock music; art cinema interests). In doing so, cinema production has cautiously begun to define itself as different from broadcast TV. It tends to be different in the kind of subjects it treats; its willingness to enter into certain controversies, even political ones; its distance from the direct control of state or para-state institutions; its attitude to the kinds of forms of narration and *mise-en-scène* that it can use. Commercial cinema can assume more of its audience than broadcast TV, or can be more exploitative, offering dubious or objectionable material. It can attempt to provide entertainment for those who are dissatisfied with broadcast TV, providing, of course, that they can afford the price of a cinema seat. However, this tendency within commercial cinema remains within the regime of a traditional conception of the film as a self-sufficient entity. It still assumes that a film should be in and of itself intelligible and not require any specific knowledges on the part of its audience other than a diffuse cultural awareness gathered from everyday life. In this sense, all that has happened is that commercial film-making has realized something of the diversity of modern culture, and has begun to realize that "mass culture" is composed of many specific facets, attitudes and knowledges rather than being a single monolith (as the pessimistic theorists of the Frankfurt School feared).

Equally, the commercial cinema in its diversified form has entered into a close relationship with the institutions of broadcast TV. In this area, there is not a distinct separation of terrains: broadcast TV dealing with a mass audience, and cinema catering to a more specified and distinct set of audiences. Instead, broadcast TV uses cinema as a central aspect of its own output; and commercial cinema looks towards broadcast TV as a vital source of finance. Broadcast TV looks to cinema to provide a particular conception of "film": not only the self-sufficient, generally intelligible entertainment, but a work at a particular budgetary level and creation of narrative image that broadcast TV institutions can only rarely afford to provide directly. Commercial cinema has tended to integrate the expectation of sale to TV in the overall financing of film production; sometimes this has gone further, with joint cinema/ TV production arrangements being formalized. These tendencies keep cinema production within a particular traditional conception of a film, and compromise its moves towards catering for more diversified conceptions of possible audiences.

From *Visible Fictions: Cinema: Television: Video*. London, Boston: Routledge & Kegan Paul PLC, 1982, pp. 224-50.

Filmgoing/Videogoing: Making Distinctions

Douglas Davis

THINKING ABOUT THE DIFFERENCES between video and film—which is nothing less than thinking about the essences of each—must begin in the experience of seeing. What we see depends upon how we see, and where, and when. There is the experience of going out to see a film, an experience that begins early in our lives, with the approach of the theater marquee, the press of the crowds, the seat found in the darkness, and then the huge, overpowering screen, larger than any imaginable life, images as big as a child imagines a building to be. Later the act of perception takes place in a dwindled space, brought on by reaching adulthood, and by the change in taste. The screen may be smaller, the noises around us less exuberant, but still we have gone to this space, gone out to sit in the dark before large, moving images. We go "out" to see a painting or a drawing, too, to a public place, to a museum or a gallery, or a cathedral. Since the nineteenth century, however, since the growth of an audience that could purchase works of art and hang them in private spaces (instead of an audience limited to princes and cathedrals), we have seen in these museums or galleries works intended for small, private spaces, for city apartments, and suburban homes. We see them even in the public museum in environments grown increasingly intimate; we focus in upon these images in light directed so as to draw us further inside them: we focus, stand, and then move on, noiselessly, from one work to another, in control of our own time. The scale of man to image is equalized, particularly in this century, when the epic or public painting has only lately begun to appear again. And then there is the experience of seeing video.

Think about this act, this totality of perception. It falls somewhere between the experiences I have just described, between film and painting. A small screen, lit from within, its moving images paradoxically built, as E.H. Gombrich points out, on the physical limitation of our vision; our eyes cannot keep up with the luminous dot that sweeps continually across the inner face of that tube. We do not go out to see video. We turn it on without any sense of occasion; often, indeed, we turn it on unconsciously and leave it there, the images moving across the screen, the sounds emerging from their tiny speakers without our knowing. The focusing, as in painting and drawing and sculpture, is inward, onto something. (While watching a film, the eye looks up and out; the mind is drawn helplessly away from itself, into a larger-than-life existence.) We give video our attention, not the reverse; even in moments of absorption the screen is left without compunction, for a drink, a phone call, an errand. There is no one around me, usually, that I do not know. Often I am alone before the screen, as I might choose to be alone before a painting. Yet there is a felt link to some larger consensus. The viewer is alone but he knows, subconsciously, that he is part of an audience, whose remaining members he can neither see nor hear.

The video experience is not, I am trying to suggest, a simple experience. It has affinities with film, painting, and theater, but there are as many contradictions. Even the experience we know, difficult enough to understand, is changing. Televisions screens are growing larger; audiences are becoming lonelier, more individuated, thanks to cable television, half-inch videotape, and videocassettes, all of which provide specialized programming choices. Our attitude toward the screen—of which this essay is a part—is becoming more self-conscious. Even so, it is clear that video's affinity with other media, and particularly with film, is conditional. *How* we see it, physically and psychically, is the major condition. Film performers, seen on the street, carry an aura; they can overpower us, in real life. Video performers remind their public— when seen in the street—of next-door neighbors; we reach out to shake their hands instinctively.

If I seem to be describing a medium that is less iconic in its nature than film, remember that I am doing so from a basis in perception. If we are going to capture video as a medium for high, difficult, and intense art, we will do so only by utilizing it for its own sake. Artist, critic, and public must act on the certain basis of how video is seen. The painter does not need to think this issue through; he knows (without knowing) the perceptual system into which his work will fit. So does the filmmaker. From the earliest age he is engaged in that perceptual system. We are all moviegoers first, even those of us who were weaned on video. For television has not yet been defined. From its inception, it has been controlled by men and women forced to pay for its existence by reaching an impossibly wide audience. We have not seen video yet.

Television until now has been made by sensibilities conditioned in popular fiction, film, and theater. I cannot think of a completely equivalent case in the history of the arts. It is the case of an enormously rich and potential medium coming to birth in the hands of people forbidden (by economics) to discover its essence.

This is precisely why artists untrained in either television, film, or the theater are beginning to show us more about video than we've yet dreamed of. This awakening has nothing to do with the technology of half-inch videotape except insofar as its appearance made personal investigations possible, as the arrival of the easel painting (as distinct from the frieze or the fresco) made another art accessible. It has to do with thinking afresh, looking at video for the first time. I cannot stress too much the necessity of this freshness. When I talk to students about video I always begin by asking them what "television" is (because I don't know myself) and we always conclude, at the end of the session, that we aren't sure of very much. The more I work in it, the less I know. Nam June Paik once told me that he always discovers more in his work when he sees it broadcast than he put into it. James Rosenquist once refused to work in experimental video because the screen wasn't large enough. "Come back when it is at least three feet by five feet," he said. He brought the conditions of painting to bear on what he saw, as a filmmaker might, who fills up the tiny screen with epic-sized images. There is nothing more intriguing to me than the size—and the variety of the size—of the video screen. I once telecast on cable in New York City a color tape (*Studies in Color Videotape II*) that focuses upon a moving red light image at the very end. Depending upon the size, shape, and nature of the receiving set, the viewers saw many different lights, in some cases highly luminous, multicolored images. The reactions depended on the condition of the set, which is a condition of the medium to be faced and used, not denied.

Let me return again to where and how we see video, to catch it there in a very special moment. Alone once more, in the home, not formally seated, or surrounded by large numbers of people. In that moment, we can also be connected to the uncertainty of real life. Film is always prepared for us, its time telescoped by the making hand. In the theater we inhabit the same time in which the players perform, but we know that the next step, and the step after that, has been predetermined by the playwright. What we have come to call "live" video links with "life" in a highly concentrated form; when we are watching "live" phenomena on the screen we participate in a subtle existentialism. Often it is so subtle that it nears boredom. Yet we stay, participating. The endless moon walk, the endless convention, the endless (in another way) *An American Family,* an open-ended *verité* documentary of a California couple telecast by the Public Broadcasting Service in 1973. In all these cases, the "live" dimension kept its audience there, before the small screen, alone, at home, waiting, because it knows that anything may happen next. I mention *An American Family* deliberately; though edited, it made less attempt to structure and pace narrative events than any popular television series yet. Often long stretches of meaningless, boring conversation were allowed to play out, unstructured. "Live" time approached life time. For this reason, and because we knew the *Family* was "real," we stayed, waiting, aware that something unpredictably "live" might occur next.

Video is not life, of course, any more than any art is. Unlike the other arts, though, it approaches the pace and predictability of life, and is seen in a perceptual system grounded in the home and the self. I do not know how we moviegoers are going to understand this, thoroughly, but we must. The link between the formal occasion that is film and the private occasion that is video must be both recognized and forgotten. There will be no video art until we approach this medium as if it had not existed before.

From *Artculture: Essays on the Post-Modern*. New York: Harper and Row, 1977, pp. 79-84.

Bibliography

Chloe Aaron. "The Video Underground." *Art in America* 59 (May 1971): pp. 74-79.

Aesthetics and Politics. Ernst Bloch, Georg Lukacs, Bertolt Brecht, Walter Benjamin, Theodor Adorno. London: New Left Books, 1977.

Albright-Knox Art Gallery. *Vasulka. Steina: machine vision/Woody: descriptions*. Organized by Linda L. Cathcart. Buffalo, NY: Buffalo Fine Arts Academy, 1978.

Louis Althusser. *For Marx*. Trans. Ben Brewster. New York: Vintage Books, 1970.

Louis Althusser. *Montesquieu, Rousseau, Marx: Politics and History*. Trans. Ben Brewster. London: Verso Editions and New Left Books, 1982.

Louis Althusser and Etienne Balibar. *Reading Capital*. Trans. Ben Brewster. London: New Left Books, 1970.

The American Federation of Arts, New York. *A History of the American Avant-Garde Cinema* (exhibition catalogue), 1976.

American Film Institute. *National Video Festival 1981—*. Washington, DC: The American Film Institute, 1981—.

Victor Ancona. "Nam June Paik: Portrait of an Electronic Artist." *Videography* 1, No. 4 (1976).

David Antin. "Television: Video's Frightful Parent." *Artforum* 14 (December 1975): pp. 36-45.

Rudolf Arnheim. *Film as Art*. Berkeley: University of California Press, 1967.

Artscanada. "The Issue of Video Art." XXX, No. 4 (October 1973).

Arts Magazine. "Video." 49, No. 4 (December 1974).

Art-Rite. "Video." No. 4 (Autumn 1974).

Avalanche Newspaper. "Video Performance." (May/June 1974).

Erik Barnouw. *Documentary*. London: Oxford University Press, 1974.

Erik Barnouw. *The Sponsor*. New York: Oxford University Press, 1978.

Erik Barnouw. *Tube of Plenty*. London: Oxford University Press, 1975.

Roland Barthes. *Camera Lucida*. Trans. Richard Howard. New York: Hill and Wang, 1981.

Roland Barthes. *Critical Essays*. Trans. Richard Howard. Evanston, IL Northwestern University Press, 1972.

Roland Barthes. *Image, Music, Text*. Trans. Stephen Heath. New York: Hill and Wang, 1972.

Roland Barthes. *Mythologies*. Trans. Annette Lavers. New York: Hill and Wang, 1972.

Fred Barzyk. "TV as Art As TV." *Print* 26 (January-February 1972): pp. 20-29.

David Bathrick. "Affirmative and Negative Culture: Technology and the Left Avant-Garde." In *The Technological Imagination: Theories and Fictions*. Madison: Coda Press, Inc., 1980: pp. 107-122.

Gregory Battcock. "Explorations in Video." *Art and Artists* 7 (February 1973): pp. 22-27.

Gregory Battcock. "Nam June Paik Exhibition in New York." *Domus* 559 (June 1976): p. 52.

Gregory Battcock, editor. *The New American Cinema*. New York: E.P. Dutton, 1967.

Gregory Battcock, editor. *New Artists Video: A Critical Anthology*. New York: E.P. Dutton, 1978.

Jean Baudrillard. "Beyond the Unconscious: The Symbolic." *Discourse* 3 (Spring 1981): pp. 60-87.

Jean Baudrillard. *In the Shadow of the Silent Majorities ... or The End of the Social*. Trans. Paul Foss, Paul Patton, John Johnston. New York: Semiotext(e), 1983.

Jean Baudrillard. *The Mirror of Production*. Trans. Mark Poster. St. Louis: Telos Press, 1975.

Jean Baudrillard. *Simulations*. Trans. Paul Foss, Paul Patton, Philip Beitchmann. New York: Semiotext(e), 1983.

Jean Louis Baudry. "Writing, Fiction, Ideology." *Afterimage* (London) 5 (Spring 1974): pp. 22-39.

André Bazin. *What is Cinema?* Essays selected and trans. by Hugh Gray. Berkeley: University of California Press, 1967.

Walter Benjamin. *Charles Baudelaire: A Lyric Poet in the Era of High Capitalism*. Trans. Harry Zohn. London: New Left Books, 1973.

Walter Benjamin. *Reflections*. Ed. Peter Demetz. New York: Harcourt, Brace, Jovanovich, 1978.

Walter Benjamin. *Understanding Brecht*. Trans. Anna Bostock. London: New Left Books, 1973.

John Berger. *About Looking*. New York: Pantheon Books, 1980.

John Berger. *The Look of Things*. New York: Viking Press, 1972.

John Berger. *Ways of Seeing*. London: British Broadcasting Corporation and Penguin Books, 1972.

David Bordwell. "Textual Analysis, Etc." *Enclitic* (Fall 1981/Spring 1982): pp. 125-36.

Pierre Bourdieu. *Outline of a Theory of Practice*. Trans. Richard Nice. Cambridge: Cambridge University Press, 1977.

Pierre Bourdieu and Jean-Claude Passeron. *Reproduction*. Trans. Richard Nice. London: Sage Publications, 1977.

Paul A. Bové. "Celebrity and Betrayal: The High Intellectuals of Post-modern Culture." *The Minnesota Review*, No. 21 (Fall 1983): pp. 72-91.

Paul A. Bové. "Intellectuals at War: Michel Foucault and the Analytics of Power." *Substance 37/38*, XI, No. 4/XII, No. 1 (1983): pp. 36-55.

Paul A. Bové. "Mendacious Innocents, or, The Modern Genealogist as Conscientious Intellectual: Nietzsche, Foucault, Said." *Boundary 2*, IX, No. 3; X, No. 1 (Spring/Fall 1981): pp. 359-388.

Bertolt Brecht. "Radio as a Means of Communication, A Talk on the Function of Radio." Trans. Stuart Hood. *Screen 20,* No. 3/4 (Winter 1979/80): pp. 24-28.

John Brenckman. "Mass Media: From Collective Experience to the Culture of Privatization." *Social Text* 1 (Winter 1979): pp. 94-109.

John Brenckman. "Theses on Cultural Marxism." *Social Text* 7 (Spring/Summer 1983): pp. 19-33.

Susan Buck-Morss. *The Origin of Negative Dialectics*. New York: Free Press, 1977.

Barbara Buckner. "Light and Darkness in the Electronic Landscape." *The Cummington Journal* (1979).

Noël Burch. "Avant-Garde or Vanguard." *Afterimage* (London), 6 (Summer 1976): pp.52-63.

Noël Burch. "Charles Baudelaire v. Dr. Frankenstein." *Afterimage* (London) 8/9 (Spring 1981): pp. 4-21.

Noël Burch and Jorge Dana. "Propositions." *Afterimage* (London) 5 (Spring 1974): pp. 40-66.

Noël Burch. *Theory of Film Practice*. Trans. Helen R. Lane. New York: Praeger, 1973.

Peter Bürger. *Theory of the Avant-Garde*. Trans. Michael Shaw. Theory and History of Literature, vol. 4. Minneapolis: University of Minnesota Press, 1984.

Victor Burgin, editor. *Thinking Photography*. London: Macmillan Press, 1982.

Jack Burnham. "The Aesthetics of Intelligent Systems." In *On the Future of Art*. New York: Viking Press, 1970.

Jack Burnham. *Beyond Modern Sculpture: The Effects of Science and Technology on the Sculpture of This Century*. New York: Praeger, 1972.

Jack Burnham. "Problems of Criticism: Art and Technology." *Artforum* 9 (January 1971): pp. 40-45.

Jack Burnham. *The Structure of Art*. New York: Braziller, 1970.

Jack Burnham. "Systems Aesthetics." *Artforum* 7 (September 1968): pp. 30-35.

Eric Cameron. "The Grammar of the Video Image." *Arts Magazine* 49 (December 1974): pp. 48-51.

Raymond Carney. *American Dreaming: The Films of John Cassavetes and the American Experience*. Berkeley: University of California Press, 1984.

Noël Carroll. "Joan Jonas: Making the Image Visible." *Artforum* 12 (April 1974): pp. 52-53.

Cornelius Castoriadis. *Crossroads in the Labyrinth*. Trans. Kate Soper and Martin H. Ryle. Cambridge: MIT Press, 1984.

Stanley Cavell. *The World Viewed*. Cambridge: Harvard University Press, 1979.

Michael de Certeau. *The Practice of Everyday Life*. Trans. Steven F. Randall. Berkeley: University of California Press, 1984.

Michael Chanan. *The Dream that Kicks*. London: Routledge & Kegan Paul, 1980.

Sue Clayton and Jonathan Curling. "On Authorship." *Screen* 20, No. 1 (Spring 1979): pp. 35-61.

David Curtis. *Experimental Cinema*. New York: Delta, 1971.

Peter D'Agostino, editor. *Transmission*. New York: Tanam Press, 1985.

Fred R. Dallmayr. *Twilight of Subjectivity*. Amherst: University of Massachusetts Press, 1981.

Arthur C. Danto. *The Transfiguration of the Commonplace*. Cambridge: Harvard University Press, 1981.

Douglas Davis. *Art and the Future: A History/Prophecy of the Collaboration Between Science, Technology and Art*. New York: Praeger, 1973.

Douglas Davis. "Art and Technology: The New Combine." *Art in America* 56 (January 1968): pp. 28-47.

Douglas Davis. "Media/Art/Media: Notes Toward a Definition of Form." *Arts Magazine* 46 (September 1971): pp. 43-45.

Douglas Davis. "Television's Avant-Garde." *Newsweek* (February 9, 1970).

Douglas Davis. "Video Obscura." *Artforum* 10 (April 1972): pp. 64-71.

Douglas Davis and Allison Simmons, editors. *The New Television: A Public/Private Art*. Cambridge, MA: MIT Press, 1977.

Régis Debray. *Teachers, Writers, Celebrities.* Trans. David Macey. London: Verso Editions and New Left Books, 1981.

Gilles Deleuze and Félix Guattari. *Anti-Oedipus: Capitalism and Schizophrenia.* Trans. Robert Hurley, Mark Seem, Helen R. Lane. New York: Viking Press, 1977.

Gilles Deleuze and Félix Guattari. *On the Line.* Trans. John Johnston. New York: Semiotext(e), Inc., 1983.

Helen DeMichiel. "Speculations: Narrative Video by Women." *The Independent* 8, No. 3 (April 1985): pp. 12-14.

George Dickie. *Art and Aesthetic.* Ithaca: Cornell University Press, 1974.

David Dickson. "Radical Science and the Modernist Dilemma." In *Issues in Radical Science.* Radical Science 17. Edited by the Radical Science Collective. London: Free Association Books, 1985: pp. 117-37.

Stephen Dwoskin. *Film Is.* Woodstock, NY: Overlook Press, 1975.

Terry Eagleton. "Capitalism, Modernism and Postmodernism." *New Left Review* 152 (July/August 1985): pp. 60-73.

Terry Eagleton. *Criticism and Ideology.* London: Verso Editions, 1978.

Terry Eagleton. "Ideology, Fiction, Narrative." *Social Text* 2 (Summer 1979): pp. 62-80.

Terry Eagleton. *Walter Benjamin, or, Towards a Revolutionary Criticism.* London: Verso Editions and New Left Books, 1981.

Bernard Edelman. *Ownership of the Image.* Trans. Elizabeth Kingdom. London: Routledge & Kegan Paul, 1979.

Roy Edgley and Richard Osborne, editors. *Radical Philosophy Reader.* London: Verso Editions, 1985.

Jacques, Ellul. *The Technological Society.* New York: Knopf, 1964.

Hans Magnus Enzensberger. *Politics and Crime.* New York: Seabury Press, 1974.

The Everson Museum of Art. *Everson Video Revue.* Organized by Richard Simmons. Syracuse, NY: Everson Museum of Art, 1979.

John Fekete. *The Critical Twilight: Explorations in the Ideology of Anglo-American Literary Theory.* London: Routledge & Kegan Paul, 1978.

John Fekete, editor. *The Structural Allegory.* Theory and History of Literature, vol. II. Minneapolis: University of Minnesota Press, 1984.

John L. Fell, editor. *Film Before Griffith.* Berkeley: University of California Press, 1983.

John Fisher, editor. *Perceiving Artworks.* Philadelphia: Temple University Press, 1980.

Philip Fisher. "Pins, A Table, Works of Art." *Representations* 1, No. 1 (February 1983): pp. 43-57.

John Fiske and John Hartley. *Reading Television*. London: Methuen, 1978.

Neil Flax. "Fiction Wars of Art." *Representations* 7 (Summer 1984): pp. 1-25.

Hal Foster, editor. *The Anti-Aesthetic*. Port Townsend, WA: Bay Press, 1983.

Michel Foucault. *The Foucault Reader*. Paul Rabinow, editor. New York: Pantheon Books, 1984

Richard Wightman Fox and T.J. Jackson Lears, editors. *The Culture of Consumption*. New York: Pantheon Books, 1983.

Hollis Frampton. "The Withering Away of the State of the Art." In *Circles of Confusion*. Rochester, NY: Visual Studies Workshop Press, 1983: pp. 161-70.

Hermine Freed. "Video and Abstract Expressionism." *Arts Magazine* 49 (December 1974): pp. 67-69.

Michael Fried. "Art and Objecthood." *Artforum* 5 (Summer 1967): pp. 12-23.

Paul H. Fry. "The Image of Walter Benjamin." *Raritan* 2, No. 4 (Spring 1983): pp. 131-152.

Lucinda Furlong. "Getting High Tech: The 'New Television.'" *The Independent* 8, No. 2 (March 1985): pp. 14-16.

Lucinda Furlong. "A Manner of Speaking: An Interview with Gary Hill." *Afterimage* 10, No. 8 (March 1983): pp. 9-16.

Lucinda Furlong. "Notes Toward a History of Image-Processed Video: Eric Siegel, Stephen Beck, Dan Sandin, Steve Rutt, Bill and Louise Etra." *Afterimage 11, Nos. 1&2, (Summer 1983): pp. 35-38.*

Lucinda Furlong. "Notes Toward a History of Image-Processed Video: Steina and Woody Vasulka." *Afterimage* 11, No. 5 (December 1983): pp. 12-17.

Peggy Gale, editor. *Video by Artists*. Toronto: Art Metropole, 1976.

Margaret Ganahl and R.S. Hamilton. "One Plus One: A Look at *Six Fois Deux*." *Camera Obscura* 8, 9, 10 (Fall 1982): pp. 89-115.

Raymond Geuss. *The Idea of a Critical Theory*. Cambridge: Cambridge University Press, 1981.

Martha Gever. "An Interview with Martha Rosler." *Afterimage* 9, No. 3 (October 1981): pp. 10-17.

Martha Gever. "Meet the Press: On Paper Tiger Television." *Afterimage* 11, No. 4 (November 1983): pp. 7-11.

Martha Gever. "Pomp and Circumstances: The Coronation of Nam June Paik." *Afterimage* 10, No. 3 (October 1982): pp. 12-16.

Martha Gever. "Underdeveloped Media, Overdeveloped Technology." *The Independent* 8, No. 7 (September 1985): pp. 15-17.

Martha Gever. "Video Politics: Early Feminist Projects." *Afterimage* 11, Nos. 1 & 2 (Summer 1983): pp. 25-27.

Florence Gilbard. "An Interview with Vito Acconci: Video Works 1970-78." *Afterimage* 12, No. 4 (November 1984): pp. 9-15.

Johanna Gill. *Video: State of the Art*. New York: Rockefeller Foundation Working Papers, June 1976.

Frank Gillette. *Video Process and Meta Process* (catalogue). Ed. Judson Rosebush. Syracuse: Everson Museum of Art, 1973.

Frank Gillette. *Between Paradigms*. New York: Gordon and Breach, 1973.

Todd Gitlin. *Inside Prime Time*. New York: Pantheon Books, 1983.

Global Village Video Documentary Festival. New York: Global Village Video Resource Center, 1975—.

Jean-Luc Godard and Anne-Marie Miéville. "France/Tour/Detour/Two/Children." *Camera Obscura* 8, 9, 10 (Fall 1982): pp. 61-73.

Erving Goffman. *Frame Analysis*. Cambridge: Harvard University Press, 1974.

Debra Goldman. "A Decade of Building an Alternative Movement." *The Independent* 6 (September 1983): pp. 18-24, 30.

Malcolm LeGrice. *Abstract Film and Beyond*. Cambridge: MIT Press, 1977.

Peter Grossman. "The Video Artist as Engineer and the Video Engineer as Artist." *Videography* 3, No. 10 (September 1978).

Nicos Hadjinicolau. *Art History and Class Struggle*. Trans. Louise Asmal. London: Pluto Press, 1978.

Charles Hagen and Laddy Kite. "Walter Wright and His Amazing Video Machine." *Afterimage* 2, No. 10 (April 1975):pp. 6-8.

Paul Hammond. *Marvelous Méliès*. New York: St. Martin's Press, 1975.

John G. Hanhardt. *Nam June Paik*. New York: Whitney Museum of American Art in association with W.W. Norton, 1982.

Josué V. Harari, editor. *Textual Strategies*. Ithaca: Cornell University Press, 1979.

Neil Harris. "Who Owns Our Myths? Heroism and Copyright in an Age of Mass Culture." *Social Research* 52, No. 2 (Summer 1985): pp. 241-67.

Stephen Heath and Patricia Mellencamp, editors. *Cinema and Language*. American Film Institute Monograph Series, vol. 1. Frederick, MD: University Publications of America, 1983.

Stephen Heath and Gillian Skirrow. "Television, a World in Action." *Screen* 18, No. 2 (Summer 1977): pp. 7-59.

Martin Heidegger. *The Question Concerning Technology and Other Essays*. Trans. William Lovitt. New York: Harper Colophon Books, 1977.

Brian Henderson. *A Critique of Film Theory*. New York: E.P. Dutton, 1980.

David R. Hiley. "Foucault and the Question of Enlightenment." *Philosophy and Social Criticism* II, No. 1 (Summer 1985): pp. 63-83.

James Hindman. "A Survey of Alternative Video." Part 1. *AFI Educational Newsletter* 4, No. 2 (1980).

James Hindman. "A Survey of Alternative Video." Part 2. *AFI Educational Newsletter* 4, No. 3 (1980).

Ralph Hocking. "Video Experiments." *Print* (March/April 1972).

Peter Uwe Hohendahl. *The Institution of Criticism*. Ithaca: Cornell University Press, 1982.

Stuart Hood. "Brecht on Radio." *Screen* 20, Nos. 3/4 (Winter 1979/80): pp. 16-23.

Max Horkheimer and Theodor W. Adorno. *Dialectic of Enlightenment*. Trans. John Cumming. New York: Seabury Press, 1977.

Bill Horrigan, editor. *The Media Arts in Transition*. Minneapolis: Walker Art Center, 1983.

Brice Howard. *Videospace and Image Experience*. San Francisco: National Center for Experiments in Television, 1972.

Kathy Rae Huffman, editor. *Video: A Retrospective*. Long Beach: Long Beach Museum of Art, 1984.

Don Ihde. *Technics and Praxis*. Boston Studies in the Philosophy of Science, vol. 24. Boston: D. Riedel, 1979.

Institute of Contemporary Art, University of Pennsylvania. *Video Art*. Ed. Suzanne Delehanty. Philadelphia: Institute of Contemporary Art, 1975.

Fredric Jameson. "Reification and Utopia in Mass Culture." *Social Text* 1 (Winter 1979): pp130-48.

Martin Jay. *The Dialectical Imagination: A History of the Frankfurt School and the Institute of Social Research, 1923-1950*. Boston: Little, Brown, 1973.

Martin Jay. "Habermas and Modernism." In *Habermas and Modernity*. Ed. Richard J. Bernstein. Cambridge, MA: MIT Press, 1985: pp. 125-39.

Bruce Jenkins. "A Case Against 'Structural Film.'" *Journal of the University Film Association* XXXIII, 2 (Spring 1981): pp. 9-14.

E. Ann Kaplan, ed. *Regarding Television*. The American Film Institute Monograph Series, vol. II. Frederick, MD: University Publications of America, 1983.

Allan Kaprow. "Video Art: Old Wine, New Bottle." *Artforum* 12 (June 1974): pp. 46-49.

Peter Kemp. "Death and the Machine: From Jules Verne to Derrida and Beyond." *Philosophy and Social Criticism* 10, No. 2 (Fall 1984): pp. 75-96.

Michael Kirby. *The Art of Time*. New York: Dutton, 1969.

Billy Kluver. "E.A.T.: Experiments in Art and Technology." *Paletten Sweden* (February 1968).

Stephen Koch. *Stargazer: Andy Warhol's World and His Films*. New York: Praeger, 1973.

Siegfried Kracauer. *Theory of Film*. New York: Oxford University Press, 1965.

Rosalind Krauss. *Passages in Modern Sculpture*. Cambridge, MA: MIT Press, 1981.

Annette Kuhn. *Women's Pictures*. London: Routledge & Kegan Paul, 1982.

Bruce Kurtz. "Artists Video at the Crossroads." *Art in America* 65 (January 1977): pp. 36-40.

Bruce Kurtz. "Video is Being Invented." *Arts Magazine* 47 (December/January 1973): pp. 37-44.

Jacques Lacan. *The Four Fundamental Concepts of Psychoanalysis*. Ed. Jacques-Alain Miller. Trans. Alan Sheridan. New York: W.W. Norton, 1978.

Teresa de Lauretis. *Alice Doesn't*. Bloomington: Indiana University Press, 1984.

Teresa de Lauretis, Andreas Huyssen, Kathleen Woodward, editors. *The Technological Imagination*. Madison, WI: Coda Press, 1980.

Teresa de Lauretis and Stephen Heath, editors. *The Cinematic Apparatus*. New York: St. Martin's Press, 1980.

Henri Lefebvre. *Everyday Life in the Modern World*. Trans. Sacha Rabinovitch. New Brunswick, NJ: Transaction Books, 1984.

Frank Lentricchia. "Reading Foucault (Punishment, Labor, Resistance) Part I." *Raritan* 1, No. 4 (Spring 1982): pp. 5-32.

Frank Lentricchia. "Reading Foucault." Part II. *Raritan* 2, No. 1 (Summer 1982): pp. 41-70.

Les Levine. "Camera Art." *Studio International* 190 (July/August 1975): pp. 52-54.

Les Levine. "The Information Fallout." *Studio International* 181 (April 1971): pp. 264-267.

Jay Leyda. *Kino: A History of the Russian and Soviet Film*. Princeton, NJ: Princeton University Press, 1983.

Lightworks: The Video Issue. (Ann Arbor, MI) 1, No. 5 (June 1976).

Barbara London. "Independent Video: The First Fifteen Years." *Artforum* 9 (September 1980): pp. 38-41.

Barbara London and Lorraine Zippay. "A Chronology of Video Activity in the United States: 1965-1980." *Artforum* 9 (September 1980): pp. 42-45.

Long Beach Museum of Art. *California Video*. Organized by Kathy Huffman. Long Beach, CA: Long Beach Museum of Art, 1980.

Long Beach Museum of Art. *Southland Video Anthology 1976-77*. Organized by David Ross. Long Beach, CA: Long Beach Museum of Art, 1977.

Richard Lorber. "Epistemological TV." *Art Journal* 34, No. 2 (Winter 1974-75): pp. 132-134.

Catherine Lord. "It's the Thought that Counts." *Afterimage* 11, No. 3 (October 1983): pp. 9-11.

Catherine Lord. "Video, Technology, and the Educated Artist." *The Independent* 8, No. 5 (June 1985): pp. 14-16.

Donald M. Lowe. *History of Bourgeois Perception*. Chicago: University of Chicago Press, 1982.

Michael Löwy. "Revolution against 'Progress': Walter Benjamin's Romantic Anarchism." *New Left Review* 152 (July/August 1985): pp. 42-59.

Eugene Lunn. *Marxism and Modernism*. Berkeley: University of California Press, 1982.

Jean-François Lyotard. "The Dream-Work Does Not Think." Trans. Mary Lydon. *The Oxford Literary Review* 6, No. 1 (1983): pp. 3-34.

Jean-François Lyotard. *Driftworks*. Ed. Roger McKeon. New York: Semiotext(e), 1984.

Jean-François Lyotard. "Les Immateriaux." *Art and Text* 17 (April 1985): pp. 47-57.

Jean-François Lyotard. "Philosophy and Painting in the Age of their Experimentation: Contributions to an Idea of Postmodernity." *Camera Obscura* 12 (Summer 1984): pp. 111-25.

Jean-François Lyotard. *The Postmodern Condition: A Report on Knowledge*. Trans. Geoff Bennington and Brian Massumi. Theory and History of Literature, vol. 10. Minneapolis: University of Minnesota Press, 1984.

Jean-François Lyotard. "Theory as Art: A Pragmatic Point of View." *Image and Code*. Ed. Wendy Steiner. Michigan Studies in the Humanities, No. 2 Ann Arbor: University of Michigan, 1981: pp. 71-77.

Colin MacCabe. "Principles of Realism and Pleasure." *Screen* 17, No. 3 (Autumn 1976): pp. 7-27.

Pierre Macherey. *A Theory of Literary Production*. Trans. Geoffery Wall. London: Routledge & Kegan Paul, 1978.

Stephen Mamber. *Cinema Verité in America: Studies in Uncontrolled Documentary*. Cambridge, MA: MIT Press, 1974.

Jerry Mander. *Four Arguments for the Elimination of Television*. New York: William Morrow, 1978.

Stuart Marshall. "Television/Video: Technology/Forms." *Afterimage* (London) 8/9 (Spring 1981): pp. 70-85.

Stuart Marshall. "Video Art, the Imaginary and the *Parole Vide.*" *Studio International* 191 (May 1976): pp. 243-47.

Stuart Marshall. "Video—Technology and Practise." *Screen* 20, No. 1 (Spring 1979): pp. 109-119.

Micki McGee. "Artists Making News, Artists Re-making the News." *Afterimage* 10, No. 4 (November 1982): pp. 6-9.

Marshall McLuhan. *The Gutenberg Galaxy*. Toronto: University of Toronto Press, 1962.

Marshall McLuhan. *Understanding Media: The Extensions of Man*. New York: McGraw-Hill, 1964.

Marshall McLuhan. *Verbi-Voco-Visual Explorations*. New York: Something Else Press, 1967.

Jonas Mekas. *Movie Journal*. New York: Collier Books, 1972.

Colin Mercer. "Culture and Ideology in Gramsci." *Red Letters*, No. 8 (1978): pp. 19-40.

Christian Metz. "The Fiction Film and Its Spectator: A Meta-psychological Study." *New Literary History* VIII, No. 1 (Autumn 1976): pp. 75-105.

Annette Michelson, editor. *Kino-Eye: The Writings of Dziga Vertov*. Trans. Kevin O'Brien. Berkeley: University of California Press, 1985.

Annette Michelson, editor. *New Forms in Film* (exhibition catalogue). Montreux, 1974.

Dorine Mignot, editor. *The Luminous Image*. Amsterdam, Holland: Stedelijk Museum, 1984.

John Minkowski. "The Videotape Collection at Media Study/Buffalo." *Afterimage* 5, No. 7 (February 1978): pp. 4-5.

Alan Moore. "Peter Campus, Andy Mann, Ira Schneider, Tom Marioni at the Everson Museum of Art." *Artforum* 12 (June 1974): pp. 77-79.

Franco Moretti. *Signs Taken for Wonders*. Trans. Susan Fischer, David Forgacs, David Miller. London: Verso Editions and New Left Books, 1983.

Steve Neale. *Cinema and Technology*. Bloomington: Indiana University Press, 1985.

David F. Noble. *Forces of Production*. New York: Alfred A. Knopf, 1984.

David F. Noble. "Present Tense Technology." *Democracy* 3, No. 2 (Spring 1983): pp. 8-24; 3, No. 3 (Summer 1983): pp. 70-82; 3, No. 4 (Fall 1983): pp. 71-93.

Christopher Norris, "Philosophy as a Kind of Narrative: Rorty on Post-modernism Liberal Culture." *Enclitic* VII, No. 2 (Fall 1983): pp. 144-159.

John O'Kane. "Theory and Cultural Politics: Althusser's Intervention." *Thesis Eleven*. No. 10/11 (1984/85): pp.250-54.

John O'Kane. "Althusser, Ideology, and Oppositional Practice." *Enclitic* VII, No. 1 (Spring 1983): pp. 104-116.

Michael O'Pray. "Modernism, Phantasy and Avant-Garde Film." *Undercut*, No. 3/4 (March 1982): pp. 31-33.

Barbara Osborne. "New Wave on the Airwaves." *The Independent* 8, No. 9 (November 1985): pp. 14-17.

Nam June Paik. "Random Access Information." *Artforum* 19 (September 1980): pp. 46-49.

Nam June Paik. "Stimulation of Human Eyes by Four Channel Stereo Videotaping." *E.A.T./L.A. Survey* (Fall 1970).

Constance Penley. "Les Enfants de la Patrie." *Camera Obscura* 8, 9, 10: (Fall 1982): pp. 33-58

Jeff Perrone. "Ins and outs of Video." *Artforum* 14 (June 1976): pp. 53-57.

Robert Pincus-Witten. "Nam June Paik at the Bonino Gallery." *Artforum* 12 (April 1974): pp. 67-70.

Robert Pincus-Witten. "Open Circuits: The Future of Television." *Artforum* 12 (April 1974): p.70.

Mark Poster. *Foucault, Marxism and History*. Cambridge: Polity Press, 1984.

Jonathan Price. *Video Visions: A Medium Discovers Itself*. New York: New American Library, 1977.

Hilary Putnam. "Reason and History." *Reason, Truth and History*. Cambridge: Cambridge University Press, 1981: pp. 150-73.

John Rajchman. "The Postmodern Museum." *Art in America* 73, No. 10 (October 1985): pp. 110-117, 171.

John Rajchman and Cornel West, editors. *Post-Analytic Philosophy*. New York: Columbia University Press, 1985.

Jacques Ranciére. "On the Theory of Ideology—Althusser's Politics." *Radical Philosophy Reader*. Ed. Roy Edgeley and Richard Osborno. London: Verso Editions, 1985: pp. 101-136.

Klause Reinke. "Video Artists." *Studio International* 183 (February 1972): pp. 84-85.

Shelley Rice. "Conjunctions: The Video Installations of Lauren Ewing." *Afterimage* 11, Nos. 1 & 2 (Summer 1983): pp. 31-34.

Shelley Rice. "Francesc Torres: The Tyranny of the Past." *Afterimage* 10, No. 5 (December 1982): pp. 4-7.

Shelley Rice. "Mythic Space: The Video Installations of Rita Myers." *Afterimage* 9, No. 6 (January 1982): pp. 8-11.

Richard Rorty. "Habermas and Lyotard on Postmodernity." *Habermas and Modernity*. Ed. Richard J. Bernstein. Cambridge, MA: MIT Press, 1985: pp. 161-75.

Richard Rorty. "Deconstruction and Circumvention." *Critical Inquiry* II, No. 1 (September 1984): pp. 1-23.

Barbara Rose. "Switch-On Art." *New York Magazine* (December 20, 1971).

Judson Rosebush, editor. *Nam June Paik: Video 'n' Videology 1959-73.* Syracuse, NY: Everson Museum of Art, 1974.

Harold Rosenberg. *The Dedefinition of Art.* New York: Horizon Press, 1972.

David Ross. "Douglas Davis." *Flash Art* (May 1975).

David Ross. "Douglas Davis: Video Against Video." *Arts Magazine* 49 (December 1974): pp. 60-62.

David Ross. "A Provisional Overview of Artists' Television in the United States." *Studio International* 191 (May/June 1976): pp. 265-72.

Robert Russett and Cecile Starr, editors. *Experimental Animation.* New York: Van Nostrand and Reinhold, 1976.

Michael Ryan. *Marxism and Deconstruction.* Baltimore: Johns Hopkins University Press, 1982.

Paul Ryan. *Cybernetics of the Sacred.* Garden City, NY: Anchor Books, 1974.

Paul ·Ryan. "Videotape: Thinking About a Medium." *Media and Methods* (December 1968).

Edward Said. "Secular Criticism." *Raritan* 2, No. 3 (Winter 1983): pp. 1-26.

Herbert I. Schiller. *Communication and Cultural Domination.* White Plains, NY: International Arts and Sciences Press, 1976.

Herbert I. Schiller. *Information and the Crisis Economy.* Norwood, NJ: Ablex Publishing, 1984.

Herbert I. Schiller. *The Mind Managers.* Boston: Beacon Press, 1973.

Paul Schimmel and Nam June Paik. "Abstract Time." *Arts Magazine* 49 (December 1974): pp. 52-53.

Ira Schneider and Beryl Korot. *Video Art: An Anthology.* New York: Harcourt, Brace, Jovanovich, 1976.

Alfred Schutz. *The Phenomenology of the Social World*. Trans. George Walsh, Frederich Lehnert. Chicago: Northwestern University Press, 1967.

Allan Sekula. *Photography Against the Grain*. Halifax: Press of the Nova Scotia College of Art and Design, 1984.

Michael Shamberg and Raindance Corporation. *Guerilla Television*. New York: Holt, Rinehart, and Winston, 1971.

Alan Sheridan. *Michel Foucault*. London: Tavistock, 1980.

P. Adams Sitney, editor. *The Essential Cinema*. Anthology Film Archives, Series 2, vol.1. New York: New York University Press, 1975.

P. Adams Sitney, editor. *Film Culture Reader*. New York: Praeger, 1970.

P. Adams Sitney. *Visionary Film*. New York: Oxford University Press, 1974.

Situationist International Anthology. Ed. and trans. by Ken Knabb. Berkeley, CA: Bureau of Public Secrets, 1981.

Joel Snyder. "Benjamin on Reproducibility and Aura: A Reading of 'The Work of Art in the Age of its Technical Reproducibility.'" *The Philosophical Forum* XV, Nos. 1-2 (Fall-Winter 1983-84): pp. 130-145.

Alfred Sohn-Rethel. *Intellectual and Manual Labor*. London: Macmillan Press, 1978.

Janet Staiger and Douglas Gomery. "The History of World Cinema: Models for Economic Analysis." *Film Reader* 4 (1979): pp.35-44.

Marita Sturken. "The Aesthetics of the Subject: James Byrne's Video Projects." *Afterimage* 10, No. 9 (April 1982): pp. 7-11.

Marita Sturken. "Denman's Col (Geometry): Mary Lucier." *Afterimage* 9, No. 7 (February 1982): pp. 10-11.

Marita Sturken. "Feminist Video: Reiterating the Difference." *Afterimage* 12, No. 9 (April 1985): pp. 9-11.

Marita Sturken. "An Interview with Barbara Buckner." *Afterimage* 12, No. 10 (May 1985): pp. 6-9.

Marita Sturken. "An Interview with George Stoney." *Afterimage* 11 No. 6 (January 1984): pp. 7-11.

Marita Sturken. "A Narrative Conceit." *Afterimage* 9, No. 9 (April 1982): pp. 10-11.

Marita Sturken. "Temporal Interventions: The Videotapes of Bill Viola." *Afterimage* 10, Nos. 1 & 2 (Summer 1982): pp. 28-31.

Marita Sturken. "TV as a Creative Medium: Howard Wise and Video Art." *Afterimage* 11, No. 10 (May 1984): pp. 5-9.

Colin Summer. *Reading Ideologies*. New York: Academic Press, 1979.

Manfredo Tafuri. *Architecture and Utopia*. Trans. Barbara Luigia La Penta. Cambridge, MA: MIT Press, 1976.

Charles Taylor. "Foucault on Freedom and Truth." *Philosophy and the Human Sciences*. Philosophical Papers, vol. 2, pp. 152- 84. Cambridge: Cambridge University Press, 1985.

Charles Taylor. "Legitimation Crisis?" *Philosophy and the Human Sciences*. Philosophical Papers, vol. 2, pp. 248-88. Cambridge: Cambridge University Press, 1985.

Patricia Thomson. "Independents on Television." *Afterimage* 11, Nos. 1 & 2 (Summer 1983): pp. 28-30.

Patricia Thomson. "Video and Electoral Appeal." *Afterimage* 12, No. 7 (February 1985): pp. 8-11.

Calvin Tompkins. "Profile: Nam June Paik." *The New Yorker* 51, No. 11 (May 5, 1975) pp. 44-79.

Alan Trachtenberg. "Albums of War: On Reading Civil War Photographs." *Representations*, No. 9 (Winter 1985): pp. 1-32.

Maurice Tuchman. *Art and Technology*. Los Angeles: Los Angeles County Museum of Art, 1971.

Maureen Turim. "Desire in Art and Politics: The Theories of Jean-François Lyotard." *Camera Obscura* 12 (Summer 1984): pp. 91-106.

Parker Tyler. *Underground Film—A Critical History*. New York: Grove Press, Inc. 1969.

Gregory L. Ulmer. *Applied Grammatology*. Baltimore: Johns Hopkins University Press, 1985.

Raoul Vaneigem. *The Revolution of Everyday Life*. Trans. Ronald Nicholson-Smith. London: Aldgate Press, 1983.

Woody Vasulka. "Syntax of Binary Images." *Afterimage* 6, Nos. 1 & 2 (Summer 1978): p. 20.

Woody Vasulka and Scott Nygren. "Didactic Video: Organizational Models of the Electronic Image." *Afterimage* 3, No. 4 (October 1975): pp. 9-13.

Videography. "The Movement Within: Images Created on a Video Synthesizer," 4, No. 12 (December, 1979): pp. 32-33.

Bill Viola. "Some Recommendations on Establishing Standards for the Exhibition and Distribution of Video Works." *The Media Arts in Transition*, pp. 50-57. Minneapolis: Walker Art Center, 1983.

Vision and Television (catalogue). Ed. Russell Conner. Waltham, MA: Rose Art Museum, Brandeis University, 1970.

Amos Vogel. *Film as a Subversive Art*. New York: Random House, 1974.

Wolf Vostell. *Happening und Leben*. Berlin: Hermann Luchterhand Verlag, 1970.

Marx W. Wartofsky. *Models*. Boston Studies in the Philosophy of Science, vol. 48. Boston: D. Riedel, 1979.

Marx W. Wartofsky. "The Paradox of Painting: Pictorial Representation and the Dimensionality of Visual Space." *Social Research* 51, No. 4 (Winter 1984): pp. 863-884.

Stephen Watson. "Jürgen Habermas and Jean-François Lyotard: Post Modernism and the Crisis of Rationality." *Philosophy and Social Criticism* 10, No. 2 (Fall 1984): pp. 1-24.

Dennis Wheeler, editor. *Form and Structure in Recent Film*. Vancouver: Vancouver Art Gallery, 1972.

Robin White. "Great Expectations: Artists' TV Guide." *Artforum* 20 (June 1982): pp. 40-47.

John H. Whitney. "A Computer Art for the Video Picture Wall." *Art International* 15 (September 1971): pp. 35-38.

Raymond Williams. *Culture*. Glasgow: Fontana Paperbacks, 1981.

Raymond Williams. *Television: Technology and Cultural Form*. New York: Schocken Books, 1974.

Langdon Winner. *Autonomous Technology*. Cambridge, MA: MIT Press, 1977.

Janet Wolff. *The Social Production of Art*. New York: New York University Press, 1984.

Richard Wolin. "The Bankruptcy of Left-Wing Kulturkritik: The 'After the Avant-Garde' Conference." *Telos*, No. 63 (Spring 1985): pp. 168-73.

Richard Wolin. *Walter Benjamin, An Aesthetic of Redemption*. New York: Columbia University Press, 1982.

Peter Wollen. *Readings and Writings*. London: Verso Editions and New Left Books, 1982.

Ann-Sargent Wooster. "An Armory of Mirrors: Juan Downey." *Afterimage* 10, Nos. 1 & 2 (Summer 1982): pp. 24-27.

Jud Yalkut. "Art and Technology of Nam June Paik." *Arts Magazine* 42 (April 1968): pp. 50-51.

Jud Yalkut. "TV as a Creative Medium at Howard Wise Gallery." *Arts Magazine* 44 (September 1969): p. 18.

Robert Young. "Post-Structuralism: The End of Theory." *The Oxford Literary Review* 5, Nos. 1 & 2 (1982): pp. 3-20.

Gene Youngblood. "The Videosphere." *Show* (September 1970).

The Contributors

LOUIS ALTHUSSER is a leading French philosopher whose writings have made influential contributions to philosophy, economics, psychology, aesthetics, and political science. Books include *For Marx* and *Reading Capital*.

DAVID ANTIN is an artist, poet, and critic who resides and teaches in La Jolla, California. His books include *Definitions, Autobiography, Talking at the Boundaries, Dialogue*, and *Who's Listening Out There?*

JEAN BAUDRILLARD, professor of sociology at the University of Paris, is the author of *The Mirror of Production* and a contributing editor to *Artforum*.

WALTER BENJAMIN was a cultural critic whose essays on all aspects of modernism have been enormously influential. "The Work of Art in the Age of Mechanical Reproduction" is one of the seminal essays in contemporary thinking on film and media and culture in the twentieth century.

BERTOLT BRECHT, in addition to his plays and writings on the theater, wrote a highly influential essay on how radio truly could serve as a communications and cultural medium. Its application to television further established its influence in our time.

JACK BURNHAM is professor of art at Northwestern University and the author of *Beyond Modern Culture: The Effects of Science and Technology on the Sculpture of this Century*.

STANLEY CAVELL is Walter M. Cabot Professor of Aesthetics and the General Theory of Value at Harvard University. His books include *Must We Mean What We Say?* and *The World Viewed* (on film).

DOUGLAS DAVIS is an artist working in videotape, printmaking, and performance. He is author of *Art and the Future: A History/Prophecy of the Collaboration between Science, Technology and Art* and art editor of *Newsweek*.

JOHN ELLIS teaches film studies at the University of Kent at Canterbury. He is a member of the editorial board of *Screen* magazine, chairperson of the Greater London Arts Film and Video Panel, co-author of *Language and Materialism*, and a contributor to *Screen* and *Screen Education*.

HANS MAGNUS ENZENSBERGER is one of the foremost contemporary German poets and essayists. His essays have appeared in *Partisan Review, Encounter*, and *The New York Review of Books*.

JOHN G. HANHARDT is curator of film and video and head of the Film and Video Department of the Whitney Museum of American Art. His publications include *Nam June Paik, A History of the American Avant-Garde Cinema*, and *Shigeko Kubota/Taka Iimura: New Video*.

ROSALIND KRAUSS is associate professor of art history at Hunter College, an editor of *October*, and author of *Passages in Modern Sculpture*, a history of modern American sculpture.

NAM JUNE PAIK is the leading artist in the history of video as an art form. A major retrospective of his work was organized at the Whitney Museum of American Art in 1982.

DAVID ROSS is director of the Institute of Contemporary Art in Boston. He was previously curator of video at the Everson Museum and curator at the Long Beach Museum of Art and the University Art Museum, Berkeley, CA.

GENE YOUNGBLOOD, the author of *Expanded Cinema*, teaches at the California Institute of the Arts.

Index